BLOOMSBURY PIE

THE MAKING OF
THE BLOOMSBURY BOOM

REGINA MARLER

A *Virago* Book

Published by Virago Press 1998

First published in Great Britain by
Virago Press 1997

First published in the United States
by Henry Holt and Company,
New York, 1997

A CIP catalogue record for this book
is available from the British Library.

ISBN 1 86049 384 X

Typeset in Fournier
Printed and bound in Great Britain by
Clays Ltd, St Ives plc

Virago
A Division of
Little, Brown and Company (UK)
Brettenham House
Lancaster Place
London WC2E 7EN

FOR M. DUBOSE

ACKNOWLEDGEMENTS

I WOULD LIKE to thank the many scholars, collectors, dealers, and friends who made this book possible, especially Angelica Garnett, for her insight and encouragement, Tony Bradshaw, for his constant generosity, and Olivier Bell and the late Quentin Bell, for their many kindnesses over the past ten years. For interviews, crucial information, permissions, and/or hospitality, I am indebted to Cressida Bell, Frances Bradshaw, Mary Ann Caws, Caroline Cuthbert, Louise De-Salvo, Jane Emery, Sarah Fox Pitt, Bernadette Fraser, Debo Gage, Barbara and Howard Ginsberg, Christopher Hampton, Julian Hartnoll, Michael Holroyd, Elizabeth Inglis, Cecily Langdale, Hermione Lee, Judith Lowry, Janet Malcolm, Jane Marcus, Madeline Moore, Richard Morphet, Christopher Naylor, Virginia and Bill Nicholson, Nigel Nicolson, Robert Reedman, Clarissa Roche, S. P. Rosenbaum, Alison Samuel, Frances Spalding, Peter Stansky, Lester and Eileen Traub, Polly Vaizey, J. J. Wilson, Roma Woodnutt, Jean and Cecil Woolf, and Marlya Woolf.

My agent, Maia Gregory, supported me through many delays and crises, and my editors, Ray Roberts at Henry Holt and Alan Samson at Little, Brown, London, were unfailingly patient and good-humoured. For research help, I would like to thank (and, someday, to pay) Renée Guillory, David Berberick, and Paige Tuhey.

BLOOMSBURY PIE

EACH SUMMER, THE water meadows behind Monk's House, Virginia and Leonard Woolf's country home, are dotted with devotees, mostly female, mostly American, lovingly retracing Virginia Woolf's path across those meadows to the River Ouse, where she drowned herself on the morning of 28 March 1941. Her earlier house, Asheham, had to be boarded shut to discourage trespassers. Many of the faithful broke in anyway, hoping to absorb the atmosphere in which a great writer lived and worked. Some, hearing a door creak shut, an old curtain rustle, tore from the house in horror, convinced that the ghost of Virginia Woolf pursued them.

The cult of Virginia Woolf is not the only curious product of the Bloomsbury boom, although it may, in its extravagance, be the central expression of a movement driven by nostalgia, adoration, and antipathy. The Bloomsbury Group has always inspired fierce emotion. Its peak of influence in the 1920s was followed by forty years of sustained sidelong derogation and occasional frontal attack. Some of these attacks are legendary, like those of D. H. Lawrence, who told David Garnett that his homosexual Bloomsbury friends had made him dream of black beetles ("It is this horror of little swarming selves," Lawrence added in a letter to Lady Ottoline Morrell), and the famously hostile Wyndham Lewis, whose gargantuan satire, *Apes of God* (1930), was the culmination of a lifetime campaign against the Group.

Not in his darkest nightmare could Wyndham Lewis have imagined that the 1994 Gay Mardi Gras parade in Sydney, Australia, would feature a wild elaboration of the love scenes from Sally Potter's film of Virginia Woolf's novel *Orlando*, involving a canopied bed and some forty costumed lesbians, or that Charleston Farmhouse, where Vanessa Bell and Duncan Grant once lived, would attract over 15,000 visitors each year, or that in 1995 an Englishman named Jonathan Pryce would win Best Actor at Cannes for his impersonation of Lytton Strachey in Christopher Hampton's film *Carrington*, based on Strachey's largely platonic love affair with an obscure artist on the fringes of the hallowed Group. Since the early 1960s, when Michael Holroyd accepted an advance of just fifty pounds for his two-volume biography of Lytton Strachey, Bloomsbury has exploded in the public imagination from a marginal and mainly academic field of inquiry to an almost mass-market phenomenon. A major exhibition of Carrington's work opened at the Barbican in London to coincide with the release of Hampton's film. A new collection of Carrington's lovely "drawing" letters is being prepared. By 1998, there will have been four new full-length biographies of Virginia Woolf published within a three-year period. Even the Merchant-Ivory films based on the novels of E. M. Forster and the British television production of Nigel Nicolson's *Portrait of a Marriage* (and its sanitized American broadcast, with thirty-six minutes of sex deleted) are ancillary products of the Bloomsbury boom, of the perception that what this group of friends said and felt seventy years ago can still affect us.

Or make us money. A 1902 Beresford portrait photograph of the young Virginia now carries such cultural resonance—of what, exactly, it is hard to say—that the makers of Bass Ale think it helps sell their brew. The Hotel Russell in Russell Square, Bloomsbury, boasts the Virginia Woolf Restaurant. Nearby, the Bloomsbury Crest Hotel offers the Lady Ottoline Room, flush with photographs of the illustrious dead. Cressida Bell, Vanessa Bell's granddaughter, opened a London shop in 1995 filled with her textiles and other decorated objects, many of which draw directly from Omega and Bloomsbury wallpaper patterns, pottery, and fabric designs. Another shop in London, the Bloomsbury Workshop, is entirely devoted to the art and books of the Bloomsbury Group. In Minneapolis, two women have opened a combination gallery and garden shop called Bloomsbury Market, in which, alongside photographs of Sissinghurst, Charleston, and Monk's House, they sell original metalwork garden arches, fencing, and trellises, "in the spirit of Bloomsbury, for reasonable prices."

For thirty years, journalists have been struggling to explain the fascination with Bloomsbury. Their arguments are often cast in economic terms, with talk of exploitation and debasement, of values and commodification. Bloomsbury is evaluated on "the stock exchange of culture" and found to be a volatile investment. Market analysis does not preoccupy the Bloomsbury enthusiast, however, whose experience is more like unrequited love. All the materials for obsession are in place: letters, snapshots, sacred places, and—critically—the absence (but so recent presence!) of the object of desire, whether this is an individual Bloomsberry, a state of being, or a way of life. This may explain the incomprehension of the Bloomsbury boom by those who cannot hear the sirens calling.

To complicate matters, a layered response to Bloomsbury operates even among the Group's enthusiasts, of a similar nature to the "double tradition" in Samuel Johnson studies, first noticed by Bertrand Bronson in the 1950s and described here by Paul Fussell:

Venerators and close readers—the two establish the polarities of the Johnsonian "double tradition": . . . the tradition, on the one hand, of "Doctor Johnson," the folklore *domine* and Tory projected in Boswell's *Life*, and the tradition, on the other hand, of Samuel Johnson, writer, poet, critic, and foremost literary intelligence of his day.[1]

Popular conceptions of the Bloomsbury Group have often vexed scholars and critics, while scholarly investigations of the Group and its works have been the subject of mocking editorials in the *Times* and cartoons in *The New Yorker*. And to further confuse the issue, there are readers enthralled with the lives of the members of Bloomsbury who do not read the novels of Virginia Woolf or E. M. Forster. There are scholars of Woolf, Forster, and Keynes who dislike the Group as a whole and lament the Bloomsbury revival. There are art historians who find value only in the prewar paintings of Duncan Grant and Vanessa Bell and blame the later decline of their work on something called "Bloomsbury."

Bloomsbury Pie is the story of the Bloomsbury revival—its scholars, collectors, dealers, enemies, heirs, fanatics—dating from about 1960, when the first clear signs of a resurgence of interest in the Group became evident. This is not a book about the Bloomsbury Group so much as the emotions surrounding the idea of Bloomsbury, and the industry that fuels those emotions. It is the social history of a tenacious and unwieldy cultural phenomenon.

BY ANY OTHER NAME . . .

Some of the most pained and soporific passages in modern letters have gone toward defining the original members of the Bloomsbury

---

1. Paul Fussell, *Samuel Johnson and the Life of Writing* (New York: Norton, 1971), 42.

Group, the terms of their membership, and the philosophy that united them. Simply put, Bloomsbury is the best-documented literary and artistic coterie in twentieth-century Britain. Its philosophical cornerstone was personal liberty, especially sexual liberty and freedom of expression, coupled with an emphasis on personal relationships and an appreciation for the arts. When Thoby Stephen, the eldest son of Leslie Stephen, went up to Trinity College, Cambridge, in 1899, Leonard Woolf, Clive Bell, Lytton Strachey, and Saxon Sydney-Turner were among the first students he met. By 1902, most of these men had been elected to the Apostles, a secret society of intellectually stellar undergraduates from Trinity and King's Colleges. E. M. Forster left Cambridge in 1901 but kept his connection with the Apostles, as did the artist and critic Roger Fry and the critic Desmond MacCarthy, two names associated with Bloomsbury but of an older generation. In 1903, John Maynard Keynes was elected to the Apostles, and—with the later addition of Thoby's sisters Vanessa and Virginia, his brother Adrian, and the artist Duncan Grant, a cousin of Lytton Strachey's—the nucleus of Bloomsbury was complete. Its name came afterward, of course, from the district in London where the Stephen children chose to settle after the death of their father in 1904.

That naming was central to the Group as we understand it, and perhaps as they understood themselves. It is said that Molly MacCarthy coined the term "Bloomsberries" in a private letter in 1910. Before this year, the habitués of Gordon and Fitzroy Squares were like any other informal circle of friends and relatives; they included such obviously non-Bloomsbury figures as Charles Tennyson, the poet's grandson, and Margery Snowden, Vanessa's artist friend. With the exception of Forster, who had published five novels by 1910, none of these young people was famous or exceptionally accomplished.

Once named, however, the Group appeared to spring miraculously into being; 1910 ushered in the Bloomsbury era or, more specifically, the public life of the Bloomsbury Group. The *Dreadnought* hoax that February and Roger Fry's *First Post-Impressionist Exhibition* at the close of the year were the unsettling events by which Bloomsbury came to be characterized in the press and elsewhere.[2] Many of their more respectable friends fell away in this period, further defining the central group. The term "Bloomsbury" remained a private joke, used ironically, and often in quotation marks, until about 1920, when it began to appear in newspapers and take on the sparkling independent life that so irked the original members of the circle. In later years, whenever the surviving Bloomsberries wrote about their early milieu, they took the opportunity to lament not only the bad press it was receiving but "the name by which it unfortunately came to be known." They spoke of the name as something separate from themselves, something imposed on them, like an unflattering light through a window. If they could have, they would have got up and moved.

We are a naming species, eager to take up and defend even an accidental signifier. Yet any name at all for this circle implies fixity where there was flux, and uniformity where there was conflict and innovation. What made the friends important is such an awkward blend of private and public achievements that almost no tenet of Bloomsbury can be firmly established, especially one that applies equally to every member of the Group. This was even more true at the height of

---

2. For a fuller discussion of the importance of this year, see Peter Stansky's *On or About December 1910* (Cambridge: Harvard University Press, 1996). The best introductions to Bloomsbury can be found in Quentin Bell's *Bloomsbury* (London: Weidenfeld & Nicolson, 1968) and S. P. Rosenbaum's *The Bloomsbury Group: A Collection of Memoirs, Commentary and Criticism* (Toronto: University of Toronto Press, 1975).

their influence, when "Bloomsbury" was so misunderstood that the term could be assigned to wildly diverse beliefs and attitudes and to figures as emotionally and intellectually far from Bloomsbury as F. R. Leavis, one of its chief opponents. The core membership was not described in print until 1927, when Raymond Mortimer wrote an elegiac memoir for the American journal *Dial*, referring to his friends fondly in the past tense. English readers did without a clear definition of the Group until many of its members were in fact dead. The most authoritative list of members is Leonard Woolf's, although his account bristled with frustration at the misconceptions of "Bloomsbury," many of which were hardening into fact. "We had no common theory, system, or principles which we wanted to convert the world to," he explained in his autobiography.

> We were not proselytisers, missionaries, crusaders, or even propagandists. . . . Maynard's crusade for Keynesian economics against the orthodoxy of the Banks and academic economists, and Roger's crusade for post-impressionism and "significant form" against the orthodoxy of academic "representational" painters and aestheticians were just as purely individual as Virginia's writing of *The Waves*—they had nothing to do with any group.[3]

Clive Bell so resented the broad attacks on an undefined "Bloomsbury" that he tried to suggest the Group had never existed. The term itself, he wrote in 1956, "may yet come to signify something definite,

---

3. Leonard Woolf, *Beginning Again: An Autobiography of the Years 1911 to 1918* (London: Hogarth, 1964), 25–26.

though as yet few people, so far as I can make out, understand by it anything more precise than 'the sort of thing we all dislike.' "[4]

What did the charged word "Bloomsbury" evoke? For some, a frail, cultured elite, aiming for "a life of retirement among fine shades and nice feelings," for others, "ill-mannered and pretentious *dilettanti.*" Having endured abuse of Bloomsbury for two or more decades, the surviving members took the flawed, hopelessly compromised name of their circle as their first line of defence in the 1950s and 1960s. This was the prelude to the Bloomsbury revival. If they could shrug off the term, with its painful connotations (not all of which—they must have realized—entirely missed the mark), they would be free again. They had entered the room through ethics but would leave it through semantics. The French scholar Jean Guiguet took up the cry in his 1965 study of Virginia Woolf, arguing that "Bloomsbury" was a term so sloppy and misleading that it should be banished from critical discourse.

A collective name must have been useful in the early years, encouraging or even forcing self-definition. It was slightly absurd, as well, as Virginia Woolf liked to point out in the 1930s by threatening to call her younger friends "Maida Vale" or "Hampstead." But it also made Bloomsbury seem, to outsiders, an unbreachable clique, a junta or "malefic cabal," especially as many Bloomsberries attained powerful positions in the London art and literary worlds. They were assumed to hold a corporate attitude, known as "the Bloomsbury party line." As critics, Clive Bell, Desmond MacCarthy, and the secondary Bloomsberries Raymond Mortimer and David Garnett were each

---

4. Clive Bell, *Old Friends* (London: Cassell, 1988), 128. E. M. Forster came closest to committing himself to the term when, in 1929, he described Bloomsbury as "the only genuine movement in English civilization." He stopped short of committing himself to that movement.

thought at times to represent the Group as a whole. This gave their individual pronouncements a strange weight. As one observer put it:

> If, say, Mrs. Woolf had held her nose on the mention of a bad
> novel that passed for good, and the author heard of it, he
> would suffer. . . . He would think of the whole coterie hold-
> ing their noses and their friends and friends' friends follow-
> ing their example.[5]

Since few patterns in their critical judgments could be determined, it
came to seem that Bloomsbury dismissed or favoured writers and
artists arbitrarily, perhaps on the merit of a handshake or a lock of
hair tastefully arranged. The Cambridge critics F. R. and Queenie
Leavis, Bloomsbury's most influential detractors, argued that the
Group had replaced critical values with "social-personal values."
Later, along the same lines, Irene Simon wrote that, despite Clive
Bell's assertions, "Bloomsbury" had a definite meaning, denoting not
only a sceptical, secular philosophy but "the use of coterie power for
the advancement of literary reputations."[6] The homosexuality of
many Bloomsberries, their pacifism during World War I, their feminism, their private incomes, their championship of French art and literature—all were black marks. By the early 1930s, "Bloomsbury" had
become a term of abuse, suggesting everything from giggling effem-
inacy to political indifference. Peter Stansky, who applied to study at
King's College, Cambridge, in the 1950s, was told that his letter ex-

---

5. Paul Bloomfield, *Uncommon People: A Study of England's Elite* (London: Hamish
Hamilton, 1955), 181.

6. Irene Simon, "Bloomsbury and Its Critics," *Revue des Langues Vivantes* 23. 5 (1957):
414.

pressing interest in the Bloomsbury Group had elicited laughter among the dons.

For writers of the 1940s and 1950s, especially, so many disparate elements in English life and culture smacked of "Bloomsbury" that it seemed they could never claim a patch of virgin ground. There was also an unhelpful emphasis on social privilege in much 1950s writing on the Group, from Noel Annan's frequently quoted essay "The Intellectual Aristocracy" to Paul Bloomfield's Bloomsbury chapter in *Uncommon People: A Study of England's Elite*, both of which assigned elaborate pedigrees to the Bloomsberries and downplayed their unconventionality. These essays had the effect of suggesting that useful connections, even more than inherited ability or hard work, were responsible for the Bloomsberries' successes. The first book-length study of the circle, J. K. Johnstone's *The Bloomsbury Group* (1954), did little to dispel the image of a charmed circle, preoccupied with "the inner life of the soul" and the leisurely pursuit of "truth and beauty." In an April 1958 article in *Esquire* called "Class War in British Literature," Leslie Fiedler described a new, more rugged group of writers—Kingsley Amis and his contemporaries—who defined themselves in opposition to Bloomsbury, which they associated with "the ideal of the gentleman." Fiedler had clearly read Clive Bell on Bloomsbury.

What "Bloomsbury" was historically, even the question of whether it existed at all, does not matter: it has become a *myth*, a handy label for a hated world. To the new writers, it means quite simply a society pledged before all else to an ideal of elegant style in conversation, art, life itself; a society in which the liberal and aristocratic are subtly blended; an in-

ternational society bounded by Oxford and Cambridge on
the one side and London on the other.

Although Bloomsbury has had some prominent advocates, it is the
fixity of opposition that stands out, decade after decade. Opponents,
too, have bloodlines, and it is illuminating to trace Roy Campbell,
who devoted a long satirical poem called *The Georgiad* (1931) to the
viragos and nancy boys of Bloomsbury, and, later, Geoffrey Grigson,
Geoffry Wagner, John Rothenstein, and Hugh Kenner to Wyndham
Lewis, whose appetite for conflict overwhelmed his devotion to his
art, and who seized at Bloomsbury as the source of his personal misery. (It is hard not to pity a man who published a book called *The
Jews, Are They Human?*—a play on the title of a popular book, *The
English, Are They Human?*—in 1938. And this was the book in which
Lewis hoped to recant his support of Hitler.) All but Rothenstein
wrote biographies of Wyndham Lewis, but it was Rothenstein's ac-
count of Lewis and his dealings with Bloomsbury in *Modern English
Painters* (1952) that has most coloured subsequent depictions of the
Group.

Most of the "Angry Young Men," on the other hand, are the intellectual offspring of F. R. Leavis and his magazine *Scrutiny*, for as
Fiedler noted, it was in large part Leavis's worldview that they
adopted, "a-religious yet moralistic, nonpolitical yet aggressively
class conscious. . . . They are, indeed, secular puritans." The Leavis
legacy lives on in the widely circulated *Pelican Guide to English Literature* (1955–58; reprinted 1982–83), edited by Boris Ford, a student of
F. R. Leavis's. About one-third of the contributors to the *Pelican
Guide* had also written for *Scrutiny*. Today, when students read in the
Pelican Guide that Virginia Woolf produced only one lasting contri-

bution to fiction, *To the Lighthouse*, that she was a minor talent, wielding a "fragmentary and inconclusive" technique, and that her feminist polemics *A Room of One's Own* and *Three Guineas* are marred by muddled thinking and hostility toward men, they are reading paraphrases of the *Scrutiny* position, over fifty years after these views were first published. The 1982 reprint of the *Pelican Guide* offered surprisingly little revision of its earlier take on Bloomsbury, and no comment— even negative—on Virginia Woolf's new status as a cultural icon. A former *Scrutiny* contributor praised Forster's intellectual shrewdness, delicacy, and responsibility, then told us that these virtues bore no relation to Bloomsbury. Another former *Scrutiny* contributor mentioned the "danger of the clique spirit" with regard to Virginia Woolf and asserted that in her first novel, *The Voyage Out*, she was "merely being clever in a Bloomsbury kind of way." In place of critical discussion of Bloomsbury, readers were offered G. H. Bantock's essay "L. H. Myers and Bloomsbury," an appreciation of a neglected writer who satirized the Group in one of his out-of-print novels. G. H. Bantock was also a contributor to *Scrutiny*.

The sympathies of a few anti-Bs, like the novelist Angus Wilson, appear to have altered midstream, following the course of the revival itself from the 1950s to the 1970s. As a young man, Wilson had delivered a stern but courteous broadcast on Virginia Woolf's failures as a novelist, finding her first and most glaring limitation her inability "to extend her sympathies outside a narrow class range," and tying this weakness not only to the moral severity of her Calvinist ancestors but to "the intuitive sense of a clique society."[7] Wilson's first novel, *Hem-*

---

7. Angus Wilson, "Sense and Sensibility in Recent Writing," *The Listener* 24 Aug. 1950: 280.

lock and After (1952), included several swats at Bloomsbury and Virginia Woolf. In lectures, he derided the Group for being out of touch with social reality and argued that Woolf herself offered "a withdrawn kind of sensibility which had little to impart to the modern novelist and the modern reader of novels." But these remarks were made at a time of fairly uniform opposition to "Bloomsbury" and all it was thought to represent. Twenty years later, in an interview in the *Iowa Review,* Wilson confessed that he had modified these views "to such a great degree that I am utterly ashamed to think that I ever said such a thing."

> I was fighting at this time, I suppose, on behalf of a re-look at the Victorian novel. . . . I had read Virginia Woolf enormously as an adolescent, and therefore the first talk I ever gave on radio was an attack on her; and I said then, you know, that one must bite the hand that feeds one. She has continually fed me and my work, sometimes when I may not have been aware that this was so.[8]

"I think for me [the feeling for Bloomsbury] is all about how writing, at its most intense, merges with living, at the top of your—what is it? sensitivity?" wrote Mary Ann Caws, who has written extensively on Woolf and her friends, "How could any living breathing suffering intense reader not find *To the Lighthouse* one of the most powerful influences possible? And everything Virginia Woolf wrote about reading, and about writing." Caws stayed at Monk's House in Rod-

---

8. Frederick P. McDowell, "Interview with Angus Wilson," *Iowa Review* 3 (Fall 1972): 288.

mell in the early 1970s, sleeping in Virginia's bedroom, with its tiled fireplace by Vanessa Bell, and has travelled several times to St. Ives, where the Stephen family kept their summer house.

> I spent (and still spend) time in Cassis [where Vanessa took her family in the 1920s], and that lighthouse, as well as the chateau at Fontcreuse there, were always among the intense connecting points of my stay there. . . . When I was doing one of my first pieces on Virginia Woolf, on framing in *The Waves*, I felt its origins there, in those moths around that lamp, so nearby.[9]

Monk's House and Charleston are recognized places of pilgrimage for Bloomsbury enthusiasts, but their potent atmosphere may still seduce the unwary. My own attachment to Bloomsbury grew from a chance visit to Rodmell—the road sign looked familiar—and a chance meeting with Quentin Bell.

Most recently the Bloomsbury Group has found an unlikely champion in the novelist Jeanette Winterson, who has moved beyond the touchy ambivalence of Angela Carter, her immediate forebear, to ally herself with Virginia Woolf and Bloomsbury. In Roger Fry's writing, especially, she claims to find "a life-delighting, art-delighting approach, unashamed of emotion, unashamed of beauty." But Woolf provokes a rapturous response in Winterson—pages about waterfalls and wine and the inexhaustible energy of art. "It may seem hopelessly old-fashioned to have returned to Bloomsbury," Winterson admits, "but I do not care about fashion, only about

---

9. Letter to the author, 19 Feb. 1996.

permanencies, and if books, music and pictures are happy enough to be indifferent to time, then so am I."[10]

Enchantments of this nature are at the heart of the Bloomsbury revival: poised between longing and resistance, exuberance and shame. How, and why, and at whose benefit, are the questions that motivated this book.

---

10. Jeanette Winterson, *Art Objects: Essays on Ecstasy and Effrontery* (London: Jonathan Cape, 1995), 5–6.

PART ONE

A myth is not about something: it is that something itself.

——SAMUEL BECKETT

THIS PART OF the story, at least, lays itself down in orderly rows. The seeds of the Bloomsbury revival were sown in a classical mode. Since the advent of copyright in about the eighteenth century, there have been heirs and executors to literary estates, more and less willing keepers of mouldering manuscripts, diaries, letters, and fragments, eager to print unpublished material, or not to print, or sometimes, simply, desperate to burn the stuff. Among the risks of literary ownership is the tendency of hidden papers—hidden stories—to exert uncanny gravitational pull. The locked door whines for its key; the secret sends up flares. If Henry James's *The Aspern Papers* is the model of the literary property drama, A. S. Byatt's *Possession* is the epic remake, the version "for our time." The protagonists of these stories tend to be scholars or would-be biographers, devoted souls whose desire seems to gradually erode their scruples. Rarely is the hero the literary executor.

Hence the charm of Leonard Woolf and his importance in the history of English letters and the story of the Bloomsbury revival. The mantle falls a little unevenly, as perhaps it should. Anyone familiar with Quentin Bell's biography of Virginia Woolf or with Leonard's own writings, or with Vanessa Bell's much-reproduced photographs, can call to mind the characteristic stoicism of his deeply lined mouth, the trembling hands. "He was a thorny old thing," an archivist of his papers has remarked. A more common epithet among Bloomsbury memoirists was "rabbinical." Cynthia Ozick, examining one of those early, now iconic Bloomsbury snapshots, contrasted the "incredibly tall and Vikinglike" Adrian Stephen and the young Leonard Woolf.

> Leonard's forehead is an attenuated wafer under a tender black forelock, his nose is nervous and frail, he seems younger and more vulnerable than his years (he was then thirty-four) and as recognizably intellectual as—well, how does one put the contrast? . . . He looks like a student at the yeshiva.[1]

As heir and custodian of the Virginia Woolf archive, along with his own voluminous personal and professional papers, Leonard Woolf assumed for nearly thirty years the role of gatekeeper to the past. There may be no exact term—steward, guardian, protector, curator, keeper—to describe Leonard's complex relationship to his wife's lit-

---

1. Cynthia Ozick, "Mrs. Virginia Woolf: A Madwoman and Her Nurse," in *Art and Ardor* (New York: Dutton, 1984): 36.

erary remains. The title "literary executor," for instance, nicely con-
jures the treasures at Monk's House, stacked manuscripts and notebooks almost glowing with scholarly significance and latent market
value, but makes Leonard seem too incidental a player, the mere func-
tionary of a last will and testament, and barely suggests his painstaking cultivation of Virginia's posthumous reputation.

For unlike most literary heirs, who are uncomfortably dependent
on editors and biographers to interpret and memorialize their dead,
Leonard was also Virginia's editor and publisher. Days after her suicide in March 1941, he met with his partner, John Lehmann, in London and, in lieu of a funeral, drew up a publishing programme for
Virginia's work. Later that year he saw her last novel, *Between the
Acts,* through the press, and for the next twenty-five years he devoted
himself to editing and publishing Virginia Woolf. Leonard is the
bridge between Bloomsbury itself ("a group of friends," as he mildly
described it) and what would become the Bloomsbury industry. He
corresponded with the earliest Woolf scholars, kept his wife's novels
in print, endured insults and scepticism, navigated a sea of anti-
Bloomsbury bias, and tirelessly promoted Virginia's interests in the
same way he had nurtured and protected Virginia herself during their
marriage. Continuity was at the heart of Leonard's patient, sometimes fretful attention to all things Virginia.

To an objective eye, the ease with which Leonard took up Virginia's flame suggests that, love and devotion apart, he was born for
the job. As a young man he had flourished in the Ceylon Civil Service,
where one of his clerical innovations—so revolutionary that it was
considered improper—was to insist that every piece of mail be answered on the day it was received. An administrator of this calibre
found the day-to-day operation of a literary estate not only manage-
able but quietly thrilling. He was answerable to no one and found his

endeavours on his wife's behalf so absorbing that his own writing slid into the background. He published only one book, *Principia Politica*, in the first nineteen years after Virginia's death, as opposed to the seventeen books (political theory, two novels, some stories, a play) he'd published during their marriage. If astute administration was Leonard's great professional skill, his great domestic skill was gardening, and there is something of the gardener, too, in his unhurried cultivation of the field and his long-term vision for Virginia's literary revival.

During the war, with paper strictly rationed, the Hogarth Press could publish little but their top priority: Virginia Woolf.[2] *The Death of the Moth* (1942) was the first of several essay collections edited by Leonard, quickly followed by a volume of short stories, *A Haunted House* (1943). In 1947, more essays appeared. While Leonard could not prevent the waning of Virginia's reputation during the 1940s, he held off total eclipse by keeping her name before the public. Due largely to these carefully timed volumes of essays, it became fashionable in the 1940s and 1950s to prefer Virginia's criticism to her novels. In this way, cultivated readers could bow to the prevailing trend against Bloomsbury writing and still appear daringly independent. It gave Leonard a useful foothold among the potential audience for her novels.

But those who owned letters from Virginia, and especially those who had been close enough to know of the diary and Memoir Club papers, knew there were further riches glimmering out of sight. The first deviation from Leonard's modest and deliberate publishing programme came in 1953, when, under increasing pressure to reveal more

---

2. Their second priority was the collected works of Freud, in the James Strachey translation. Today, once more, the Hogarth Press publishes only Freud and Virginia Woolf.

of the goods, he edited *A Writer's Diary*, an abridged and expurgated
selection from the diaries Virginia kept between 1918 and her death.
In narrowing his focus to "Virginia Woolf's intentions, objects, and
methods as a writer," Leonard managed to avoid libellous mention of
Virginia's friends and acquaintances, and just about all hint of the
Bloomsbury Group. The book was received kindly, especially in
America, but as the reviewer in the *Times Literary Supplement* noted,
"Virginia Woolf's reputation suffered, and is still suffering, from the
complex attack on 'Bloomsbury.' " This remark was borne out by an
antagonistic notice in the *Adelphi*, which found the diaries full of arrogance, "an arrogance big-boned and belligerent," deriving from
what the reviewer described as Bloomsbury's snobbish self-assurance.

The first ten years after a writer's death are crucial to the formation of her lasting reputation. Even a backlash during these years
can eventually be overcome, if manuscripts have not been scattered
and destroyed, if a handful of the faithful have kept the flame alive.
We don't know how, exactly, Leonard articulated his role to himself,
but he did become intensely preoccupied with Virginia's public image, suffering acutely from bad reviews of her posthumous books.
He remembered reviewers' names and could nurse grudges for
years. Meeting Malcolm Muggeridge in the 1960s, for instance, he
could hardly believe that this "extremely nice man" had written such
callous things about Virginia eight years earlier, and was at first rude
to him. While Leonard could not, of course, approve or censor
every piece of related scholarship or journalism that surfaced after
Virginia's death, he exerted control by judiciously spacing the essay
and story collections (no one then complained of overexposure to
Virginia Woolf) and by barring scholars access to the archive, pre-
ferring instead to answer specific questions through the post. Some
scholars, like Peter Stansky and William Abrahams, then writing

their book on Julian Bell and John Cornford, were not allowed to quote as liberally from Virginia's writings as they would have liked. While Leonard was clearly considered "the authority" on Virginia Woolf, in part because of his iron grip on those papers, he did not believe he had—or should have—the final word on her fiction. He made no secret that he thought *The Waves* her transcendent achievement, distantly followed by *To the Lighthouse* and *Between the Acts*, but he was willing to entertain a variety of interpretations of her novels, corresponding gamely with scholars of every stripe, and even sending unsolicited remarks to some, like Angus Wilson and Queenie Leavis, who had published criticism of his wife's work. As the 1960s advanced, Leonard particularly liked to quote Virginia's rising sales figures to those who dismissed her as a relic.

When it came to biography, though, Leonard made it known that the path was dark and perilous. In his review of Roy Harrod's biography of John Maynard Keynes (1951), for instance, and his later review of the first volume of Michael Holroyd's *Lytton Strachey* (1967), he took pleasure in pointing out not only factual errors but what he felt were errors of interpretation. He could relinquish Virginia Woolf's novels to the world, it seemed, but not her life, nor the lives of her friends. To discourage others, he even took a few gratuitous shots at Holroyd's youthful raptures and Harrod's pedantic little jokes.[3]

Uneasily anticipating a mixed response to *A Writer's Diary*, the first "personal" writing of Virginia's to face public scrutiny, Leonard

---

3. There was, strangely enough, one very personal area of Virginia's life that Leonard was happy to debate with scholars and doctors: her periods of mental instability. He may have hoped that science would advance to the point where these episodes could be explained, but he was, in the end, satisfied with none of the suggested diagnoses, especially that of bipolar disorder, or manic-depressive illness, although he had earlier referred to Virginia as manic-depressive in his autobiography. See Frederic Spotts, ed., *Letters of Leonard Woolf* (New York: Harcourt Brace Jovanovich, 1989).

had tried to head off at least one complaint with a disclaimer in the preface:

> At the best and even unexpurgated, diaries give a distorted or one-sided portrait of the writer, because, as Virginia Woolf herself remarks somewhere in these diaries, one gets into the habit of recording one particular kind of mood—irritation or misery say—and of not writing one's diary when one is feeling the opposite.

But this time there was another anxious voice at his elbow. On scanning *A Writer's Diary*, with its ominous ellipses and omissions, Clive Bell hurriedly tapped out a corrective, hoping, like Leonard, to dispel the notion of Virginia as a gloomy malcontent ("let me say once and for all that she was about the gayest human being I have known") but also beseeching "a vast posterity of enchanted readers to be on their guard." Well did Clive remember

> an evening when Leonard Woolf, reading aloud to a few old friends extracts from these diaries, stopped suddenly. "I suspect," said I, "you've come on a passage where she makes a bit too free with the frailties and absurdities of someone here present." "Yes," said he, "but that's not why I broke off. I shall skip the next few pages because there's not a word of truth in them."[4]

Thus one of her oldest friends, sensing perhaps that he had figured in those deleted passages, helped to perpetuate an impression of Virginia

---

4. Clive Bell, *Old Friends*, 97.

Woolf as frivolous, fantastic: not to be taken seriously.[5] Perhaps because it throws out of focus her stylistic achievements, the foundation of her claim to be remembered, it is a view with peculiar sticking power. As late as 1971, this characterization informed a BBC television programme, *A Night's Darkness. A Day's Sail,* produced by Julian Jebb, in which the interviewer, whenever a silence threatened the recording studio, fell back on the question "Was she a genius?" and then, "Was she malicious?" The first of these questions, though outwardly flattering, trivializes a lifetime of work, in effect lifting a writer's novels from her ink-stained hands and ascribing them to chance. The second, of course, hints at some core of ill will, some unwarranted (read: mad) delight in others' pain. It reinforces a suspicion—the fragrance that clings to her, that she feared would cling to her—that Virginia Woolf's novels are not the products of a sane mind. Many of these interviews were reprinted in a popular book, *Recollections of Virginia Woolf* (1972), itself much reprinted, and so passed into perpetuity, with their refrains of "Yes, she was a genius," and "Oh, malicious. I should think so," and the weary anecdotes that these questions evoked.

In the light of Leonard's concern for Virginia's reputation it is surprising that the next posthumous glimpse of his wife that he permitted was her engaging but affected correspondence with Lytton Strachey. Their letters, wrote Noel Annan, "brought out the worst

---

5. When the diaries were edited by Anne Olivier Bell and published in full beginning in 1977, she quoted Clive's anecdote and remarked, "One would like to know which passage it was that Leonard Woolf censored. I do not think that there is any substantial part of the diary of which it can fairly be said that 'there's not a word of truth' in it. . . . The editor has frequently had occasion to correct [Virginia Woolf] upon points of detail but never, I think, has she discovered a complete fabrication" (Anne Olivier Bell, ed., *The Diary of Virginia Woolf,* vol. 1 [New York: Harcourt Brace Jovanovich, 1977], xiv).

in each of them." This project, too, had been a compromise between publication of a broader and necessarily expurgated selection of Virginia's letters, urged by Vita Sackville-West and others, and continued, increasingly conspicuous silence. Over the previous ten years, several proposals for editing the letters had been rejected, Leonard always settling back on his conviction that the time wasn't right. "The difficulty," he told Vita in 1948, "is that the really personal letters are unpublishable and it seems to me that if one publishes only the impersonal ones, one gives a totally false impression of the character."[6]

But in January 1955, Leonard was forced to reconsider. The publishers Little, Brown had surprised him with proofs of the first real biography of Virginia Woolf, Aileen Pippett's *The Moth and the Star*. This was a decidedly unauthorized text, with Pippett's main resource being the conversation and papers of Vita Sackville-West, who emerged, not surprisingly, as a profoundly influential figure in Virginia's life. Relieved that someone was at last paying appropriate attention to her brilliant friend, Vita allowed herself to assume that Pippett had Leonard's blessing. In truth, Pippett had never sent Leonard her manuscript, as promised, and had never secured the right to quote Virginia's letters. Although he could deny copyright permission for those quotations, and he did prevent English publication of the biography, Leonard now realized that access to his wife's vast and far-flung correspondence was beyond his control.

"The whole subject of Virginia's letters has become very difficult," he wrote some months later to T. S. Eliot, asking him not to show scholars his letters from Virginia until a decision had been

---

6. *Letters of Leonard Woolf*, 488.

reached regarding publication.[7] Leonard weighed the matter carefully. In 1954, J. K. Johnstone's academic study *The Bloomsbury Group*, a dry piece of toast, had passed unmolested through reviewers' hands. This surprising occurrence, along with the calm reception of George Rylands's August 1956 broadcast *A Portrait of Virginia Woolf;* a steadily increasing flow of letters from American doctoral students; a well-illustrated, chatty French monograph by Monique Nathan; and Irma Rantavaara's *Virginia Woolf and Bloomsbury,* a perceptive work published in Helsinki in 1953, all made Leonard wonder if Bloomsbury's season in hell might be ending. Still hesitant, he began to collect and make copies of Virginia's letters.

Vanessa Bell had long nourished the hope of someone editing Lytton Strachey's letters, at one time proposing her son Julian, in collaboration with Janie Bussy, Lytton's niece. The risk of prosecution for obscenity was so great, however, that in the years just after Lytton's death his brother James doubted if they could even find a person willing to type the letters—let alone the "awful questions of blackmail, libel, hurt feelings, etc.," as Vanessa put it, concluding that she was "out for truth, really."[8] Now she encouraged Leonard to publish Virginia's letters. It was not unlike her. Vanessa had been almost alone, some forty years earlier, in advising Leonard to go ahead and publish his resentful roman à clef *The Wise Virgins* (1914), with its venomous depictions of himself, Virginia, Vanessa, and every member of his family. Although *The Wise Virgins* was reprinted during the Virginia Woolf boom of the late 1970s and sheds light on Leonard's courtship of Virginia, the novel seems

---

7. Ibid., 495.

8. Regina Marler, ed., *Selected Letters of Vanessa Bell* (New York: Pantheon, 1993), 409.

chiefly memorable for eliciting from Vanessa the startling assertion, "After all, feelings *aren't* very important." When her sister Virginia was researching the life of Roger Fry in the late 1930s, Vanessa remarked that "I must read [his letters] myself before giving any to her, as some might easily be indiscreet. Also some are very intimate, but perhaps one oughtn't to regard that. . . . On the whole I think one ought to disregard one's own feelings of wanting to keep things to oneself."[9] When it came to the correspondence between Virginia and Lytton, Vanessa's exceptional candour and detachment in these matters may have encouraged Leonard toward a bad decision.

For there is no doubt that the Strachey-Woolf letters, jointly edited with James Strachey, damaged both Lytton and Virginia's reputations. Even the good reviews portended evil, one critic noting that the letters depicted Bloomsbury as "lacking in feeling" and another flatly remarking that the book provided ammunition for Bloomsbury haters. The first to take aim was Geoffrey Wagner, admiring biographer of Wyndham Lewis, arch-enemy of Bloomsbury. Wagner claimed to have approached the works of the Bloomsbury Group with a certain amount of sympathy, having read so many attacks on them by Lewis and his disciple Roy Campbell. "The Bloomsburies," thought Wagner, "could not all have been pacifists, pederasts, and literary pimps." But his hopes were dashed. "The Letters exchanged between Virginia Woolf and Lytton Strachey do seem to reveal Bloomsbury at its most inessential," he quipped, adding that Strachey, "whose present correspondence shows the fantastically high opinion he held of himself . . . will go down with Roger Fry as a popularizer, a disseminator via inaccurate biogra-

---

9. Ibid., 388.

phies of precisely that torpid amateurism, that philistinism, even, which Bloomsbury boasted of opposing." Wagner found Strachey's "arch coyness" and "smug whimsy (not to mention his one poem)" at times almost unbearable, adding that "in the final analysis, Virginia Woolf's work too is robbed of real compassion and humanity. There remains, thankfully, E. M. Forster. Were it not for him the whole Bloomsbury movement would go down not merely as a 'distressing' moment in British literature, but as one scarcely 'civilized.' "[10]

It is too easy to pick apart this sort of review, which lays its writer open like a filleted fish. Suffice it to say that Wagner gave a faithful résumé of all Wyndham Lewis's views on Bloomsbury.

Malcolm Muggeridge offered a less partisan but no less painful opinion. "It is easy to laugh at this sad, foolish, rather commonplace correspondence between Lytton Strachey and Virginia Woolf," he wrote for the *New Republic*, recalling that he had recently picked up *Eminent Victorians* and found that

> the magic had all gone. It seemed meretricious, shrill and unconvincing. I heard a reedy voice across a tea-table, coming from far, far away, and breaking into an occasional snigger. Quickly I put the book away. Virginia Woolf's novels likewise made their initial impact, though how far this was authentic, and how far an acceptance of a prevailing fashion, it is difficult now to say. I should not dream of even trying to re-read them.

---

10. Geoffrey Wagner, "Bloomsbury Revisited," *The Commonweal* 8 March 1957.

It is difficult both to promote and to protect a dead writer, still more so when that writer's reputation is tangled with that of a disfavoured milieu. Skimming the press response, Leonard must have felt that all his care, his artful timing, had been wasted. Now was certainly not the moment to publish more of Virginia's letters or diary and expose her memory to further abuse.[11] Like Vanessa, he had been embarrassed by two recent Bloomsbury memoirs, Clive Bell's *Old Friends* (1956) and David Garnett's *The Flowers of the Forest* (1955), noting almost smugly the hostile reviews they received, and in September 1957 he told Vita that both books had harmed the reputation of Bloomsbury, and therefore of Virginia. Vita must have disagreed, for he wrote again a few days later:

> I feel very strongly—as do others more impartial than my-self—that there has been too much washing of intimate Bloomsbury linen lately. This has encouraged naturally the inevitable turn of the tide against what is called Bloomsbury. To publish this great mass of very intimate letters would still further encourage it and the professional writers who dislike Bloomsbury. They would not get a fair press at the present time.[12]

From this point on, Leonard was testily aware of "anti-bloomsbur-iansis" in the press and elsewhere. In 1959, he advised David Garnett

---

11. The reviews appeared in early 1957, too late to influence Leonard's cooperation with a 1956 BBC radio programme on Virginia, which featured interviews with friends and family. The year before he had also allowed a BBC broadcast of excerpts from *Mrs. Dalloway*.

12. *Letters of Leonard Woolf*, 504.

against publishing a Bloomsbury picture book, and the next year, when Margaret Lane, Countess of Huntingdon, suggested undertaking a biography of Virginia Woolf, Leonard said he had a feeling in his bones that the moment still wasn't right.

THESE, THEN, WERE the cultural circumstances into which Leonard chose to launch his autobiography. To what extent he hoped the story might clear the fog surrounding Bloomsbury and Virginia Woolf is uncertain, but it was characteristic of Leonard to want to sum up his life, pursuing a variation of the Cambridge philosopher G. E. Moore's famous and astringent query, "What exactly do you *mean*?" along the lines of "What happened? What exactly does it mean?" The five-volume autobiography has been considered the triumph of Leonard's long career, the fullest imaginable statement of his rationalist philosophy and of his tender, scrupulous character. It also marked the swing of the pendulum back in favour of Bloomsbury.

The words were slow in coming. He had begun the first volume, *Sowing,* in 1953 but stopped for unknown reasons. Did his continuing promotion of Virginia's interests conflict with this new, necessarily inward-looking venture, or was he simply gathering courage? We do know that a bitter letter from his brother Edgar in November 1953, accusing him of brutality and coldheartedness in depicting his family, from *The Wise Virgins* on, so appalled Leonard that he incorporated it into a later volume of his autobiography, as an example of how little we can know the inmost thoughts of even our nearest relations. Reaching him while he was again writing of his childhood, Edgar's letter may have stunned Leonard into silence. Five years later, he resumed work, but once more he set the manuscript aside. Finally, in January 1959, he settled to his task. *Sowing* was published the next year to immediate acclaim, two months short of Leonard's eightieth birthday. The author was inundated with fan mail and requests for interviews, articles, broadcasts, and advice. Some correspondents dazzled him with as many as four hundred letters, and he occasionally found admirers on his doorstep at Monk's House.[13]

Each volume of Leonard's autobiography dealt in some respect with Bloomsbury, and this became the principal appeal of the books, especially in the later 1960s. *Sowing* offered a chapter on Cambridge, in which he described the Group's beginnings—his version of a story that had been variously told by Clive Bell, Desmond MacCarthy, and Maynard Keynes, as well as by several historians. The book sold well in America, where reviewers found it "expectedly intellectual rather than personal." At least one English reviewer complained that, on the contrary, Woolf had abdicated thought for feeling.

The great divide in English and American evaluations of Bloomsbury dates from about this time. American critics had heard little of the Group since the death of Virginia Woolf. They had never felt diminished by Bloomsbury's power and influence in the world of arts and letters—why should they?—and they were insulated enough from the problems of a rigid class system to look mildly, even nostalgically, on Edwardian social privilege. Predictably, English reviewers were more severe, trotting out the old jibes against Bloomsbury as if answering a drill in cultural commonplaces. The *Times Literary Supplement* review, titled "Ethos of an Elite," devoted hundreds of words

---

13. It must be said that even before the publication of his autobiography, Leonard had begun to attract fans from around the world by virtue of his relationship to Virginia and his reputation as a standard-bearer for liberal causes. Frederic Spotts tells the story of Evangeline L., who sent Leonard more than five hundred letters. Determined that he should have a plant from her garden, she "flew with it on her lap from California to London, took a taxi to Rodmell, deposited the gift on the doorstep of Monk's House and immediately returned home without having seen LW, who was working in his garden" (*Letters of Leonard Woolf*, 506).

to defending Desmond MacCarthy from his chilly Bloomsbury co-horts. Frank Kermode's review in the *Spectator* defined Bloomsbury as "an expensive experiment in civility." Alan Pryce-Jones was equally unmoved. Years before, he had published an evenhanded essay called "The Frightening Pundits of Bloomsbury," in which he described the alertness and conversational range of Lytton Strachey and Raymond Mortimer, seen through the eyes of an impressionable young dinner guest in the 1920s. Leonard Woolf, as he appeared in *Sowing,* seemed far less charming: "a very cold fish," in fact. "He knew himself to be extremely clever," complained Pryce-Jones, "and he mentions this burden very frequently."

Each of these remarks, strange to say, appeared in reviews that were otherwise favourable, and by the following year, when *Growing* (covering Leonard's seven years in Ceylon) was published, it had clearly fallen out of fashion to disparage this particular manifestation of Bloomsbury. *Beginning Again* (1964) and *Downhill All the Way* (1967) contain the fullest accounts of the Group and of Leonard's marriage to a woman of genius. Both volumes were generously received, even in England. And the final volume, *The Journey Not the Arrival Matters,* published soon after Leonard's death in 1969, provoked an embarrassment of praise from everyone except a single, sour *Times Literary Supplement* reviewer, who was shouted down. "It is almost as readable as one's first love letter," gushed the critic for the *Christian Science Monitor,*

> and considerably more incisive. . . . It begins in the bow wave of onrushing world disaster, rides like flotsam into private tragedy, and finds harbor in the shadow of an endless silence. There is not a dull line in the book.

By a freakish reversal—or is it a law of cultural economy?—Virginia Woolf's *Collected Essays*, issued in four volumes by the Hogarth Press in 1967, shot from reviewers' mouths like bad milk.

Sales of Virginia's novels had benefited, nevertheless, from fresh attention to Bloomsbury. In 1963 and again in 1964, combined American and English sales for *To the Lighthouse* topped 23,000—not bad for a book first published in 1927. The vogue for *Orlando* was still years away, and it sold only a few hundred copies in England each year and was out of print in America. *Mrs. Dalloway*, however, sold 8,000 copies in 1963 and over 10,000 in 1964. And there was more to come. By 1966, over 50,000 copies of *To the Lighthouse* were selling annually. As it is for the revival of the Bloomsbury artists, 1964 is the pivotal year for Woolf studies. By that year there was enough secondary material emerging on Virginia Woolf for one critic to publish a survey entitled "L'Univers Woolfien."

Important new scholarship included Jean Guiguet's comprehensive study *Virginia Woolf and Her Works* (1963), published in England by the Hogarth Press in 1965 and still well respected; it is also memorable for a cantankerous dismissal of virtually all previous Woolf scholarship. Ralph Freedman's *The Lyrical Novel: Studies in Hermann Hesse, Andre Gide, and Virginia Woolf* (1963) was the first attempt to place Woolf in the European tradition. Monographs by A. D. Moody and Dorothy Brewster appeared in England in 1963. Publishers felt there was room even for reprints of studies originally published in the 1940s: David Daiches's somewhat deflating *Virginia Woolf* and Joan Bennett's *Virginia Woolf: Her Art as a Novelist*. Even Winifred Holtby's 1932 *Virginia Woolf*, the first book-length monograph on her life and work, was exhumed, although much of what it had to offer had been superseded, contradicted, or made impossibly tame by postwar critics.[14]

The standard bibliography of Bloomsbury studies, *Writings About the Bloomsbury Group* (1989), lists six entries for 1960, seventeen for 1961, sixteen each for 1962 and 1963, and a leap to thirty-five entries for 1964. Not all of these articles and books were pro-Bloomsbury or pro-Woolf, but the figures indicate that the subject was heating up. American universities with progressive English departments were beginning to offer seminars in Virginia Woolf. J. J. Wilson, later one of the founders of the *Virginia Woolf Miscellany*, taught the first course on Woolf at Smith College, Massachusetts in 1966 and said, "it was like putting a match to dry tinder."

Historians of Bloomsbury account for this shift in taste by pointing to the social upheavals of the 1960s, and it is reasonable, though a little dull, to do so. Less obvious influences were also at play. Imagine, for instance, your name in lights on Piccadilly and Broadway, and surfacing in conversation everywhere, buoyed by exhilarating adjectives, ever more suggestive and subtle: *your name* floating on a sea of talk. Now imagine Elizabeth Taylor repeating the precious syllables in a major motion picture and improvising a drunken ditty around them. Good for business?

Not only does it make no difference that Edward Albee's play *Who's Afraid of Virginia Woolf?* (produced in New York in 1962, and two years later in London) bears only the faintest allusive relation to Bloomsbury or Virginia Woolf, but it may actually have helped. Far fewer people would have seen the play or the 1966 movie if they thought it recounted the life of a mild-mannered English writer and

---

14. Its less promising French analogue, Floris Delattre's *Le Roman Psychologique de Virginia Woolf* (1932), was reprinted in an English translation in 1995.

her friends.[15] Instead, her name was plastered across newspapers and marquees, a weirdly detached signifier that, for vast numbers of Americans and many English people, set off no clamour of resistance in the mind, no associations apart from those of a hit play and an extended on-screen shouting match between Richard Burton and Elizabeth Taylor. People found the name lodged in their memories, ready to be teased into consciousness the next time they flipped through a college course schedule or passed a bookshop window. The title of Albee's play is certainly the first time readers of my generation encountered the name Virginia Woolf.

GIVEN THE CURRENT glut of personal detail on Woolf, it may be hard to imagine that, as recently as the summer of 1972, an admirer of her novels could complain that she was the least discussed of the "great English women writers": "Why had so much been written about her work and so little about Virginia Woolf herself?"[16] The Leonard Woolf autobiographies provided invaluable descriptions of Virginia's work habits, for instance, and other facets of their shared life, but offered little insight into her early years and barely ap-

---

15. Albee had asked Leonard's permission to use Virginia's name and had sent a copy of the play prior to its staging. In January 1965, Leonard and his friend Peggy Ashcroft saw a London production of *Who's Afraid of Virginia Woolf?* and "enjoyed it immensely. It is so amusing and at the same time moving and is really about the important things in life" (Leonard Woolf to Edward Albee in *Letters of Leonard Woolf*, 536).

    Many years later, Albee revealed he had lifted his title from the blackboard of a gay bar in Greenwich Village. Brenda Silver has argued that the reception of Albee's play "is crucial to the construction of Woolf's image." For critics' attempts to link the play with Virginia Woolf and Bloomsbury via the narrow bridge of homosexuality, see Silver's "What's Woolf Got to Do with It? Or, The Perils of Popularity," *Modern Fiction Studies*, Spring 1992.

16. Joan Russell Noble, *Recollections of Virginia Woolf* (New York: William Morrow, 1972).

proached the sources of her art. To confuse matters, memoirs from fringe Bloomsberries such as Gerald Brenan, David Garnett, and the publisher John Lehmann continued to surface, each displaying a small, sometimes eccentric piece of an unseen whole, and only whetting the appetite for more. It seemed astonishing that thirty years after her death, a major biography of Virginia Woolf had not appeared, and that the materials for such a book were so closely guarded. James Joyce had also died in 1941, but by 1959 his readers had the benefit of Richard Ellmann's masterful biography.

Leonard wrote to his nephew Quentin Bell, a professor of fine art, in November 1964:

> A surprising and ramshackle number of people approach me from time to time asking me to authorize them to write a life of Virginia which means that I should give them access to the diaries and letters. I usually have to give them lunch and politely say no. Among recent applicants have been Leon Edel, the Countess of Huntingdon, and Miss Joanna Richardson. I say no because I have so far myself felt that the time has not yet come for a life, that the aura of Bloomsbury or rather the fog which surrounds it has not yet sufficiently dissipated. . . . I think that far and away the best person to do it, if it is to be done, would be you. What would you feel about this?[17]

What Quentin Bell felt, when he assessed the prospects of undertaking his aunt's biography, was uneasiness verging on horror. He was no literary critic. And wouldn't reviewers, who had been calling Bloomsbury a mutual admiration society for some forty years, make painfully

---

17. *Letters of Leonard Woolf*, 534–35.

short work of a biography by a family member? "A filial tribute," he later wrote, "is, of all literary forms, the most difficult and the most perilous—censure is out of place and praise is discounted; impersonality is absurd and intimacy is embarrassing." He turned down the offer. "But can you bear the idea of someone else writing it?" pressed Leonard. "I must have said No," Quentin recalled, "because I found myself writing it. I have read a good deal written about my friends and it grates terribly. Whether it's hostile or friendly, you think, No—you're getting it wrong."[18] And so, after writing a short book on Bloomsbury, Quentin Bell turned his full attention to *Virginia Woolf: A Biography*, an endeavour he once called "the only big success" in his life.

EVEN THE UNWORLDLY Leonard managed to enjoy his late celebrity, and the success he had made of Virginia. An American admirer who sought Leonard out, uninvited, at Monk's House one summer day, has left a convincing picture of the octogenarian in his prime:

> We knocked at the gate. Waited, admired the old place with its profusion of flowers, trees, vines and shrubs, its winningly irregular air of having "just growed." . . . No response. Knocked again, entered cautiously. "Hallo! Is anyone there?"

A barking spaniel rushed at the intruders, then only nuzzled their hands and rolled over to be petted.

> Then around the corner came a slender old man in flannels, blue shirt, vest, heavy shoes, gardening gloves, trowel. White

---

18. From "Dear Quentin: Janet Watts Interviews Mr. Bell of Bloomsbury," *Arts Guardian* 14 June 1972.

hair like a brush and faded bleak eyes—no glasses—peering from a long, thin, tough, aristocratic, unself-pitying old face.

Leonard threw a wintry gaze on the visitors, endured their explanations and apologies, then, "not surprised, not put out," asked if they'd care to see his garden.[19]

In 1967 Leonard gave a two-part television interview with Malcolm Muggeridge and shocked both interviewer and audience by answering that no, he did not expect to meet Virginia in heaven; he still maintained a "strong disbelief" in immortality. About sixty viewers wrote to him in protest and he fastidiously answered each letter, no matter how rude or witless. In his final years, Leonard's letters and diaries show not so much a transfer of his efforts from his dead wife to himself as a subtle shift in emphasis. He wrote four to six hundred words of his autobiography each morning, finishing the last volume shortly before his death. While he continued to defend Virginia and Bloomsbury from hostile critics, and to assist scholars of her work, one can sense Leonard's relief as he handed on to Quentin Bell and others the torch he had so capably kept lit.

UNLIKE LEONARD, WHO was in a position to keep his wife's novels in print while few readers were buying them, the Bloomsbury artists desperately needed the cooperation of others—gallery support, good sales, reviews—if they hoped to continue exhibiting after the Second

---

19. Stanley Poss, "To the Woolf House," *The Nation* 6 Feb. 1967.

World War. While there had been a less violent reaction against their work than against, say, Virginia Woolf's or Lytton Strachey's, this also meant that the critical neglect they had fallen into, although precipitated by the usual shifts in fashion, seemed more profound and intractable, like the delayed enforcement of a natural law. Evidently the art world had made up its mind. There would be no reversal of fortune. Beauty was fast asleep.

Enter The Prince. Ask English art historians who rescued the Bloomsbury painters from near oblivion, and nine out of ten will point to Anthony d'Offay, a London art dealer who began to represent Duncan Grant, along with the estate of Vanessa Bell, in about 1969. Assisted by, and in turn assisting, a renewed interest in British modernist art, d'Offay exhibited Duncan and Vanessa's finest work (very often their early, little-known Postimpressionist paintings), securing numerous sales to the Tate Gallery and other important collections, arranging exhibitions in New York, educating critics, getting Duncan's paintings onto magazine covers, and in general supplying these artists with badly needed hype. By the mid-1980s, no curator would consider mounting a survey of twentieth-century English art without a nod to Bloomsbury, and in 1995, in posthumous defiance of their detractors, the Bloomsbury artists secured a precious wall, for months on end, in Room 14 of the Tate Gallery. In the bid for immortality, wall space at the Tate ranks just below being chronicled by Vasari.

Over the years since d'Offay took on the Bloomsbury painters, this version of the ascent-in-glory has muscled out competing legends, and understandably so. One man's ambition is so much sexier than a bland list of contributing factors. But d'Offay comes into the picture rather late—at the end, in fact, of a crucial decade in the fortunes of the Bloomsbury artists. The challenge then is to trace the romance of the lesser princes, that handful of young men (and a few women) who, in the mid-1960s, laid the groundwork for the revival, and made d'Offay's achievements possible.

WHAT EVERYONE AGREES on is that Duncan and Vanessa badly needed rescue. Their reputations had been sagging since the mid-1930s, and the war years, spent at Charleston, further isolated them from new movements. Decorative commissions dried up. There was talk of reviving the Omega, especially after a 1946 exhibition of Omega goods at Miller's Gallery in Lewes, but nothing came of it. Demand for Vanessa's paintings, in particular, plummeted and she had no solo exhibition between 1941 and 1956. Rumour has it that in the 1950s, at one of the major London auction houses, when experts were unable to attribute a run-of-the-mill, premodern Dutch painting, they jokingly catalogued it as a "van Esserbel." Those in the trade would immediately realize that the canvas was not only unattributed but as undistinctive as the work of that tiresome Bloomsbury painter Vanessa Bell, whose pictures so often passed through the same rooms.

These attitudes lingered well into the 1960s, perpetuated by historians and writers who knew little about the Omega Workshops or other Bloomsbury experiments before the First World War.[20] Richard Morphet, later a curator at the Tate Gallery, recalls applying for a position in the British Council Fine Arts Department in 1963, where he was interviewed by Lilian Somerville, the legendary advocate of advanced British art, of Henry Moore and Barbara Hepworth. "Do you collect art yourself?" she asked. "Yes," Morphet replied, "I've bought

---

20. The few early works that were widely known, such as Duncan Grant's *Queen of Sheba* (1912) and *Lemon Gatherers* (1910), both in the collections of the Tate Gallery by 1922, did not represent the most radical Bloomsbury experiments.

a Vanessa Bell." At this point, he later learned, Somerville crossed out his name on the list of candidates. When he added that he'd also bought a work by a young pop-associated artist, she erased her first mark, and he was eventually hired.

Educated at the Slade School of Art in the mid-1920s, Somerville was of a generation trained to dismiss Bloomsbury as the terminal blossom of a dying leisured class. It is hard to distinguish this bias from serious critical disaffection for the bulk of Vanessa's painting after the 1930s. Both still cloud her reputation. The late work is, in fact, a thorny issue among friends of Bloomsbury, like the late work of de Kooning, although there is nothing so definite as a diagnosis of Alzheimer's to divide Vanessa's audacious early work from the increasingly tentative and subdued efforts of her later years, the sort of painting that an ungenerous critic dubbed "Churchillian Impressionism."

At least one critic whom Vanessa trusted, her friend Sir Kenneth Clark, suggested that her paintings of the mid-1930s were beginning to show "some of the adverse effects of middle age."[21] The work had not atrophied, but it had evolved in ways that lessened its visual impact: Vanessa had toned down her palette, reined in her subject matter, and taken to a high degree of finish. And, except on trips abroad, she rarely looked outside her studio for inspiration. After about the 1920s, Vanessa showed little appreciation for new art or its advocates, lashing herself to the mast of Postimpressionism—or, more precisely, to her cautious later interpretation of the creed. When, for instance, the 1936 International Surrealist Exhibition caused a furore in the London art world, Vanessa grasped at once its similarity in impact to the Postimpressionist shows. But she could not be troubled to enlarge her

---

21. Quoted in Frances Spalding's *Vanessa Bell* (New York: Ticknor & Fields, 1983), 340.

sympathies, telling Julian that although she hadn't been to the show, it sounded as though the surrealists were going back to "Victorian ideas of subject and its importance." Duncan, always open to new art, did attend the private viewing, and he had an appropriately surreal experience. He found a ten-shilling note on the ground, which he tried to attach to a sculpture, to "add meaning" to it. As Vanessa recounted,

> Unfortunately someone—perhaps the owner, perhaps not— came up and pocketed it. Then as he was going out Paul Nash came up and gave him a herring, which he asked him to put outside, as he said some Philistine had attached it to a picture, but Duncan refused.[22]

Local opposition to Duncan and Vanessa's last major joint commission, the murals for the twelfth-century parish church at Berwick (completed in 1943), must have sounded familiar, almost heartwarming, to artists who had braved the public outcry over Postimpressionism. Villagers, led by a Mrs. Sandilands, complained that the colours were garish and Duncan's Christ figure too sumptuously nude.[23] Quentin, who had used Leonard as a model for Christ in *The Supper at Emmaus*, was chided for making "Our Lord" look like a middle-aged Jew. These rear-guard remarks may have obscured what would have been a fruitful inquiry for Vanessa in these years: had her painting lost its edge?

We know that none of the postwar figurative movements, with

---

22. Ibid., 414.

23. Response to these murals continues to waver; see, e.g., *The Knopf Travelers Guide to Art: Britain and Ireland* (1984): "It is difficult now to share the enthusiasm which these dull and amateurish works inspired when first unveiled."

their varied but inescapable emphases on subject matter, appealed to her. This only raises another question. Why did Vanessa, who once described herself as "certainly an impressionist," cling so religiously to the early Postimpressionist disregard for subject matter? A figurative painter refusing to explore her subject matter seems a little like a jockey maintaining that his horse is irrelevant.

Recognizing that the doctrine of significant form pointed toward pure abstraction, Quentin Bell once asked Vanessa why she had abandoned abstract painting so early. She told him that she preferred compositions found in real life to anything she could invent. In fact, her usual choices of subject matter—flowers from her garden, portraits of friends, local landscapes—were not only close at hand but often deeply personal. While she favoured nursery themes and domestic tableaux for her larger paintings, she resolutely avoided delving into their possible meanings for herself or her audience. All her working life, she deprecated what she called "literary" or dramatic content in art, preoccupying herself instead with formal qualities.[24] This put her in a unique position to appreciate her sister's writing, and she instinctively recognized what Virginia was trying to achieve in *The Waves*, her most innovative novel. "How can one explain," Vanessa wrote from Cassis after finishing the book, "but to me painting a floor covered with toys and keeping them all in relation to each other and the figures and the space of the floor and the light on it means something of the same sort that you seem to me to mean." It was a tenuous balance: subjects that resonated with the artist's life but were meant to convey only pure aesthetic emotion. This high aim called for de-

---

24. Perhaps because her paintings leave so many questions unanswered, they lend themselves beautifully to the sort of biographical and symbolic interpretations Vanessa detested. See for instance Spalding's *Vanessa Bell* and the section "Vanessa's Art" in Mary Ann Caws's *Women of Bloomsbury* (New York: Routledge, 1990).

tachment amounting to a mental discipline. She tried to explain her purpose to Julian:

> There is a language simply of form and colour that can be as moving as any other and that seems to affect one quite as much as the greatest poetry of words. At least so it seems to me but I admit that it is very difficult to be sure for of course the form and colour nearly always do represent life and I suppose any allusions may creep in.[25]

In her later years, Vanessa rarely cast around long for subjects, content to pay her grandchildren to sit, or to arrange a few dahlias against a piece of patterned silk and a window frame. The more simple and automatic her choices, however, the more she unconsciously allowed personal allusions to "creep in." Richard Shone, a friend of Duncan Grant's who became one of his and Vanessa's most insightful critics, describes Vanessa's late painting as a "slow-burning reflection of her immediate world":

> Her touch became soft and hesitant; a tendency to idealise her sitters—invariably her family—led to a sentimentality of interpretation that comes as a surprise from the ironic and amused painter of *Iris Tree* or *Mary Hutchinson*.[26]

Vanessa may have believed that her painting gave primacy to colour, pattern, line, composition—in short, to the formal elements celebrated by the proponents of significant form—while in fact she

---

25. Quoted in Spalding, *Vanessa Bell*, 312.

26. Richard Shone, *Bloomsbury Portraits* (London: Phaidon Press, 1995), 244–45.

was building an oeuvre that was relentlessly domestic, privately symbolic, and emotionally charged. She would have recoiled from this description of her work, but anyone looking now at Vanessa's warm, almost caressing portraits of her Garnett granddaughters (incidentally, among the works least accessible to others in their intensity of private affection) or the mother-and-child images that preoccupied her middle years cannot help but register their emotional tenor.

This contradiction may help explain why, although figurative art experienced a mild renaissance in England after the war, Vanessa could not benefit from the new movements,[27] and also, more pertinently, why there is scant critical interest in her late work, with the exception of a few austere self-portraits. Her 1956 show at the Adams Gallery sold well but seems to have attracted not a single review. Some of her postwar paintings were in fact badly received, such as *The Garden Room*, submitted by invitation to *60 Paintings for '51*, an Arts Council exhibition timed to coincide with the 1951 Festival of Britain. Bursting with economic optimism, or hoping to appear so, organizers had stipulated that artists work on as large a scale as possible. The show was panned, including Vanessa and Duncan's contributions, marked down by Colin Anderson, who had helped select work for the show, as "pathetic." They ended up in the Charleston attic.

In 1960, Vanessa's friend Edward le Bas persuaded the Adams Gallery to give her another show. Vanessa died before negotiations could be completed, and the show, opening in October 1961, became a memorial exhibition. I can find only one sixty-five-word notice of

---

27. Tellingly, one of the few young artists who impressed Vanessa was Nicholas de Staël, whose later work was devoted to achieving a synthesis between abstraction and figuration.

this event. "Her champion was Roger Fry," the *Arts* critic wrote, "which is exactly right":

> she was the Bloomsbury painter *par excellence* and never fails to be both intelligent and decorous. In a few paintings, *Monte Oliveto: Siena, Snow at Charleston* and a self-portrait painted in 1958, she is something more.

Tepid praise, perhaps, but in keeping with the responses her paintings earned throughout the 1960s.

DESPITE HER CONTINUED pleasure in her work ("To see her in later life, brush in hand," her daughter wrote, "was to see her happy") and the rewards of her life with Duncan, Vanessa's late years can be a source of paralysing pathos for historians of Bloomsbury. Duncan's situation after the war was more promising, for while his paintings were not in demand, he was usually able to keep a few of them in the stacks at Agnew's or the Leicester Galleries, coasting on the memory of his impressive prewar sales. When he did show a more substantial body of work, he could count on a polite, if subdued, response. A 1957 solo exhibition at the Leicester Galleries managed to earn over fifteen hundred pounds in sales without exciting critical interest. Similarly, little notice was taken of Duncan's last major decorative commission, his large, lively panels for the Russell Chantry in Lincoln Cathedral (executed 1955–59). This was a shame, since *The Wool Staple in Medieval England* and *The Good Shepherd Ministers to His Flock* have the buoyant, slightly fantastic quality of some of Duncan's best decorative painting. The clerics seem not to have had their eyes on his whimsical bags of wool, however. Art critic Simon Watney suggests that Duncan's brawny and tantalizing male figures, another feature of his finest work, may have led to the closure of the Chantry in the 1960s and its conversion to a storeroom.[28]

Vanessa Bell was a member of the committee that awarded the Russell Chantry commission to Duncan from a pool of fifty-five applicants. Where he had fewer friends, his luck was less certain. Even his 1959 retrospective at the Tate Gallery, ostensibly the pinnacle of an outstanding career, garnered only a handful of brief, mixed reviews. The *Times* review was actually titled "Artist Who Belongs to a Period Now in Disfavour." "No one falls from favour like a favorite," the critic remarked; "that this, after a decade or more of compromising adulation, has been Mr. Grant's fate was plainly enough demonstrated by the sparse attendance at yesterday's preview."[29] Raymond Mortimer, usually a champion of Duncan's, also found the show "untimely and ill-hung," which is more or less what Vanessa concluded. She blamed John Rothenstein, the Tate director, who had recently published his damning critique of Bloomsbury in volume one of *Modern English Painters* (1956). Evidently, the time was not ripe for a reappraisal of Duncan's talents.

It was only slightly more ripe five years later, when *Duncan Grant and His World* opened at the Wildenstein Gallery in London. Organized by Denys Sutton, who would later edit Roger Fry's letters, this carefully selected exhibition of over one hundred paintings is often considered the turning point in the revival of Duncan's reputation. But reviews at the time were less than ecstatic. Keith Roberts, the *Burlington* critic, was typical in denigrating Grant's

---

28. The Chantry has recently been renovated and is once more open to the public.

29. There is some question whether this assessment of the crowd is accurate. See Frances Spalding's 1997 biography of Duncan Grant.

later paintings: "Like his friend and contemporary Vanessa Bell, he reverted, after a bold flirtation with fauve principles, to a slack, rather cosy form of Impressionism." More significant, perhaps, than whether critics gave Duncan Grant his due is the fact that the Wildenstein show was the first to place Duncan's work within the context of Bloomsbury. Many portraits of Bloomsbury figures were included, and the catalogue introduction, also by Sutton, explored Duncan's connection with the Group. Playing up the link with Bloomsbury may have drawn attention from the paintings them-selves—a state of affairs that still irks Duncan Grant scholars—but it also provided possibly resistant viewers with an avenue for appre-ciating distinctly unfashionable work.

Rancour against Bloomsbury seemed to be fading among the younger art audience, replaced by a vague historical or biographical interest that cannot have much hurt an artist of Duncan's stature (Somerset Maugham's self-appraisal comes to mind: "the very first row of the second rank"). Since the vogue for Bloomsbury and the re-action against that vogue were still years away, Duncan was not yet trapped in the catch-22 that would bedevil his reputation in the 1970s and 1980s.

The lasting significance of the Wildenstein show is that it marks this shift in critical and public interest from aesthetic and art-histori-cal concerns to an increasingly personal focus. While critics of the 1940s or 1950s, looking for instance at Duncan Grant's *Tents* (1913), might have asked only whether the composition worked, or if the crisply delineated tents clashed with the cubistic splendour of the sur-rounding woodland, or might have merely dismissed the work as de-rivative of Cézanne or Picasso, they now told the story of Brandon camp, where the image was painted, and tried to determine whether Vanessa also painted this scene, and what comment Rupert Brooke tossed over his well-shaped shoulder as he skirted Duncan's easel. This process occurs to some extent with all artists worth studying, but especially so with the Bloomsbury artists, whose popular standing, for good or ill, now rests on their association with Roger Fry in those heady prewar years, and with the Bloomsbury Group as a whole.

The 1964 Wildenstein show may also seem momentous, in retrospect, because it closely followed both the Victoria and Albert Museum's fiftieth-anniversary exhibition commemorating the founding of the Omega Workshops (1963) and a second Vanessa Bell memorial exhibition, curated by Ronald Pickvance for the Arts Council in 1964. Like the writer Nevile Wallis, who published four Bloomsbury-related articles in 1964 and seems to have reached his lifetime limit, Pickvance displayed a fleeting but pivotal advocacy for the Bloomsbury artists. His catalogue introduction for Vanessa's memorial exhibition was uncommonly appreciative, concentrating on her work rather than her milieu and bemoaning art historians' "incomplete view of her achievement." His references to the much-maligned Bloomsbury Group went no further than suggesting that art historians who had been "slumming in Camden Town" for the past decade ought also to be "burrowing in Bloomsbury." Later that year he published a glowing full-page review of the Wildenstein show, openly drawing on his esteem for Duncan: "As a person he retains a remarkable physical vitality, a puckish humour and a rare unaffected charm, and these qualities inform the best of his work."

Keith Roberts, of the *Burlington*, was having none of it. Vanessa's memorial exhibition opened in London on 29 February 1964 and travelled to several English cities before closing in Brighton. "It was obviously a good *idea* to devote an exhibition to Mrs Bell," wrote Roberts, although he thought the Arts Council show suffered "from a severe case of over-exposure. But given Mrs Bell's talents, I do not see how it could have been otherwise." Roberts developed this theme for five long paragraphs, relieving his tedium with the occasional sharp jab. To give him credit, he did try to account for his aversion to Vanessa's work, recalling that Virginia Woolf once described Vanessa's pictures as reticent: "as silent as the grave."

> But this reticence [Roberts countered] is not positive as with Velasquez, or, more relevantly, as with Gwen John. It is a sapping, anaemic deficiency. It also throws a harsh emphasis on her technique.

"Of her later landscapes," he concluded, "it would be unkind to speak in any detail."

To speak at all, however, of Roger Fry's paintings seemed beyond the pale. He was the most neglected of the Bloomsbury artists in the three decades following his death in 1934. His theories were discussed, often combatively, and his influence taken for granted, thanks in part to the irresistibly quotable tribute from Sir Kenneth Clark that "in so far as taste can be changed by one man, it was changed by Roger Fry," but his canvases had begun to moulder in the cellars of municipal art galleries. There was something odd about his paintings, something dry and deliberate, that made them hard for English people to appreciate until about the 1980s. Even a fellow artist, his second cousin Anthony Fry, has stressed Roger's failure as a painter: "I hated his paintings. We in the family thought they were ghastly."[30] When Frances Spalding, researching her doctoral dissertation in the mid-1970s, sought out Roger's work in private collections, she found one

---

30. Quoted in Alan MacWeeney and Sue Allison's *Bloomsbury Reflections* (New York: Norton, 1990), unpaginated.

painting, his portrait of H. G. Wells's mistress, Baroness Budberg, that seemed especially battered and grimy. When questioned, the sitter's daughter confessed that her family had used it as a fire screen.

A small 1952 Arts Council show of Roger's paintings had failed to disturb the settling dust. Except for *Vision and Design*, his books were hard to come by, and Virginia Woolf's 1940 biography of him was unobtainable. In 1958, however, his sister Margery Fry boosted the Bloomsbury revival by bequeathing Roger's art collection to the Courtauld Institute, which became, for the next thirty years, the only place in England where one could see and study a permanent display of Bloomsbury art. And five years later Roger finally picked up an influential advocate in Quentin Bell, who presented an inaugural lecture on him at the University of Leeds. Quentin also took up the gauntlet with regard to Wyndham Lewis and his notorious break from the Omega Workshops in 1913—an event much recounted by art historians, but from Lewis's point of view. A recent scholarly edition of the letters of The Enemy (as Lewis styled himself) had raked open the wound, and Quentin, already impatient with John Rothenstein's unquestioning pro-Lewis stance in his widely read *Modern English Painters* (1956–58), decided to set down the facts as he understood them. The resulting article, "The Ideal Home Rumpus," co-written with Stephen Chaplin, sparked a fierce, lengthy debate in *Apollo*. The editor of the journal, Denys Sutton, seemed unusually open-minded toward Roger Fry, devoting an editorial to him, in part a response to Quentin's lecture at Leeds, in the same issue in which "The Ideal Home Rumpus" appeared (October 1964). In any case, Sutton emerged in the mid-1960s as a powerful spur to the revival of Roger's reputation and that of Bloomsbury in general, writing and commissioning many Bloomsbury-related articles and reviews; contributing to exhibition catalogues; promoting Roger's 1966 Arts Council show, *Vision and Design*, with a two-page colour spread in *Apollo;* and eventually editing Roger's letters in two volumes (1972). Under Sutton's lead, *Apollo* became noticeably pro-Bloomsbury, in opposition to the *Burlington,* a journal that had once, ironically, been edited by Roger Fry.[31] (He had been crucially involved in its founding.) There were other London art magazines in the 1960s, but they included only occasional, lacklustre reference to Bloomsbury. The real debate took place between the *Burlington* and *Apollo*.

Vision and Design: The Life, Work and Influence of Roger Fry was a large travelling exhibition organized by the Arts Council and the University of Nottingham. The original plan had been to devote the exhibition to the Bloomsbury Group as a whole, but someone noticed the upcoming centenary of Roger Fry's birth and the focus quickly narrowed. Perhaps for this reason, *Vision and Design* gave a reasonably good impression of Roger's family background and connection with Bloomsbury, as well as of his influences (whether accepted or fought against), but fell short of conveying his importance as the champion of Postimpressionism and the bête noire, at least briefly, of an entrenched and hostile London art world. "And I am not sure," commented the *Burlington* critic, "that Fry's cause is served by displaying quite so many of his own paintings." Nevertheless, *Vision and Design* carried the Bloomsbury banner into the provinces and stirred discussion all that summer.

VANESSA HAD ALWAYS shied from comparisons between her art and Duncan's. Not only did she worry about succumbing to "the usual female fate" of not being taken seriously in the presence of mas-

---

31. Another important advocate of Roger's work was his daughter Pamela Diamand, who tried to organize an Omega exhibition in Paris in 1960 and who eventually left a number of Roger's paintings to the Tate Gallery.

culine talent or, even worse, of being considered a follower of Duncan's, but she deeply admired his abilities. In later years she cast a misty veil of longing over almost everything he painted while subjecting her own work to an acid critique. In this light it is hard to imagine that she would have approved of the implicitly comparative focus of the exhibitions that formed an overture, in the mid-1960s, to the revival of both artists' reputations.

The 1966 show *The Paintings of Duncan Grant and Vanessa Bell* at the Royal West of England Academy, Bristol, opened in April, at the same time as *Vision and Design*, and honoured not only the artists' long collaboration but also their connection to the RWEA, where they had begun sending work for annual exhibitions in 1952. The academy had purchased several of Duncan's and Vanessa's paintings over the years, providing a basis for the show. Angelica Garnett lent many more works by Vanessa. Altogether over one hundred paintings were included, some not publicly exhibited before. Shows like this cannot often be repeated, and one wishes it had been staged two or three years later, when it might have attracted London critics and a larger audience.

In the catalogue introduction for the RWEA show, Denys Sutton argued that it was the Roger Fry show, *Vision and Design*, that was stimulating interest in "the cultural background in England during the early years of this century." But Sutton was also reflecting a general sense of excitement in the rediscovery of British modernism, which unfolded, in part, from the phenomenal international success of British pop art in the early to mid-1960s. It was becoming possible to see the British avant-garde of the early twentieth century on their own terms, and not only in deflating comparison to the European greats.

Among the art dealers turning their attention to neglected British modernists was Julian Hartnoll, in those days a close colleague of Anthony d'Offay's. Hartnoll's interest in the Bloomsbury Group had been sparked by the novels of David Garnett, and Richard Morphet introduced him to Angelica Garnett. Although the origins of Hartnoll's November 1967 show, *Vanessa Bell: Drawings and Designs*,[32] at Folio Fine Art are now vague, he well remembers driving down to Charleston with Angelica in a battered Mini Traveller to select works for the show. He found her "a person of formidable intellect,"

> and whether it was the nervousness this created in me, or the mode of transport, I was very ill by the time I arrived at Charleston! But Duncan Grant was such a warm and reassuring person that, after a beautiful lunch, my nerves were restored.

Hartnoll then went through large piles of unsigned drawings, applying a small studio stamp (with the initials "VB") under the direction of Duncan Grant. In a number of instances Hartnoll thought he'd uncovered drawings that were clearly related to Duncan's work and must have been by him, but Duncan would decline them: "Oh, that is far too good for me, give it to Vanessa."

Another 1967 exhibition, *Artists of Bloomsbury*, at the Rye Art Gallery, Sussex, was the first show to present these artists collectively and to suggest their social milieu as a defining factor in their art. This attitude evolved from Duncan's 1964 Wildenstein show, the Art Council show *Vision and Design*, and the RWEA exhibition of Dun-

---

32. The catalogue for this show, with its brief introduction by Richard Morphet, very usefully includes prices, ranging from £125 (in today's terms about £970, or $1,500) for small paintings from Vanessa's most experimental period, c. 1913–14, to £14 (now £108, or $170) for a Christmas card design.

can's and Vanessa's paintings, and was fast becoming the customary way to think of the Bloomsbury artists. Most telling is the organizers' broad definition of the Group, which substantially increased the number of Bloomsbury artists. Some of Quentin Bell's "goggle-boxes" (named by his daughter Virginia) were included, for instance, as well as works by Barbara Bagenal, who lived in Rye and may have helped plan the exhibition. In all, 101 pieces were shown. One small show for Rye, one giant leap for the Bloomsbury industry.

Hermione Lee, in her 1977 study of Virginia Woolf's novels, described how the English domesticate their rebels, plunging into their lives—which, after all, resemble mainstream lives in many ways—as a means of blunting individuality and explaining away dangerous ideas. As early as 1951, Noel Annan lodged a protest against these methods as they applied to Maynard Keynes.

> It would be wrong to talk about him as if he were an ordinary man. He was not. And I think it a part of modern cant—a form of self-flattery to which we are too prone today—to reduce great men to our own stature by telling a string of stories about them to show that they were really "human."[33]

Although Duncan and Vanessa were not great in the way that Maynard Keynes was, with his dazzling achievements in a wide range of endeavours, they are at the same risk of being reduced to English eccentrics through an obsessive preoccupation with their milieu. In 1980, Hilton Kramer wrote a sympathetic and fair-minded review of a Vanessa Bell exhibit at the Davis and Long Gallery in New York, suggesting that although she was not a major artist, her work showed

---

33. Noel Annan, "A Man of Peerless Intellect," *The Listener* 3 May 1951.

the power to outlast the current fascination with Bloomsbury. Her early abstract paintings struck "a very original note for their time," he argued, but her graphic work was more successful, her book jacket designs for the Hogarth Press "among the loveliest works of their kind produced in this century." Four years later, however, reacting against a spate of recent books on Bloomsbury, including the Spalding biography of Vanessa Bell and Angelica Garnett's *Deceived with Kindness,* Kramer published a severely critical overview of the Bloomsbury revival in the January 1984 issue of his journal *The New Criterion,* dismissing Bell and the rest of her friends as "failed writers and artists." How did the "very gifted minor painter" of the 1980 review become the "failed artist" of this later essay? Vanessa Bell's work had not changed. What had altered was the climate of opinion surrounding Bloomsbury. The sheer bulk of popular writing on the Group aroused suspicion among critics, but it was biography in particular that did the damage. Kramer complained of the decline in critical standards since the 1960s—a decline he found chiefly responsible for Bloomsbury's rise to prominence. Warming to his theme, he declared that this revival was based on biography, rather than criticism, because the Bloomsberries' shocking, muddled lives or "life-style" were all they had to offer to succeeding generations.

Here the "double tradition" makes itself felt. Although the Bloomsbury artists received far more disinterested critical attention in the 1970s and 1980s than Kramer acknowledged, it is true that a good part of the appeal of Bloomsbury art is associative, rather than aesthetic. This became increasingly evident during the 1980s, as the last few major paintings from the artists' estates found homes in museums and more-or-less stable private collections. Hundreds of sketches, fragments, and late paintings remain in circulation, few of which represent Duncan's or Vanessa's work at its best or most innovative. Cecily Langdale, co-owner of Davis and Langdale (once Davis and Long) Gallery, suspects that many of her customers are not looking for paintings or drawings so much as "souvenirs" of Bloomsbury. Davis and Long had shown the occasional Duncan Grant or Vanessa Bell painting in the early 1970s but began to pursue Bloomsbury art in earnest in 1975, when they organized Duncan's first show in America. "From day one," Langdale recalls, "the response was rabid."

Extra-artistic factors will always influence critical appraisals, as they influenced Hilton Kramer's. It is a question of degree. And membership in the Bloomsbury Group is a particularly potent extra-artistic factor. Duncan naturally enjoyed the renewed interest in his painting in the mid- to late 1960s and seems not to have worried that the word "Bloomsbury" was adhering to each canvas. Vanessa, had she lived, may have been more shrewd. Years before, she had discerned the dangers of the Bloomsbury connection, the consequences of being perceived as essentially "Bloomsbury" and therefore dismissed or favoured accordingly. What she could not have then known was that her private life, her unconventional domestic arrangements, would form so large a part of her posthumous mystique.

Which brings us to Duncan's admirers. There were many, but the three most significant for our purposes all met Duncan within the span of a few years in the mid-1960s: Richard Morphet, who would help redress a conspicuous gap in the Tate Gallery's holdings of Bloomsbury art; Simon Watney, who wrote insightfully on the English Postimpressionists and would later publish the first significant monograph on Duncan Grant; and Richard Shone, author of *Bloomsbury Portraits* (1976), the standard history of visual Bloomsbury.

Duncan's character always eludes our first, fumbling grasp, and it is easy to misconstrue these friendships, especially considering the age difference: Duncan was eighty years old in 1965, when Watney and

Shone were in their twenties. We picture dewy acolytes pouring his tea and keeping notebooks of his sayings. In truth, young people arriving at Charleston seem to have found themselves almost instantly comfortable with Duncan, with his perfect, easy manners and affectionate nature. He could be drawn out about the past but was just as happy eliciting stories from his young friends. We learn much about Duncan simply from these men's continuing loyalty to him and his painting, nearly twenty years after his death.

Simon Watney was an undergraduate at the University of Sussex when he met Duncan, shabbily dressed but with a rose from Charleston in his lapel, at a Brighton dinner party in 1968. He was asked back to Charleston the following week for tea and became a close friend, visiting Duncan almost weekly, often staying overnight in Clive Bell's old bedroom. He sat for a number of Duncan's later paintings. In his monograph *The Art of Duncan Grant* (1990), Watney suggested that his friendship with the older man prospered

> because I offered him some access to a social world from which he was, for a variety of reasons, somewhat cut off. It was certainly not as an undergraduate art historian that Duncan saw me, but as someone actively involved in the contemporary social life of the still swinging Sixties. He was ever eager to hear of one's amours, keen to meet one's friends and lovers, especially if they could be pressed into service as sitters.

About 1964, while still a schoolboy, Richard Shone became interested in Duncan's painting and took the intrepid step of writing to the artist. His first visit to Charleston was in 1965, and some decorative work of his survives there. In a 1986 radio broadcast on Charleston,

Shone reminisced about this first visit, recalling that once he had survived the car journey from Lewes station, with Duncan at the wheel, he entered a "house which was pure magic." Duncan suggested that he paint the younger man's portrait: "So the next morning I was sitting on a high stool at 10 o'clock being looked at by him, and felt completely at home from then onwards."[34] Although his most significant contribution to the Bloomsbury revival is his first book, *Bloomsbury Portraits*, written in part at Charleston and with Duncan's help, Shone shaped the discussion of these artists in a number of ways, beginning in the late 1960s, not least by his extensive research, which served the dual purpose of advancing knowledge and lending an aura of seriousness to exhibition catalogues at d'Offay Gallery and elsewhere, the crucial antidote to the Bloomsbury legend of frivolity. Shone also organized small shows, including a 1969 Arts Council show of Duncan's portraits that may have helped convince Anthony d'Offay to pursue the Bloomsbury artists. In recent years, he has worked as an associate editor at the *Burlington*.

Richard Morphet had also admired Bloomsbury art long before he met Duncan. In the late 1950s, while a student at the London School of Economics, he used to walk from his lodgings to 28 Percy Street, hoping for a glimpse of Duncan and Vanessa as they came or went from their upper-floor flat. "All I ever saw," he recalls, "were the sometimes lighted windows and the stairs and first-floor landing, as although I got as far as placing my finger on the bell marked 'BELL/GRANT' I never quite dared to push it."[35] Before the rush on early Bloomsbury, Morphet bought an exceptional Vanessa Bell, her

---

34. "Kaleidoscope: Charleston Revisited," a BBC Radio Four broadcast of 26 May 1987 transcribed in part in the *Charleston Newsletter* 15 (June 1986): 44.

35. Letter to the author, 6 Dec. 1995.

portrait of Iris Tree. He never met Vanessa, but he remembers his first meeting with Duncan in February 1964, at the private view for the Arts Council's Vanessa Bell memorial retrospective. Angus Davidson, knowing Morphet's fondness for Bloomsbury art, introduced the two, and Duncan at once invited the young man to Charleston.

Morphet also made a favourable impression on Angelica Garnett, who found him intelligent and sympathetic and suggested he write the catalogue introduction for Vanessa's show at Folio Fine Art. She brought his knowledge of Bloomsbury to the attention of Denys Sutton, who commissioned him to write "The Significance of Charleston," the first essay on this subject, which appeared in *Apollo* in November 1967, the same month as Vanessa's Folio show. Sensitive both to the visual exuberance of Charleston and its associations with remarkable people, Morphet saw the decorations as "distilled between painting and life, with an impassioned involvement in each."

> This house, curious and individual in its decoration and mood, expresses both a pattern of life and a visual style; it makes especially evident, in a way that a museum or book cannot, the fusion of these two characteristics into a single sensibility.

Long before anyone dreamed of rescuing the dilapidated house, which did not even belong to Duncan, Morphet offered a strong argument for the preservation of Charleston.

Soon after, in 1969, Morphet was able to help the Tate buy two important early works from Vanessa Bell's estate, her portrait of Helen Dudley (c. 1915) and *Still Life on Corner of Mantelpiece* (1914), and, from Duncan, his *Interior at Gordon Square* (c. 1915). The Tate had not bought a Duncan Grant in nearly twenty years and had never purchased a work by Vanessa Bell.[36]

In his capacity as Tate curator, Morphet found himself visiting a small London gallery in Vigo Street and admiring how the shows were simply and well presented, carefully chosen, and amply supported with information. He remembers telling the gallery owner, Anthony d'Offay, to take a closer look at Bloomsbury art, ripe for rediscovery. It was about 1967, and Morphet suspects that others were giving d'Offay the same advice.

ANTHONY D'OFFAY KEEPS an exceptionally low profile, especially given the high-profile artists he now shows—Gilbert and George, Anselm Kiefer, and Ellsworth Kelly, among the living, and Andy Warhol, among the recently dead. Even during the art crash of the early 1990s, d'Offay kept three, and then four, gallery spaces in London, staffed with seven or eight assistants, and in a rare interview explained that his gallery stayed afloat through hard times because "we operate in a wider context; in other words, we put on shows for the world. . . . We declare ourselves to be in the world, rather than in London."[37] This is not just a gorgeous example of gallery-speak; in 1993, d'Offay and his staff mounted eight exhibitions in Asia, and several recent shows have traveled to foreign museums.

An early puff by John Russell in *Art in America* described d'Offay's sharp ascent through the art world. He dealt in rare books while still at school, then came to London in the early 1960s and opened up

---

36. The Tate owned four Vanessa Bell paintings when Morphet arrived there. Two were bequests from Frank Hindley Smith and one was a gift from Sir Kenneth Clark. None of these paintings date from her pivotal Postimpressionist period, c. 1910–19.

37. "Anthony d'Offay, Gallerist," *Flash Art* 173 (Nov.-Dec. 1993): 67.

"in a fairly secretive way," although he "turned out to have things (like a page of handwritten notes by Baudelaire and a caricature drawing by Marcel Proust) that every one of his senior competitors would have jumped at." From manuscripts and drawings, d'Offay branched out into French Impressionist and Symbolist paintings, then, having spent time in Japan, took up Japanese prints. In about 1968, d'Offay developed a new specialty in early-twentieth-century English art, which led, the next year, to his ground-breaking Vorticist show, *Abstract Art in England, 1913–1915*. With a catalogue that was impressive and well researched ("if," according to the *Burlington* critic, "a shade pretentious"), this show went a good way toward rehabilitating the prewar English avant-garde, and established d'Offay as a formidable presence in the London art scene.

Sometime before this show, Lindy Guinness (now Lindy Dufferin), a close friend of Duncan's, introduced him to Anthony d'Offay. Duncan had not been properly represented by a gallery for many years. Neglected and lonely, with a Bloomsbury revival threatening on every side, he was an obvious find for the young dealer. D'Offay began to learn about Bloomsbury, and in 1969, when he moved his gallery to 9 Dering Street, he approached Angelica about becoming an agent for Duncan and Vanessa. She accepted, as Vanessa's executor, and encouraged Duncan to accept also, although his friend Paul Roche disagreed, and had already contacted another dealer, Andras Kalman. Looking back on their relationship, Angelica thought that Duncan didn't like Anthony d'Offay: "just an intuitive reaction, I think." Caroline Cuthbert, who worked with d'Offay in these years, thinks it was not dislike, exactly, but wariness on Duncan's part. He nonetheless encouraged d'Offay and his wife to come to Charleston for weekends, where they could spend their time in Clive Bell's old rooms. Whether d'Offay actually stayed in that damp, decaying house more than a night or two is doubtful, but Clarissa Roche, then Paul's wife, remembers d'Offay carrying away armfuls of Duncan's paintings, and Quentin Bell recalled that the dealer once had "a whole warehouse" full of family paintings.

Duncan had made a practice of painting every day. When away from his studio, he sketched on anything that came to hand—bills, meeting agendas, used envelopes. This mass of material proved something of a problem for his new gallery. Given its abundance, Duncan's work would fetch less than that of most of his contemporaries. Vanessa's could be priced higher, since there was less of it, but she sold better in America, where her connection with Virginia Woolf added a lustre it could not summon in London. D'Offay began by separating out the best work, according to the standards of the day: the most stylistically innovative paintings and drawings, usually the early pieces.

Richard Morphet, able to observe a similar process among his colleagues at the Tate and other institutions in this period, saw an unprecedented preoccupation with artistic innovation combining with a fixation on "the properties of art as pure form." This conjunction of interests is an important strand in the revival of Bloomsbury art and is reflected in a spate of Tate acquisitions from Anthony d'Offay and other dealers. Between 1971 and 1984, the Tate purchased nine pieces of Bloomsbury art (seven from d'Offay), all dating from the "radical" period, 1912 to 1919 or so. Tate curators who wanted to represent the most formally radical phase of Bloomsbury's art were at the same time advocating, unsurprisingly, the acquisition of early abstract work by Ben Nicholson, Henry Moore, and Barbara Hepworth and examples of the new minimalist art. Fashions change, but the Tate still owns no paintings from the last thirty years of Vanessa's life, or from the last thirty-four of Duncan's.

While the Bloomsbury artists had received considerable visibility in the mid-1960s and were poised for revival, d'Offay's involvement seems to have been the deciding factor. His credibility reassured curators and collectors who still remembered the "van Esserbel" jokes, and his instinct toward the Postimpressionist work, though it surprised and amused Duncan, paid off handsomely. D'Offay tested the waters with a small show, *Bloomsbury Painters,* in December 1970, then mounted an exhibition of Duncan's watercolours and drawings in April and May 1972 and one of Vanessa's paintings and drawings at the close of 1973.

With so much emphasis on Bloomsbury's origins, its sexual escapades, and its early radicalism, it is easy to overlook its quieter but equally remarkable endings: the productive and vigorous old age of so many Bloomsberries and their capacity, often, for disarmingly up-to-date attitudes. Even when his reputation was at its lowest, Duncan had been respected by his fellow artists: "for his integrity and sweetness," Angelica recalls, "if not for his painting." Now his presence had a quickening effect on the revival. His curiosity about new art, for example, brought him in contact with many younger people and reinforced the impression that, as Clive James put it, "these Bloomsbury people were the ur-hippies, if you can figure that." Duncan accepted his mild celebrity as others accept product samples in a shop, with good manners but not much change in his routine. In 1970 Christopher Mason, the husband of Joanna Carrington (the artist Carrington's niece), made a short colour film for British television, *Duncan Grant at Charleston,* in which Quentin Bell, shy but resigned to his task, interviews an affable and engaging Duncan Grant. Grant was then about eighty-five. Frances Spalding remembers a similar scene from a few years later, when, in the midst of her work on the Roger Fry biography, Quentin took her to Charleston for tea. She had brought a camera and tripod and took photographs in the house, then entered the studio to meet Duncan. As he half-rose from his chair, she was struck first by his extreme shabbiness and then by his "extraordinary gentleness in speaking." She felt there was something cheeky in coming to tea and asking her hosts to pose for a photograph, but "Duncan loved it and Quentin was quite happy for it to happen. They didn't seem to mind at all. And I took this wonderful photo of them— Quentin, with his long white beard, looking 108, and Duncan looking really quite youthful."[38]

BEFORE 1967, IT would have required psychic abilities to foresee that the breakthrough in the Bloomsbury revival would be a two-volume critical biography of Lytton Strachey. None of the Bloomsberries had fallen farther. Historians and critics had long since dismantled his claims as a biographer and prose stylist, his books were unread, but his squeaky voice and elongated physique lived on as quick, amusing copy for memoir writers. The voice, especially, persisted, as not only a vital part of his legend but a subject in its own right, the emblem of a fascinating but defeated culture. "It had a life of its own," recalled Frances Partridge, "starting low and soft, rising to a faint scream, stopping altogether, swallowing itself, and then sinking to the depths again."[39] Frank Swinnerton, a skilled antagonist of Bloomsbury, described Lytton's voice as "normally low,"

---

38. Interview with the author, 20 Feb. 1995.

39. Frances Partridge, *Memories* (London: Robin Clark Ltd., 1982), 66.

but in discussion or elaboration it would fly up to a strange falsetto which some describe as a squeak, and certain curious changes of stress, as well as the speed with which he gathered phrases, gave his speech a character which unfriendly ears found affected. The falsetto, or squeak, being infectious, became habitual with attendant males, so that it was afterwards known as "the Bloomsbury voice."[40]

Osbert Sitwell lavished over a page of his memoir *Laughter in the Next Room* (1949) to this voice by which "true citizens of Bloomsbury" could be recognized. His earwitness account is to the Bloomsbury voice what Quentin Bell's biography is to Virginia Woolf:

The tones would convey with supreme efficacy the requisite degree of paradoxical interest, surprise, incredulity: in actual sound, analysed, they were unemphatic, save when emphasis was not to be expected; then there would be a sudden sticky stress, high where you would have presumed low, and the whole spoken sentence would run, as it were, at different speeds and on different gears, and contain a deal of expert but apparently meaningless syncopation. . . . Experts maintain that it originated as an appanage of the Strachey family—of Lytton Strachey, that is to say, and of his brothers and sisters, in whom it was natural and delightful—and that from them it spread and took captive many. . . . The adoption by an individual of the correct tones was equivalent, I apprehend, to an outward sign of conversion, a public declaration of faith.

---

40. Frank Swinnerton, *Figures in the Foreground* (London: Hutchinson, 1963), 138–39.

Sitwell remembered a Bloomsbury dinner party when a young friend of his "took the plunge" and adopted the voice: "I heard his tongue suddenly slide off sense, making for a few moments meaningless but emphatic sounds that somehow resembled words, and then, as quickly, creak into the Bloomsbury groove, like a tram proudly regaining its rails!"[41]

Leonard Woolf, returning from Ceylon in 1911, was amused to find half the undergraduates at King's College talking in "the Stracheyesque voice." Many tried to trace the infection. "It is my belief," wrote Frances Partridge, "that the Bloomsbury voice was a product of the Strachey family and the Cambridge intellectuals combined, although the Cambridge strain had a special quality, being softer, more monotonous and less violently emphatic than the original virus." Quentin Bell, however, who was not above imitating the voice for dinner guests, denied its infectious quality. To him, it seemed that

> no one who was not a Strachey ever spoke like a Strachey. My incredulity proves very little; brought up with the accents of Bloomsbury continually in my ears I should, naturally, be deaf to their peculiarities. No doubt I too speak in this manner. It is, I must confess, a painful thought.[42]

Clive Bell wrote of his friend's "squeaky notes." To Lady Ottoline Morrell, they were small and faint. In what circle of hell are our words cast from us and our manner of speaking richly preserved? Although there were one or two American scholars doggedly ped-

---

41. Quoted in S. P. Rosenbaum, *The Bloomsbury Group*, 251–52.

42. Quentin Bell, *Bloomsbury*, 10.

dling Lytton Strachey in the 1950s (the Maytag repairmen of post-war letters), he was chiefly useful as a bad example—a careless and partial historian, a sentimentalist, a popularizer; he was also, strangely, considered an elitist, a coldhearted classicist, "sterile" and austere—in short, the bizarre embodiment of the very worst of what Bloomsbury was thought to offer. His influence had been so routinely derided that it ceased to seem genuine, and was eventually forgotten.

But this preoccupation with Lytton Strachey's vocal peculiarities is in fact a veiled tribute to his powers, for each of his biographical in-novations—the irreverence and iconoclasm of his polemic *Eminent Victorians* (1918), the intimacy of *Queen Victoria* (1922), the psycho-analytic subtext of *Elizabeth and Essex* (1928)—can be read as a vari-ation of a hitherto unthinkable tone of voice. It was never his research skills that set Lytton apart, but his bloody cheek. The general's son lampoons the British Empire. The arch-bugger of Bloomsbury beds down with Queen Victoria. Not perhaps a major achievement, this unseemly tone of voice, but it was, in its day, a potent subversion of the self-satisfaction, religiosity, and doe-eyed patriotism (the will to worship) that characterized Victorian biography.[43] To carry this voice, Lytton cultivated an engaging and readable style that did not seem, on the surface, the least transgressive. Reaching a large audience was his best means of undermining the status quo. In time, England took its revenge on Lytton Strachey, as it had on his magnificent precursor, Oscar Wilde.

---

43. In an especially purple passage in *Queen Victoria*, Strachey quoted Disraeli: "Everyone likes flattery; and when you come to royalty you should lay it on with a trowel." Strachey then commented, "In those expert hands the trowel seemed to assume the qualities of some lofty masonic symbol—to be the ornate and glittering vehicle of verities unrealised by the profane" (346–48).

HUGH KINGSMILL WAS among those iconoclastic biographers of the 1920s and 1930s said to have been fatally influenced by Lytton Strachey. In 1961, when Michael Holroyd, then in his early twenties, approached the publishing firm of Heinemann with his manuscript of a biography of Kingsmill, a kind editor explained that "were his firm to make a practice of bringing out books about almost unknown writers by totally unknown authors, it would very soon be bankrupt." Was there a better-known figure he might like to write about? So it happened that one of the most widely disparaged twentieth-century writers was resuscitated by a scholar who would, perversely, become one of the most widely liked and respected literary figures in England. In the field of Bloomsbury studies, not many scholars brought into conversation are so often described as *nice*.

Part of this admiration for Holroyd is due to his geniality, which carries over into print, and a sort of spry, self-deprecating humour that makes those who deal with him feel uniquely charming. It helps that he is not a university professor. In a world of harassed academics, now paying for their own chalk and teaching classes of forty, Holroyd retains the aura of the man of letters—the inverted values of art. He breaks into delighted laughter when he finds the right word in conversation, and he once told a journalist that he did not really live alone in his flat since—gesturing toward stacks of files—"I have the dead with me." During a lonely childhood and adolescence, spent mostly with his grandparents in England, Holroyd read a great deal. Eventually coming upon biographies in the public library, he picked up the heartening message that many people who do rather well in life had difficult or unorthodox childhoods. His first subject, Hugh Kingsmill, was the one for whom he felt the most affinity. "I think he was a lonely person," he explained,

which in those days I certainly was, and he compartmental-
ized his life. One friend would be in that compartment, another friend in that compartment, and I think lonely people
do that—I think Dr. Johnson did it—and I noticed a similarity to myself, and I was attracted to him. And he had a philosophy that attracted me very much, about will versus
imagination. It made all my laziness seem rather imaginative.[44]

In interviews, Holroyd dutifully tells the stories he is expected to, but
he is always shaping his phrases, looking for a slightly new joke at the
end. He keeps his pale hands folded across his chest until he needs
them for narrative emphasis.

In the preface to the paperback edition of *Lytton Strachey* and in
the new preface accompanying the revised version, Holroyd gives an
account of how his project expanded from one to three to six years,
from a slim survey to a "baggy monster" of a half million words, a
modern biography intended to provide excerpts from Strachey's vast
and virtually untapped correspondence, a reappraisal of his work, and
a panoramic view of Bloomsbury life. Also—and this decision still
carried a legal risk—it would be indiscreet. Lytton's loves were the
mainstay of his existence. To the extent that it made him a pariah, and
an indignant one, his homosexuality informed both his critical stance
and his biographical practice. There was no use proceeding without
complete disclosure. This, Lytton's literary executor was only too
willing to grant. James Strachey believed that his brother had intended, had he lived a little longer, to declare his homosexuality and
to shine forth, presumably unemployed and very likely in exile, as a

---

44. Interview with the author, 15 April 1994.

model of courage and human dignity, a spur toward legal reform and social understanding. In retrospect, it seemed to Holroyd that James hoped the biography would "offer as a subtext the unfulfilled life he had foreseen."

Scholars working now rarely have to please or cajole elderly Bloomsberries and their heirs to get access to old papers. There are fewer awkward interviews. Most of the letters, diaries, and manuscripts have been published, and the originals sold or bequeathed to museum archives, libraries, and colleges. Microfilm or photocopies can be purchased. Routine requests to quote are not even mentioned to heirs. In 1962, however, when Michael Holroyd pressed the doorbell at James and Alix Strachey's house in Marlow Common, almost all these papers were in private hands. Leonard was still alive, as were Duncan Grant, Clive Bell, Barbara Bagenal, E. M. Forster, David Garnett, Raymond Mortimer, Harold Nicolson, Bertrand Russell, Lydia Keynes. While this generation could provide a fantastic potential quarry of reminiscence and opinion, they might as easily join together to exclude him from the sacred precinct. He knew there was no hope of a worthwhile biography unless he could woo James and Alix, who would, in turn, urge their friends to help.

His first visit to the Stracheys was unpromising. James, who had spent the last twenty years on an exquisite translation of all Freud's works, looked like an exact replica of the master, down to his pointed white beard. The bulbous nose, perhaps, showed a hint of Lytton. He soon displayed a more disconcerting Strachey quality: long, ambiguous silences. "To fill the vacuum," Holroyd recalled, "I began jabbering nonsense." After a frugal lunch of Spam and cold potatoes, the food issuing from cold storage or numbered tins, swathed in layers of protective cellophane, James led Holroyd to a building in the garden, where he kept most of his brother's library and papers. Beside a bookcase filled with French and English volumes dating back to 1841 (Roger Senhouse, Lytton's last love, had inherited the older books), two large wooden tables overflowed with boxes and files. Piled on the floor were countless trunks and suitcases, all containing letters, diaries, typescripts, and miscellanea, and all under thick, discouraging dust. The work had already broken several men. And there was more inside the house, in James's study. At the far end of that room

> stood a desk on which lay the intimidating engines of James Strachey's *oeuvre*. Two massive metal radiators, to which I politely extended my hands, turned out to be stereophonic loudspeakers. . . . Above the fireplace hung a portrait of Lytton relaxing in a deck-chair, painted by Carrington. Next to the fire was an armchair, draped in cellophane.[45]

Further papers and microfilms were brought out. At length, James asked his guest if he still wanted to write about Lytton. Holroyd replied that he did. "I see" was the only comment.

But he had convinced the Stracheys, and in October 1962 he settled down to the first stack of papers in the dining room at Marlow. He soon realized the immense significance of the archive. Like Virginia and Vanessa, Lytton had never grown accustomed to the telephone, and had continued to write long letters nearly every day. Many answers were also preserved. Here were the internecine struggles of the Cambridge Apostles at the turn of the century, and Lytton's momentary engagement to Virginia, and his unhappy passion for the artist Henry Lamb. Here, too, in tantalizing fragments, was the story

---

45. Michael Holroyd, *Lytton Strachey: The New Biography* (New York: Farrar, Straus and Giroux, 1995), xv.

of Carrington. Sometimes Holroyd was able to add to the collection. At 51 Gordon Square, a Strachey residence for nearly fifty years, he unearthed a 1928 letter from Freud, his response to *Elizabeth and Essex*. The house was being vacated after its purchase in 1963 by University College, London. In the basement, Holroyd won a battle with the dustmen for Lytton's long-lost fellowship dissertation on Warren Hastings.

But papers were not enough. Holroyd's plan to write frankly about Lytton "depended on the cooperation of a band of mercurial octogenarians." He visited Bertrand Russell at Plas Penrhyn, his remote house in North Wales, and Harold Nicolson, well-meaning but senile, at the Albany club. At Cambridge, he had sherry with E. M. Forster, who had once told Lady Ottoline that he thought Lytton's life could never, perhaps should never, be written. "He was on his guard," Holroyd remembers. "Gave me one or two letters. He was not unhelpful. He was not obstructive, but he was not jovially forthcoming."[46] Leonard, on the other hand, was jovially obstructive. James had asked him to show Holroyd the many letters he'd received in Ceylon from Lytton, which he'd recently drawn on for the first two volumes of his autobiography. Leonard consented to see Holroyd, but when it came to the letters, he couldn't put his hands on them, or he felt doubtful about lending them, or he'd read through them and found nothing that would be of any use to a biographer. Only after Leonard had read and approved the second volume of the Strachey biography did he offer Holroyd "those letters" the younger man had asked about years earlier.

Duncan Grant, as one of Lytton's early loves, had more at stake than most of those consulted. Although his decision to permit the

---

46. Interview with the author, 15 April 1994.

story of their involvement to be published in full now seems characteristically generous, it was not his immediate response. Realizing that Duncan's politeness might put him at a disadvantage, friends tried to intervene. "It puts Duncan in a rather awkward position," Quentin Bell explained to Holroyd in July 1966.

> He is certainly not an enemy of historical truth or, I think, at all ashamed of his erotic adventures; but I don't think that anyone could fail to be rather taken aback by contemplating the publication of such very intimate details of his early loves, and, what is more, of his very youthful expressions of feeling. . . . He is very much torn between a desire not to be unfair and obstructive and a natural reluctance to see very private emotions made so very public.[47]

As Holroyd has since remarked, it took him many years to fully appreciate the courage and integrity of Duncan Grant and Roger Senhouse, old men who still had friends and public esteem to lose from the disclosures in the Strachey biography.

"Relatives," as Janet Malcolm mordantly observed, "are the biographer's natural enemies; they are like the hostile tribes an explorer encounters and must ruthlessly subdue to claim his territory."[48] Holroyd appeared to have won over the natives, but in autumn of 1964, when he brought the Stracheys his draft of volume one, it was his turn to be subdued. Alix, reading the opening chapters of the typescript, told Holroyd that she found them "frog-like and unfeeling." James's reaction was more severe. He objected violently to many passages,

---

47. Holroyd, *Lytton Strachey: The New Biography*, xxvii.

48. Janet Malcolm, "The Silent Woman," *The New Yorker* 23 and 30 Aug. 1993: 87.

finding evidence throughout of an unconscious dislike of Lytton, perhaps "on moral grounds." What could they do, short of abandoning the project altogether?

Over the next two and a half years, the biographer and Lytton's loving brother struggled through both volumes, sentence by sentence, twice. They exchanged a hundred letters. James sent sheaves of closely written notes. "Nothing escaped his attention," wrote Holroyd:

> One character had "short" not "small" shin bones; "extrovert" was a word that derived from Jung and was meaningless. . . . These notes, queries and comments took up an infinite amount of James's time. But they were of incalculable value to me. By nature he was uncommunicative, yet now he was being provoked into divulging all sorts of information known to almost no one else that would greatly enrich the biography.[49]

Exhausted, but increasingly sure of his efforts, Holroyd circulated the finished typescript among the surviving Bloomsberries. Reactions were swift and hostile, and centred on the telling of a worn, already semi-public secret.[50] Frances Partridge, who agreed in principle with Holroyd's aims, read his typescript with "a sort of horror." "Perhaps he has probed too unmercifully," she wrote in her diary on 28 March 1966; "even the bedrooms and beds are explored for data."[51] Angelica Garnett, thinking of Duncan in particular, argued that "one couldn't

---

49. Holroyd, *Lytton Strachey: The New Biography*, xxi.

50. Adverse criticism of the 1930s had all but spelled out Strachey's homosexuality.

51. Frances Partridge, *Other People: Diaries 1963–66* (London: HarperCollins, 1993), 206.

publish such things about living people."[52] Some felt the dead needed similar protection. Years before, Geoffrey Keynes had tried to convince James Strachey to destroy the "sodomitical" correspondence between Maynard and Lytton in their Cambridge years. They finally agreed to put the letters under embargo at the King's College library until 1986. Fearing the destruction of the letters, however, James had made a secret microfilm, which he allowed Holroyd to see. From this, Holroyd judiciously quoted, keeping himself well within the fair usage clause of the Copyright Act. Explaining the salacious nature of the correspondence, he argued in his biography that "in a society which regarded homosexuality as more grave than murder, what Lytton and Keynes were looking for almost as urgently as love itself, was a discreet and sympathetic source of disclosure."[53] And disclosure they got. When the book appeared, Geoffrey Keynes blamed Holroyd for a sniggering review by Malcolm Muggeridge. "Your book has done just as much harm to my brother's image as if you had infringed copyright," he later wrote.[54]

David Garnett called for immediate suppression. Never, in his own well-spiced memoirs, had he even hinted at unnatural passions within Bloomsbury. Now they would all be stained lavender. Alix, with a trace of condescension, reported his "red-faced truculence and talk about libel actions." We can suppose "Bunny" would have rejected James's vision of Lytton as a homosexual crusader, and indeed he had his own modest ambitions for his dead friend: "Lytton, if he had lived, would have spoken for mankind on Auschwitz, Hi-

---

52. Partridge, 248.

53. Holroyd, *Lytton Strachey: The Unknown Years, 1880–1910* (London: William Heinemann Ltd., 1967), 212.

54. Holroyd, *Lytton Strachey: The New Biography*, 696.

roshima, the nuclear bomb and torture in France with a clarity and force with which the political leaders of the world would have had to reckon."[55]

Bunny's appalled reaction to the Holroyd biography points out the limits of Bloomsbury's famous candour and is worth scrutinizing. If Lytton's conduct had been discovered while he lived, he would have faced the same criminal code under which Oscar Wilde received two years' hard labour. At that time, discretion was only prudent. But Lytton was long dead. To conceal his homosexuality in the mid-1960s, even at the nominal risk to his surviving friends, would only be bowing to prejudice. Or had Bunny and some of the latter-day Bloomsberries come to feel less tolerant of Lytton's orientation? The legend, ironically, is that a reading of Lytton's story "Ermyntrude and Esmerelda" at Christmas 1914 first convinced Bunny, otherwise ardently heterosexual, to throw off his inhibitions and go to bed with Duncan Grant. And once, at Wissett, in the thick of his romance with Duncan, Bunny sat on a garden bench kissing Lytton, having first cast a nervous glance in the direction of the house.

This incident in the garden was only alluded to, as "a tremulous flirtation," in the Holroyd biography, but four years later, when Holroyd edited the collection *Lytton Strachey by Himself: A Self Portrait* (1971), he included the experimental diary-essay "Monday June 26th 1916," in which the kissing scene appears, ostensibly with Bunny's permission. The essay had been read by Lytton to the Memoir Club some years after its composition, long after the Wissett ménage had dissolved and the fires of romance between Duncan and Bunny had presumably been quenched. Given the grounds of his opposition to

---

55. Holroyd, *Lytton Strachey: The Years of Achievement 1910–1932* (London: William Heinemann Ltd., 1968), 416.

the Holroyd biography, we may wonder why Bunny permitted the publication of this essay. Not only does it effectively "out" him as a willing recipient, at least, of another man's embraces, but it demonstrates that Bunny's affair with Duncan was not a single bisexual aberration, as he wished to characterize it in later life. The true purpose, it would seem, of Bunny's code of debauchery—the aromatic fruit of "Ermyntrude and Esmerelda"—was to permit Bunny to desire men. (He had not needed a doctrine to sleep with women.)

The laws in England had changed, of course, since Bunny first perused the Holroyd typescript. In 1967, the recommendations of the Wolfenden Report of 1957 were finally adopted as the Sexual Offences Act, which legalized homosexual acts in private between consenting adults. Raymond Mortimer called *Lytton Strachey* "the first post-Wolfenden biography," and it is still considered one of the seminal works of that hopeful moment for civil liberties. It may be that Bunny felt ready, by 1971, to enjoy this reminder of his licentious past. The text is littered with descriptions of his manly beauty—more reason for a fond, forgiving glance. And, he might have argued, sexual ambivalence was in the air. Duncan, after all, divided his love between Bunny and Vanessa. Even Lytton, who devotes pages of this essay to his futile attempt to meet a fresh-faced country postman, spares a few sentences for "the puzzle" of his own relations with women, and wonders why he did not make a pass at Maria Nys at Garsington while the dear thing was bent over her Latin text.

But not all the dots have been connected in this essay. Readers can easily discern that Vanessa loves Duncan, whom Lytton once loved, and who now seems attached to Bunny, but the relationship between Bunny and Vanessa remains hazy. Some of Bunny's own writings move beyond haziness to hint at an affair. Angelica Garnett has speculated in *Deceived with Kindness* that Bunny's outrageous vow, leaning over her cradle, to marry her one day and his subsequent, carefully plotted courtship were motivated in part by revenge at Vanessa for rejecting his advances. Reading his old friend's essay selectively, Bunny may have appreciated the ambiguity in its depiction of the Wissett ménage. There is evidence, in any case, that Bunny hoped to subtly disavow the kissing scene. His comment on the essay, which appeared as a note in the book, was that what he remembered of Lytton's long-ago visit to Wissett was the two of them taking a walk along the edge of a cornfield and Lytton confessing that he was in love, "or more than a little in love," with Carrington. He made Bunny promise not to tell anyone.

> I kept my promise. . . . I suppose it was the reassurance I had given him which led him to confide in me and he was also perhaps more ready to confide a hetero-sexual attachment to me than a daydream about the post-man which would have strained my powers of sympathy![56]

Recounting this memory, and with this odd retrospective gloss on it, not only drags Lytton a few steps closer to legitimate passions but implicitly negates the embraces he shared with Bunny. Readers are encouraged to find it natural, inevitable, that Lytton would come to Bunny, of all his friends, for the real man-to-man about Carrington. We can see Bunny waving his arms in the cornfield, frantic to distract us from his male lover in the house and his faithless kisses in the garden.

---

56. Quoted in Rosenbaum, 19.

JAMES STRACHEY DIED of a heart attack in April 1967, soon after Holroyd received his final comments on the typescript. During their work together, James had said many unpleasant things to and about the younger man, but in the end he told Holroyd that he approved his seriousness of purpose. To express his respect for James without yielding what he felt were important points, Holroyd decided to publish the most vehement of James's objections as footnotes in his text. Holroyd's portrayal of Lytton is so convincing, and so scrupulously documented, that his brother's grievances rarely sway the reader. What does emerge from this commentary is an acute and sometimes startling self-portrait of James Strachey. In one instance, when Holroyd quoted Desmond MacCarthy's description of Lytton's "small rather dismal moustache," James retorted: "What do you think you mean by this?"

> What can you mean? A wispy moustache which grew with difficulty? One like Hitler's? It certainly wasn't like Sir Gerald Nabarro's. Not an R.A.F. moustache. Nor a cavalry moustache. But, as you might see from photographs, a thick one, not in the least straggly. In those days far from unusual. This is a good example of your unceasing desire to run Lytton down—in this case to make people think he was impotent—which, believe me, he wasn't.[57]

When advance copies of *Lytton Strachey: The Unknown Years, 1880–1910* reached reviewers in August 1967, the long-simmering Bloomsbury revival burst into full boil, flaring up again the following

---

57. Holroyd, *Lytton Strachey: The Unknown Years*, 129.

February, when the second volume appeared. A May 1968 interview
with Holroyd in the *New Yorker* referred to the "literary commotion
in London" and forecast a similar reaction in America. Critical response shuttled between admiration, trepidation, and disdain. As
usual, reviewers unsympathetic to Bloomsbury took the opportunity
to air their prejudices, often while praising Holroyd's industry (two
volumes! 1,229 pages!) in uncovering this reprehensible character. No
serious writer missed the importance of Holroyd's candid treatment
of Lytton's sexuality, however, and discussion soon focused on two
interrelated questions: what did *Lytton Strachey* mean for biography
as a discipline? And what did Lytton's homosexuality mean for his
writing, for Bloomsbury, for England?

Leonard Woolf found the emphasis on Lytton's love life absurd,
arguing in the *New Statesman* that Holroyd, apparently deficient in
humour, had been misled by Lytton's "loud lamentations and jubilations." "I do not think," he continued,

> that [Lytton] had any very strong passions or emotions. He
> loved to dramatise himself, his friends, and his loves. And he
> was hardly ever completely serious when he had his pen in
> hand, writing the tragedy or comedy of his perpetual love af-
> fairs. . . . Mr. Holroyd is taken in by all this, and Lytton is al-
> ways dying of love at the top of his voice.

Noel Annan, a Kingsman, the biographer of Leslie Stephen, and as
nearly a B as a non-B can be, agreed with Leonard and wrote to
congratulate him on his sound evaluation of the Holroyd biography.
Annan wondered how it is that "all the letters and juvenilia" available to biographers of the recently dead seem to impede, rather than
aid, understanding. He had felt the same way, he recalled, reading

Christopher Hassall's portentous 1964 biography of Rupert Brooke. "I think biographers should be warned that letters, & even diaries, do *not* necessarily reflect the inner man," he added, praising Leonard for managing "to puncture a lot of biographer's shibboleths—especially dear to them is the notion that if only you dig deep enough you will always find a man of profound and tragic depth of emotion."[58] Leonard wrote back that he regretted having consented to review the biography: "I tried to say as much as I could in favour of it, but it really is a bad book." He, too, tried to account for the misleading nature of letters and diaries, raising again, as in his preface to *A Writer's Diary*, the issue of the writer's state of mind: "It is partly the deadness of the dead. All these things dashed off in half a minute by a living hand and mind are served up to us as if they were carved in stone. . . . It is a curious fact that Pepys is almost the only intelligent diarist who does not go to his diary only or mainly when he is miserable."[59]

In a 1968 *Spectator* article, "A Problem of Discretion," Nigel Nicolson warned that were the tell-all trend in biography to continue, those likely to be the objects of such scrutiny would burn their most intimate letters and censor their diaries. Perhaps Holroyd had brought undue attention to his methods and materials by mentioning in his preface the thirty-thousand-odd letters he had read for the biography. Along with the much-repeated praise of Holroyd's industry, the *Times Literary Supplement* reviewer also chose to pin his essay on the matter of saving letters, especially such letters as those between Lytton and Maynard as undergraduates: "Alas! for the reputation of Lytton Strachey, the silly nonsense has survived to be

---

58. *Letters of Leonard Woolf*, 560.

59. Ibid., 560–61.

scrutinized by a silly world as if it had the consequence of a roll of papyrus." Since the correspondence existed, the reviewer conceded, Holroyd was plainly right to use it, although "the perceptive reader will notice that [it] reveals only a side—and not perhaps a very important side—of Lytton Strachey's character."

The difference between pronouncements carved in stone or inscribed on papyrus and Lytton's correspondence with Maynard is not only the relative speed at which Lytton's letters were composed but their rough passage from private into public record. They do not read like the letters of a great man, or even a man of great achievement. Their scale of values is unsettling. The trouble is not Lytton's preoccupation with bodily functions (though someone should look into digestion as a recurring theme in literary correspondence) or with winsome lads or even his obscenities—we have seen these elsewhere—but that characteristic tone of voice: arch, epigrammatic, mannered. On Lady Ottoline, for example: "Her bladder is now gone the way of her wits—a melancholy dribble." And on Duncan Grant, at the height of their affair: "His features were moulded by nothing intermediary, but by the hand of God itself; they are plastic like living marble, they clothe a divinity, a quintessential soul. I rave; but I weep too." Pure camp: so pure that Cynthia Ozick, trying to explain the difference in sensibility between Lytton Strachey and E. M. Forster, once declared that Lytton Strachey invented homosexual manners.

If Lytton's epistolary style was—and this is something of a leap—saturated with a homosexual sensibility (specific, furthermore, to his class and his moment in English history), it may explain the exasperation of so many reviewers. They could not tell what, exactly, Lytton was up to, but they knew it was not quite manly. In the *Listener*, Geoffrey Grigson, an advocate of Wyndham Lewis, brought up the few quotes from Eliot that appear in the biography and noted with relief that "suddenly one comes for a while on a man and not a confectioner." This is not so far from the reaction of his fellow Lewisite, Geoffrey Wagner, to the Lytton Strachey–Virginia Woolf correspondence: "one is forced to stop reading, to ask oneself how any man could write this stuff."

Even reviewers favourable to the Holroyd enterprise or to Lytton himself deplored the liberal quotation from his letters, some complaining, like Leonard, that Holroyd lacked sufficient distance from these documents, with their suspect assertions and spot eloquence, and others arguing that the letters misrepresented Lytton. Some of the underlying reasoning here on the relation of style to personality is beyond the scope of this study, but it is interesting that these critics seem to recognize that Lytton's "lamentations and jubilations"—his camp style, in other words—reduced his literary stature for many readers. Lytton's letters persistently undermined the task at hand: the reclamation of his reputation as a serious writer.

"The parade of these things," wrote the *Times Literary Supplement* reviewer, "tilts the balance against the real man." When reviewers of the Holroyd biography argued that the author placed too much emphasis on Lytton's homosexuality, they may have been helpfully pointing out a narrative flaw. Or they may have meant that Lytton's homosexuality offended them, or that they were willing to accept it only in the abstract. "There are homosexuals and there are homosexuals," as one reviewer put it. In the reaction against Bloomsbury, there has always been a strong vein of sexual anxiety. The Holroyd biography, by providing the first uncensored details of the Bloomsberries' sex lives and attitudes,[60] opened the door for a better-informed but

---

60. Holroyd had suppressed nothing but Lytton's erotic poems, which contained, in Holroyd's terms, "a truly phenomenal amount of copulation" and "a compulsive

sometimes hysterical debate on these matters and on the broader implications of Bloomsbury's sexual radicalism. Did it lead, for instance, directly to the Burgess spy ring?

The *Times Literary Supplement* reviewer of volume two thought the biography revealed in the end "a puzzling picture, and a singularly revolting one."

> While no one would condemn Strachey for being attracted to his own sex, the indulgence of his fancies at the cost of the happiness of those he loved (and—what is surely worse—at the cost of the happiness of those they loved) can only be condemned.

Of course some would condemn Strachey for being attracted to his own sex. Some still would. This disclaimer only helps the reviewer establish his own, seemingly more tenable condemnation. Note that Lytton's desires are downgraded to "fancies" and there is an implicit argument that Lytton should have sacrificed his search for a mate to spare Carrington's feelings. A few reviewers were more blatant. Quoting a letter in which a lonely young Lytton complained about his sister Dorothy's nuptial bliss ("Two people loving each other so much—there's something devilishly selfish about it"), Geoffrey Grigson remarked in the *Listener*, "How nasty, how insolent the tone is!"

---

preoccupation with the male reproductory and excretory organs." Even without the prejudicial verse, Lytton inspired little bonhomie in readers. Adjectives used to describe him include, in descending order: clever, entertaining, spiteful, epicene, snooty, pitiable, odious, self-loving, self-hating, nauseating.

And to be plain, that is one kind of homosexual: spiteful and ungenerous, and against those who do not share his condition. From the situation, the condition, arise, I should think, both the substance and the essentially coarse style of *Eminent Victorians* and *Queen Victoria*.

Gertrude Himmelfarb, a Victorianist with a grudge (understandable, to a degree) against Lytton Strachey for having reduced the beloved figures of Florence Nightingale, Victoria and Albert, and others to such petty proportions, went much further in discrediting Lytton's work and life. She wielded the words "homosexual" and "homosexuality" as if they were damaging in themselves.

One would not want to do to Strachey what he did to others—reduce the whole of an acting, thinking life to a single aspect of personality. Yet how important this single aspect of personality is in understanding his work! This is not to suggest that only a homosexual could have been so destructive of authority, suspicious of morality, venomous towards the father (and mother) figures representing that moral authority, cavalier in respect to truth, arch in innuendo, and tiresomely fey in rhetoric. But knowing about Strachey's homosexuality, we can better understand the quality of his writing, the perfect apposition of style and substance.[61]

"Not to suggest" is the light armour Himmelfarb slips on when she means, in fact, to suggest. She adds later, "This is not to suggest that homosexuality created the culture that we think of as Bloomsbury. It

---

61. Gertrude Himmelfarb, review of *Lytton Strachey* in the *New Republic* 18 May 1968.

may well be that the culture created, or at least encouraged, the homosexuality that was so congenial to it." No matter. She has neatly conflated "Bloomsbury" and "homosexuality" for her wide-eyed readers and managed to posit Bloomsbury as the mother of all iniquity. We cannot know whether Himmelfarb believes her own rhetoric, only that she is happy to engage her readers' prejudices as an instrument of criticism.

It would be unfair to hold these reviewers to today's standards of apparent indifference, and in fact their comments are useful precisely because they are so glaringly intolerant and, in Himmelfarb's case, so vituperative. While this attitude toward Bloomsbury's unconventionality in love still lingers, it rarely reaches print now except in the form of nudge-and-wink jokes (a favourite device of English critics of the Right and Semi-Right) and batty letters to the editor. Among Bloomsbury scholars, especially feminists, it sometimes shows up as antagonism toward the mostly homosexual men to whom Carrington and Vanessa devoted their lives and in a tendency to quote and requote Virginia's few remarks about the boredom of "buggers' talk."

When the smoke cleared after publication of the second volume, a few thoughtful pieces of journalism lay intact on the battlefield. In the *New York Review of Books,* Noel Annan had provided a dispassionate overview of the cult of homosexuality in Europe at the beginning of the century and called for historical inquiry into this neglected topic. In *Encounter,* Goronwy Rees had addressed each viable objection to the Holroyd biography (not always deciding in Holroyd's favour, especially with regard to his convoluted prose) and, like Annan, tried to put the sexual revelations in context. He seems to have read Lytton's letters with a delight almost unknown among reviewers. And among several writers who bridled at the contradiction between the candour espoused by Old Bloomsbury and the reticence of the memoirs and biographies that followed, Rees provided the only evenhanded discussion of this paradox. His was an essay that could not have been written ten or even five years earlier. Struck by Rees's arguments, Melvin Lasky, the editor of *Encounter*, asked several biographers and memoir writers, including Roy Harrod and Leonard Woolf, why they did not deal frankly with homosexuality in their books. Only Leonard responded, giving an answer divided, à la Moore's *Principia Ethica*, into dry, numbered assertions: "(1) not being a homosexual myself it was irrelevant to my relation to them; (2) it was irrelevant to the subject treated by me in my autobiography; (3) when I wrote, it was still unusual to reveal facts which might be painful to living people unless it was absolutely vital to mention them."[62]

In retrospect, the critical response to the Holroyd biography seems exceptionally unguarded, like the first words after a slap. Truth yielded truth, or at least a sort of coarse authenticity. Reviewers would never again be startled, though, by Bloomsbury misconduct. After *Lytton Strachey*, there were no more virgins.

MICHAEL HOLROYD WENT on to write his acclaimed biographies of Augustus John and George Bernard Shaw and to become a spirited advocate for writers, campaigning for Public Lending Right (a scheme to give writers a penny or two in royalties each time one of their books is borrowed from a public library), serving on the Arts Council and as chairman of the writers' organisation PEN. After the initially bumpy reception of his Lytton Strachey biography among critics and surviving Bloomsberries, he was embraced as a community asset. At least his weighty volumes had produced something other than a slow, fitful revival, like that of the Bloomsbury artists, or a

---

62. *Letters of Leonard Woolf*, 564.

minutely plotted recovery, like that of Virginia Woolf. Here was the stuff of legend—a Herculean effort to reinstate a despised and outdated writer. Holroyd can also be said to have founded the Bloomsbury industry, making his initial investment in Strachey yield many times his fifty-pound advance from Heinemann: editing Lytton's "Ermyntrude and Esmerelda" for *Playboy* (1969), for example, as well as *Lytton Strachey by Himself* (1970) and, with Paul Levy, *The Shorter Strachey* (1980); writing on the Bloomsbury artists; broadcasting on Virginia Woolf's novels; helping establish the Strachey Trust; lecturing; reviewing; and, most recently, selling film rights to the Carrington story to his friend Christopher Hampton. The initial English release dates of *Carrington* coincided with the publication of Holroyd's newly revised biography of Lytton Strachey.

Among the immediate effects of the Holroyd biography on the critical and popular perception of Bloomsbury was that it managed to make the Group seem revolutionary again, and at a moment when rebellion of every kind was most likely to find a receptive audience. Certainly by 1968, when the second volume appeared, Carolyn Heilbrun and others had begun to remark on the similarities between early Bloomsbury and the new generation of youth. Readers found and embraced what was radical in Bloomsbury. Only a few hypersensitive sorts, Leonard for one, noticed that Holroyd had in fact played Lytton off against the Group (a tactic we shall see again), allowing an amorphous "Bloomsbury" to carry the burden of malice customarily distributed between its members. At this distance, and more problematically, the book can also be seen to have provided the raw materials, both in documents and intensity of focus, for the cult of personality that makes up such a large part of the response to Bloomsbury today.

It is frequently said that Holroyd sparked the vogue for Bloomsbury, that he made possible a renewed appreciation of Lytton Strachey's achievements, and that, like his subject, he altered the scope and tenor of biography. Whether Holroyd succeeded in rescuing Lytton's works, in bringing new readers to *Queen Victoria*, for instance, is less certain. Style, as Elizabeth Hardwick wrote, is to some degree a decision, but it is also a fate.

ACROSS THE FIRST page of the manuscript of *Maurice*, his novel of homosexual love written in 1913–14, E. M. Forster, perhaps as late as 1960, scrawled: "Publishable, but worth it?" An ambiguous remark, but we can suppose that Morgan feared the loss of his quiet life, of his cosy and sheltering reticence; he viewed the prospects for homosexual emancipation with considerable pessimism. He tinkered with *Maurice* every few years, adding a "Terminal Note" in 1960 that explained the circumstances of its composition, but the novel remained unpublished at his death and entered the collections of the British Museum. What in fact occurred when *Maurice* reached reviewers in autumn 1971 would have surprised its author. The homosexual theme shocked almost no one, but the novel was declared so wretchedly, heartbreakingly bad that it threw into question his entire body of work.

Forster's aim was explicitly moral: to trace, without blame or shame, the sexual coming-of-age of Maurice Hall, a hearty, complacent, middle-class youth—a character Forster intended to be as unlike himself as possible—who happens to be homosexual. Maurice has a torrid platonic affair with his friend Clive Durham at Cambridge, but Clive shakes off the episode and marries a limp-petalled English rose named Anne. Maurice tries to overcome his desires, consulting a Harley Street doctor and a hypnotist without effect. Visiting the newlyweds at the Durham estate, he has a disturbing encounter with the gamekeeper, who refuses his tip and glares at him enigmatically. Throwing open his window that night and sighing into the darkness ("Come!"), Maurice is surprised by the thud of a ladder on the sill. Alec, the gamekeeper, enters. A series of misadventures follow, Alec and Maurice finally agreeing to flout convention and live happily ever after, away from the jeers of society, in what Forster calls "the greenwood," as woodcutters.

Maurice is one of those novels that inspire brilliant demolition. Critics objected to the inflated language, the unreal characters, the implausible ending, and the curiously sexless quality of what purported to be a defence of homosexuality. In her *Listener* review, Brigid Brophy juxtaposed love scenes from *Maurice* and from the works of the nineteenth-century popular novelist Marie Corelli, stripping names and other identifying features, to devastating effect and concluded that at the time of its composition "its homosexual theme made *Maurice* unpublishable, at least with Forster's name attached. Now, I imagine, it would be unpublishable without." For those whose respect "for the first half of *A Passage to India*" encouraged them to seek out all Forster's work, she offered the reassurance that "*Maurice* is not nearly as bad as bad Forster can be. Pan is not among the characters." Both she and Cyril Connolly, who actually liked *Maurice*, pounced on what seemed like unconscious slips, allusions to the erotic ferment so conspicuously absent in the text. At one point Clive suggests that Maurice behave in public as though nothing had changed between them and says this will be "a public convenience." And can it be unintentional, Connolly wondered, when, after Clive's marriage, the Master makes him say, "Anne's dear little hole may grow in the night"? (Clive meant to refer to a leak in the ceiling.)

Brophy and Connolly were among the few critics who did not

use *Maurice* as a springboard for pseudocritical musings on Forster's homosexuality (although Brophy did manage to slip in a twelve-line argument for vegetarianism), and it is worthwhile to compare these remarks with those meted out to Lytton Strachey after the Holroyd biography. With echoes of Grigson and Himmelfarb, a reviewer in the *Times Literary Supplement* asserted that "to say that [Forster] was homosexual is to define not only his private nature, but the nature of his imagination." This is not to regret Forster's homosexuality or, alternatively, society's disapproval of it, the review continued, because "the spiritual and imaginative restraints of a suppressed and guilty sexuality . . . made his literary and social existence possible." I do not know whether this is true of Forster, or of any writer; it sounds like a sinister but well-meaning assessment in the post-Freudian vein. The reviewer went on, however, to attribute "the most serious limitations—the blind spots and imaginative failures" of Forster's work to his sexual orientation, in particular, his inability "to imagine any aspect of the range of experience between men and women." Here, perhaps, the inherent violence of biographically based criticism begins to make itself felt. According to this formula of limitation, *The Longest Journey* makes sense only as "a crypto-homosexual story," and no scene between the lovers in *A Room with a View* is treated as vividly as the all-male bathing scene. Boldly pursuing his theme, the reviewer declared that "ordinary emotional states were beyond Forster."

What happens, then, when E. M. Forster casts aside the doubts and restraints that cripple his other novels and tries to put, in his own words, "the private lusts and aches" of his sexuality into fiction? The answer is that, like a long-term prisoner suddenly handed his own clothes and thrust into daylight, Forster is no longer Forster. Like others, the *Times Literary Supplement* reviewer lamented the sacrifice of

Forster's characteristic distance, his ironic tone and humour and shrewd wisdom, and noted instead a "poverty of feeling," which the reviewer read as evidence of Forster's ambivalence toward his homosexuality. This critic also discovered in Forster a sense of sordidness: "He could not imagine sex that was neither furtive nor repulsive. Love for him may have been a Beloved Republic, but it was never an innocent act."

Forster had noted with satisfaction that *Maurice* was "not pornographic," considering this a mark in its favour. Late in life, he told Noel Annan: "If you let a prick in, it comes between you and art." This absence of a prick—the pricks, perhaps, having fled to the more welcoming Holroyd biography—does tend to defeat Forster's high purpose. He substituted a pained lyricism for the missing lovemaking: "O for the night that was ending, for the sleep and the wakefulness, the toughness and the tenderness mixed, the safety in darkness. Would such a night ever return?" Quoting this passage in the *New York Review of Books*, Noel Annan remarked that it called to mind Radclyffe Hall's *The Well of Loneliness*, another famously bad book,[63] and interjected: "I suspect that Forster had never had a sexual affair until he was in his forties."

Cynthia Ozick, in some ways the reviewer most devoted to E. M. Forster, was also the most stung by *Maurice* and what it implied of its author's inner life. Stressing that she did not intend the pun, she declared *Maurice* "a fairy tale" of a classic type, in which the hero is "struck with an ineradicable disability."

---

63. Vanessa Bell's crushing appraisal of *The Well of Loneliness* could easily be applied to *Maurice:* "perfectly decent . . . and as dull as ditch water and incredibly bad and very sentimental."

The essence of a fairy tale is that wishing does make it so: the wish achieves fulfillment through its very steadfastness of desire. . . . Consequently *Maurice* is a disingenuous book, an infantile book, because, while pretending to be about social injustice, it is really about make-believe, it is about wishing; so it fails even as a tract.[64]

In Forster's abdication of authorial rigour and his refusal to describe even a kiss, Ozick, like the *Times Literary Supplement* reviewer, found evidence that he disapproved of homosexuality. The half-baked character of Maurice is, for Ozick, "the ghost of undepicted, inexplicit coitus." She pointed out that the only viable reason for the book was a "fresh and potent interest in all those matters that did *not* get written: the caresses in detail, the embraces, the endearments precisely depicted." If readers put down Ozick's essay at this point, they would be left with a sad impression of *Maurice*. But Ozick went further, announcing that, with the appearance of this book, it became clear that "Forster's famous humanism is a kind of personal withdrawal rather than a universal testimony, and reverberates with despair. Does it devalue the large humanistic statement to know that its sources are narrowly personal? Yes."

This is the most severe statement of a disappointment that pervades the critical response to *Maurice*. The surface argument avowed that E. M. Forster's homosexuality cut him off from "ordinary emotional states" and from the universal stream. If the novelist's job is to locate the pulse of humanity, to clap a hand smack on the carotid artery, Morgan could only place a languid finger on the wrist. At another level, critics suggested that his acquiescence, his complicity in

64. Cynthia Ozick, "Morgan and Maurice: A Fairy Tale," *Art and Ardor*, 64.

his own suppression (what might today be called his internalized homophobia) tainted, in Ozick's words, "the candor of his liberalism with a hidden self-interest." Even Cyril Connolly, who argued for clemency in judging *Maurice,* thought Forster should have taken the risk and published the novel in the 1920s or 1930s, especially since, like Gide and Proust (and unlike Strachey), he was of independent means: "the lot of the consenting adult could well have been improved and legislation undertaken much earlier. . . . Was it a failure of nerve? It looks like it."

IN THE FIVE years after the Holroyd biography, publishers and other arbiters of taste could be seen carefully—and somewhat incredulously—stoking a small fire that had sprung up on what educated opinion had so recently declared a wasteland. From what had seemed, two years earlier, only disparate compliments for Leonard Woolf's autobiography and a schoolgirl following for *To the Lighthouse,* an audience had materialized. There was a palpable sense of excitement about Bloomsbury, especially in America. In those years, and in the absence of a Virginia Woolf biography, it was not clear which aspects of the subject most appealed to this new audience, only that demand had begun to outstrip supply. Carolyn Heilbrun's first essay on Bloomsbury appeared, an early approach to her provocative argument that the androgynous nature of the group was its "most threatening and most distinguishing characteristic,"[65] along with the first seminars on Bloomsbury in American universities (Stanford for one) and, in England, caustic articles on the occasion of Leonard Woolf's death (rebutted by Noel Annan), caustic responses to *Mau-*

---

65. Carolyn Heilbrun, "The Bloomsbury Group," *Midway,* Aug. 1968.

rice (also rebutted by Noel Annan), and Paul Levy's more or less gay collection *Lytton Strachey: The Really Interesting Question and Other Papers* (1972). Producers began to clamour for film and stage rights to the Strachey-Carrington story. In 1970, the first show of Carrington's art opened in London. David Garnett edited *Carrington: Letters and Extracts from Her Diaries* in the same year, and although he expressed regret that the men Carrington loved did not encourage her painting, the opening lines of his preface are a lesson in priorities for women artists.

> The reader may ask: "Who was this woman Carrington any-way?" And when I reply that he should read this book to find out—for all her qualities good and bad are revealed in these letters—he may be annoyed and ask: "But to look at? Was she beautiful?"

Bunny then devoted a tightly printed page to Carrington's physical charms. In the winter of 1971–72, Gallery Edward Harvane in London held a series of Bloomsbury-related exhibitions with unusual topics—Clive Bell and Ottoline Morrell, for instance.

Much of this increased activity centred on Virginia Woolf. Sales figures for her novels shot up, but the most convincing evidence of a resurgence of interest, reader by reader, may be found in small events like a 1969 talk on Woolf by J. J. Wilson at the San Francisco Public Library, part of a lecture series on underrepresented women writers. To the organizers' surprise, common readers turned up in the hundreds, among them the writer Tillie Olsen. "All of them," Wilson recalled, "were friends I hadn't met yet, fascinating private people who claimed Woolf as their personal saviour and were almost dismayed to find her become so popular."[66] It is easier, of course, to trace Woolf's revival in these years in American universities, where the women's movement and the student movement were making slow advances against moribund curricula and critical approaches that favoured the work of male modernists. Women graduate students struggled to get Virginia Woolf's novels onto reading lists for Ph.D. exams, when just a few years earlier her name had been cropping up on lists of exhausted dissertation topics. (To those who had inherited a disdain for Bloomsbury, it seemed that the Virginia Woolf revival had all the cultural endurance of the hula hoop. In any case, after Jean Guiguet's comprehensive study, what else could be written about the woman?)

In 1970, J. J. Wilson sent out a call for Woolf enthusiasts to convene at the Modern Language Association's annual convention. Over thirty scholars turned up early one morning in a "squeezed-in little room atop some vast New York hotel," she has written, followed by a party that evening at the poet Sharon Olds's Riverside Drive apartment, to which Wilson lugged a Virginia ham. "That event," Wilson observed, "became the model for the Virginia Woolf Society MLA party tradition. It seemed an imperative because we all so craved to talk with colleagues who did not immediately assume we meant the Albee play or who did not say as someone once did to me . . . 'And just who are these Blueberries you are working on?' "[67] By 1976, a full day of Woolf sessions and events was scheduled at the MLA conven-

---

66. J. J. Wilson, "From Solitude to Society Through Reading Virginia Woolf," *Virginia Woolf: Emerging Perspectives: Selected Papers from the Third Annual Conference on Virginia Woolf* (New York: Pace University Press, 1994), 15.

67. Ibid.

tion. Returning from one of these conferences in the early seventies, Thomas Flanagan, then chair of the English Department at Berkeley, is said to have remarked that one-third of the people there were in English literature, one-third were in American literature, and one-third were in Virginia Woolf.

Joan Russell Noble's *Recollections of Virginia Woolf by Her Contemporaries* (1972) was among the best-received books to emerge in the preboom period, since, as well as gathering recent interviews and memoirs, the editor elicited a number of slight but endearing stories that would otherwise be lost. Barbara Bagenal, for instance, remembered a day when she and her small daughter Judith ran into Virginia Woolf in Lewes High Street. Virginia asked the child, "Will you come with me to Woolworth's to buy a very large india-rubber? I want to rub out all my novels." Noble also approached Louie Mayer, the Woolfs' cook-general at Rodmell from 1934 until Leonard's death, and Mayer's kind, commonsense description of daily life at Monk's House may be the most emotionally affecting portion of this book. How many critics since have betrayed their recollection of it by sniping at Virginia Woolf's bread-making? The incongruous image of Virginia kneading away in her sloping kitchen has entered popular culture via, among other sources, an Elizabeth David cookery book (1987), and even there it remained startling enough to inflame critics. "Although otherwise an indifferent cook," wrote Angela Carter in a demolition of the David book,

Virginia could certainly knock you up a lovely cottage loaf. You bet. This strikes me as just the sort of pretentiously frivolous and dilettantish thing a Bloomsbury *would* be good at—knowing how to do one, just one, fatuously complicated kitchen thing and doing that one thing well enough to put the cook's nose out of joint.[68]

Amid this welter of renewed enthusiasm and reaction, Anne Olivier Bell (known since her marriage as Olivier) was sedulously reading, dating, and summarizing the contents of the Stephen family papers in preparation for her husband's biography of Virginia Woolf. Her notes are still kept with those papers at the Berg Collection in New York, and scholars who have read Vanessa and Virginia's letters there forever associate them with Olivier's handsome, no-nonsense script. Although she takes no credit for the actual writing of the Bell biography, it was truly a collaborative venture, Olivier's organizational and research endeavours supporting Quentin's elegant narrative, as a wall might support a flowering vine. So much was the biography part of Bell family life that their daughter Virginia finally protested the confusion in names, and the Bells thereafter referred to their subject as "Mrs. Woolf."

Trained as an art historian and employed before marriage in archival and curatorial jobs, Olivier has written that "the common element in all the various activities of my career was the commitment to an ideal of perfection in whatever I was doing. I was always employed to do things properly, to get things right."[69] The first document Quentin had carried away from Monk's House in 1966 was Virginia's diary—not the thirty manuscript volumes, which were kept at Westminster Bank in Lewes until Leonard's death, nor even the typed tran-

---

68. Angela Carter, review of Elizabeth David's *English Bread and Yeast Cookery*, reprinted in *Expletives Deleted* (London: Chatto & Windus, 1994), 98.

69. Anne Olivier Bell, *Editing Virginia Woolf's Diaries* (London: Perpetua Press, 1989), 9.

script Leonard had had made of the original, but a tattered carbon copy of the typescript, from which the old man had snipped whatever he planned to include in *A Writer's Diary*. Leonard sent along these excerpts in a bundle of manila envelopes, with his explanation that the Bells now had "the complete text," and Olivier set herself the task of determining where these largely undated shreds of paper belonged. She then devised a series of four-by-six-inch card indices, beginning with one card for each month of the diary and adding further cards for letters, as they became available—green for letters from Virginia, yellow for letters to Virginia, and so forth—and eventually for names. Research began in earnest after the Bells moved from Leeds to Sussex in 1967 and they could ferret at will through bundles and boxes at Monk's House and Charleston. Leonard would occasionally show up at their door with his pocket bulging—fifteen letters to Virginia from Katherine Mansfield, for instance. In the end, Olivier filled four long boxes with these cards, which Quentin spread out before him, beside his own notes, as a spare scaffolding while he wrote. Olivier's formidable mastery of facts—the bane and blessing of a generation of Woolf scholars—could be unnerving. "Quentin," she recollected, "who naturally had a far greater imaginative grasp of Virginia's life and character than I had, was often tempted to strike me dead. But somehow our marriage survived, the biography was written, and was perhaps none the worse for being factually accurate."[70]

Quentin Bell's *Bloomsbury* (1968), written in the course of his research for the biography, is a humorous, humane, and very slightly plaintive introduction to the Group. Its principle virtue is authority (the book is still in print), but one senses that, as in his 1964 article "The Ideal Home Rumpus," an answer to John Rothenstein's attacks

---

70. Ibid., 12.

on Bloomsbury, Quentin was out to settle some scores. Knowing, for instance, that D. H. Lawrence's dislike of Bloomsbury had fortified two generations of anti-B scholars, he made short work of Lawrence (the favourite modernist, not incidentally, of F. R. Leavis), arguing that Lawrence's loathing for David Garnett's Bloomsbury friends, the men he famously labelled "black beetles," was a reaction against his own emerging homosexual impulses.[71] Quentin took issue once more with John Rothenstein, who, he claimed, regarded Bloomsbury as "not so much an artistic as a criminal association." He allowed himself a poke at Rothenstein's "violent fantasies," but only at the close of a sympathetic, well-reasoned discussion of Wyndham Lewis's treatment by Roger Fry and Bloomsbury. He then delivered an exasperated rebuttal of Keynes's much-quoted memoir "My Early Beliefs," avowing that the essay cannot be understood outside the context of the Memoir Club, or as much more than a carefully phrased provocation of the young Marxists in the room, Quentin Bell and Janie Bussy. In these sane, eloquent rejoinders, and in his patient elucidation of the character and ideas of the Group, Quentin betrayed a conviction dear to many friends of Bloomsbury: that objections to the Bloomsbury Group are based on misunderstanding. Explain all, and objection will vanish. Reason, one remembers, was the magic dust of Bloomsbury.

On second thought, Quentin seems to have taken into account at least one profound, irrational reaction to the Group. The facet of

71. This position has been more or less accepted by Brenda Maddox, Lawrence's most recent biographer, with the proviso that Lawrence cannot be neatly categorized as a suppressed homosexual, despite his fierce attraction to John Middleton Murry: "Homosexuality, for Lawrence, threatened more than the criminality and social ostracism of the time. It meant being locked in the tomb of himself and his own sex, shut off from Woman, the unknown and the current of life" (*D. H. Lawrence: The Story of a Marriage* [New York: Simon & Schuster, 1994], 203).

Bloomsbury most discussed in after years was its sexual reticence. Quentin knew he might be challenged on this point—he also knew that the Holroyd biography would reveal much that he omitted—and in his introduction conceded that he had left out a good deal that he knew and much more at which he could guess concerning the private lives of the Bloomsberries. "This is, primarily, a study in the history of ideas," he explained,

> I am not required nor am I inclined to act as Clio's chamber-maid, to sniff into commodes or under beds, to open love-letters or to scrutinize diaries. On the present occasion I shall leave Bloomsbury linen, whether clean or dirty, un-aired.[72]

Since sexual liberty was in fact so central to the "ideas" of Bloomsbury, one regrets Quentin's lost opportunity to shape the debate on Bloomsbury's sexual radicalism. But it is likely that exposure of the unconventional amours of his friends and family seemed to him incompatible with his mission and that he sensed he would only lose more sympathy for the cause. From his allusion to beds and love letters, he plunged almost immediately into a discussion of the complex opposition to the Group. Later, attempting to describe the sexual bravado of early Bloomsbury, he was forced to present a miserably neutered piece of evidence: a paraphrase of Vanessa Bell's now famous 1914 letter to Maynard Keynes on the pleasures of "Sucking Sodomy," and so on, stripped of names (even of writer and recipient) and of obscenities, sanitized and anonymized, a telling reference to the [   ] that dare not even [   ] its [   ].

---

72. Quentin Bell, *Bloomsbury*, 9.

Bloomsbury was politely received, but it clearly paled beside the more arresting Holroyd biography. In the *Times Literary Supplement* the book was for some reason reviewed jointly with a biography of the Irish writers Somerville and Ross, and the reviewer made awkward attempts to find common ground. *Studio* magazine of July 1968 contained a bland appraisal, seemingly preoccupied with definitions and descriptions of the Group, in which only the last sentence crackled with life: "The fact that the writings and paintings are exceedingly English, and provincial and unsophisticated by European standards, in most cases, and also slightly priggish is striking; however much Bloomsbury is revalued this will surely have to be recognized." "I cannot remember any reaction from Duncan or Morgan," Quentin wrote recently, "I suspect that neither of them read the book."[73]

The bulk of the Virginia Woolf biography was composed during a sabbatical year, 1967–68. Quentin made the usual rounds among surviving friends of Virginia, travelling also to the Berg Collection at the New York Public Library in 1970 and informing the curator, John D. Gordan, that he would need to see their prized possession, the Virginia Woolf diaries, but only to check certain passages against the transcripts Leonard had given the Bells. The existence of these illicit copies came as a mortal blow to Mr. Gordan. "The face of that chap at the Berg was a treat," Quentin remembered, "when he discovered what had happened. He was furious. I thought he would never speak to me again. Nor did he."[74] That was on a Friday. On Monday morning, on his way to the Berg Collection, Quentin opened a copy of *The New York Times* in the subway and saw, under "Obituaries," John D. Gordan.

---

73. Letter to the author, 19 Oct. 1995.

74. Interview with the author, 26 April 1994.

Virginia Woolf was Quentin's sixth book and a comparatively joyless undertaking. His initial ambivalence never dissipated. He seems to have sensed sharks circling as he wrote. Something of this anxiety comes through in the text; he understood that his relation to his subject was both an advantage—it made him a primary source—and a serious liability. Interviewed in the *Guardian* on the verge of publication in June 1972, he admitted that the last few years had been "something of a nightmare."

> I now realize more what Virginia went through with *The Years*—the despair. . . . I was appalled when I read the first draft. It's partly the feeling that this is something from which a splendid book should have been written. . . . Therefore the sense of failure is very acute.

Early notices were brilliant. Reviews for the second volume, four months later, were even better. The biography was an immediate best-seller on both sides of the Atlantic and won several prizes. Reprints were so rapid that Quentin could not even insert a correction until the seventh printing. He had received no advance, having made some sort of gruff handshake agreement with Leonard and the Hogarth Press, but he soon pulled in an embarrassment of royalties, with which the Bells, amused and delighted, bought a new car, a Greek holiday, and a pied-à-terre in Islington, where their daughter Cressida now lives.

Despite his misgivings, the Quentin Bell biography is a masterpiece of spare, graceful prose. What the author chose to include (Virginia's sexual molestation, for instance, and speculations on whether she bedded Vita Sackville-West) jarred some readers, but rereading the biography now, when these revelations have spawned entire books, we can see how cautiously he approached Virginia's private life, anxious to neither censor nor sensationalize material that would, ten years earlier, have been suppressed by any official biographer. He "struggled hard," as Elizabeth Hardwick wrote, "between piety and indiscretion." In *Vogue*, however, Rebecca West announced that "Virginia Woolf's official biography is to me a scene of carnage." And Cynthia Ozick, still reeling from *Maurice*, remarked, "It is possible to be too 'modern,' if that is what enables one to read a sensual character into every exuberant or sympathetic relationship between women."[75]

Quentin did not spurn the occasional first-person comment—it gave an opportunity, after all, for voicing his characteristic self-doubt (for example, "But, in fact, I myself know too little")—but what remains of himself, the author, the nephew, is like the faint impression left after a vigorous erasing. "The biography," one reviewer observed, "is a model of tact and self-effacement." Angelica Garnett recently called it "a monument of restraint, truthfulness and good writing."[76] Restraint, tact, and self-effacement may be admirable qualities, but are they fully necessary to this enterprise? When we praise these attributes of *Virginia Woolf*, do we not agree with Quentin Bell that his authority as a biographer (he who studies, considers, constructs) conflicts with his authority as a nephew (he who remembers), and that one of these roles must be suppressed? Only every third or fourth chapter, for a sentence or two, can we hear the murmurings and

---

75. *Art and Ardor*, 42–43. Ozick could not know, of course, that some months later Nigel Nicolson's *Portrait of a Marriage* (1973) would confirm Quentin's conclusion that there was "some caressing, some bedding" between Virginia and Vita. "Virginia is not the sort of person one thinks of in that way," Vita wrote to her husband, somewhat primly, in August 1926. "There is something incongruous and almost indecent in the idea. I *have* gone to bed with her (twice), but that's all."

76. Letter to the author, 13 Sept. 1995.

indecorous jokes of Charleston after dinner—and we come to long for them. Virginia had a point when she teased Quentin, then seventeen, that he should "throw up his career" to become a writer: "if you can write as well as all that, with abandonment to devilry and ribaldry—for I don't believe a word of what you say—how in God's name can you be content to remain a painter? Surely you can see the infinite superiority of the language to the paint?"[77]

Not all critics, I should add, have found the Quentin Bell biography self-effacing. In what is by far the most searching review of the book, Cynthia Ozick argued that Quentin offered "the particular intimacy of perspective—of experience, really—which characterizes not family information, but family bias." Ozick supplied the critique Quentin most feared and which he may, by his anxious exertions, have brought on himself. "Every house," she continued, "has its own special odor to the entering guest, however faint—"

> it sticks to the inhabitants, it is in their chairs and in their clothes. The analogy of bias to scent is chiefly in one's unconsciousness of one's own. Bell's *Woolf* is about Virginia, but it has the smell of Vanessa's house.[78]

The fatal flaw of the book, in Ozick's view, was that it was not about a writer's whole self—and not even about a writer, in the last analysis, but about "a madwoman and her nurse." Ozick turned to an examination of Leonard Woolf's Jewishness, his disassociation from his roots, and his enchantment with a certain segment of English society.

---

77. Nigel Nicolson and Joanne Trautmann, eds., *The Letters of Virginia Woolf*, vol. 3 (New York: Harcourt Brace, 1980), 492–93.

78. Ozick, *Art and Ardor*, 29.

She suggested, in short, and with blistering skill, that in his access to Bloomsbury and to his wife's creative genius, Leonard was more than compensated for all those breakfast trays he had carried to Virginia.

The Ozick review reflects one of the fundamental reappraisals that the Quentin Bell biography made possible: the birth of suspicion that Leonard Woolf's care of his wife was self-interested where previous observers had found it selfless, and crippling where it had once been thought sustaining.[79] These shifts in attitude toward the Woolfs' marriage arose in part from new material in the biography (Quentin's narrative varies just enough from Leonard's to suggest that the old man's memory was selective) and in part from Quentin's saintly characterization of Leonard, which invited reaction. Naturally these new concerns cast shadows, by implication, on the machinery of Virginia Woolf's posthumous fame. In later writings, Leonard would increasingly be portrayed as controlling, small-minded, tightfisted, and dogmatic, first as a husband, then as a literary executor, and Virginia's heirs—one of whom had presumed, after all, to pen the official version of her life—would be subjected to the same censorious critiques.

Adverse reactions to the Bell biography can tell us much about the burgeoning Virginia Woolf community. Her readers had waited over thirty years for a full biography and were, in the event, angered by Quentin's failure to discuss the novels. "How satisfactory can the biography of a writer be," wrote Michael Rosenthal in the *New York Times Book Review*, "if the author is unwilling (or unable) to grapple

---

79. In a general reaction against such attacks, Harold Fromm wrote that "Ozick's assault on Leonard Woolf . . . exhibits the all-too-familiar way in which political positions develop as emanations of private psychological needs and then are projected as binding morality upon a resisting outside world" ("Recycled Lives: Portraits of the Woolfs as Sitting Ducks," *Virginia Quarterly Review*, 61. 3 [Summer 1985]: 396–417).

with the crucial facts of her imaginative life?" Quentin had explained in the preface that he knew too little about English literature to tackle such a job, adding that even if he had "the equipment," he did not have the inclination. But his reluctance recalls the anxiety with which he approached the Virginia Woolf biography as a whole. He found something unseemly in writing "objectively" of his aunt—a stance even more fundamental to criticism, as he saw it, than to biography. Not only was he unqualified, he felt, to perform literary criticism: he was disqualified. His decision seemed a mark against Virginia's writing, however, an admission that her novels were difficult, and a suggestion that they were less than central to her life. As one critic complained, "It makes no more sense to talk of her as a woman without discussing her writing than it would to talk of her as a writer without mentioning she was a woman."[80]

Some reviewers found Quentin's sexual attitudes simplistic, even chauvinistic, and it is true that his depiction of Virginia's sexual development was tinged with bewilderment and disapproval. The son of Vanessa Bell may not, after all, prove the best interpreter of a less robust sexuality. Most troubling to feminists was the conjunction of Quentin's baffled response to Virginia's "frigidity" with his harrowing descriptions of her mental breakdowns and, again, his refusal to discuss her work or ideas in any depth. In so doing, argued Ellen Hawkes Rogat, "he implies a vague causal relationship between her sexual anxiety, her fear of life, her mental breakdowns, and her creative talent." Putting the point even more strongly, some years later, Jane Marcus wrote that Quentin Bell's Virginia Woolf "is a bogey

---

80. Ellen Hawkes Rogat, "The Virgin in the Bell Biography," *Twentieth Century Literature* 20.2 (1974): 98.

which frightens American women readers ... an Ophelia of the Ouse, a woman who is a failure as a woman, a cautionary figure."[81]

Nevertheless, so loud and abundant was the praise of *Virginia Woolf* that the Bells, asked recently if there was any negative reaction to the book, could recall only a single bad review. If the Bell biography was in fact a "monument of restraint," this review was its murky reverse image: a monument of unrestraint, a model of tactlessness and self-assertion. Although published in a short-lived journal, the *Virginia Woolf Quarterly*, and not widely read, Suzanne Henig's review of the biography merits discussion here because it expressed, in an extreme manner, the discontent that would inform the Woolf debates of the later 1970s and 1980s.

Henig began by announcing that *Virginia Woolf* "must be written again before the decade is over and preferably as soon as possible" and moved on to deride Quentin, "a potter and painter," for accepting the job in the first place. Like other reviewers, she felt the book should have incorporated criticism of Virginia's novels and more detailed discussion of her professional life, and she tagged Leonard as "the true hero of the book," with "Mama Vanessa" as the heroine. Henig was so intent on demolition, however, that she piled together substantive and trivial objections, weakening her argument, and tossed in bizarre declarations based on her readings at the Berg Collection—in one instance asserting that "Virginia's unpublished diaries reveal a virulent anti-Semitism such as later flourished unreasonably and insanely in Nazi Germany." She was among the first American Woolf scholars to suggest that the Bells had too much control over documents in the

---

81. Jane Marcus, "Quentin's Bogey," *Art and Anger* (Columbus, Ohio: Miami University, 1988), 204.

Berg. The Bells were not permitting note-taking from the Virginia Woolf diaries during Quentin's work on the biography, which may explain in part Henig's misinterpretation of these documents.

But the great irony of this review, considering the later controversy over Louise DeSalvo's book on Virginia Woolf's childhood sexual abuse, is Henig's revulsion at the incest story. She claimed that Quentin arranged the book in two volumes so as to provide in each "a titillating scandal guaranteed to make it an instant commercial best seller"—incest, in the first volume; in the second, lesbianism. The author, she protested, was "ready to believe the worst, sexually, of everyone he writes about," and, moreover,

> quick to embrace without any satisfactory documentary evidence the notion that George Duckworth, a man whose many kindnesses and solicitations both Virginia and Vanessa continually accepted even after the purported sexual advances, was a sexually maladjusted individual whose particular vice was incest. His obvious source was his mother Vanessa who dutifully recounted Virginia's versions of purported incidents. He never records the exact date, place and witnesses to such incidents. In view of Virginia's own sexual maladjustment and uncertain mental states, is it not possible that she might have imagined or even wished her elder half-brother's interest to be more than it was?[82]

Again, like those who objected to the hints of lesbianism in the Bell biography, Henig could not have known of every document available

---

82. Suzanne Henig, review of Quentin Bell biography in *Virginia Woolf Quarterly* 2 (Summer 1972): 58.

to Quentin, in this case Virginia's Memoir Club essay "22 Hyde Park Gate," in which she described George's malefactions for an audience that would have included her sister, unlikely to sit silently through a patently false account of their childhood.[83] Henig's suggestion that Virginia may have "imagined or even wished" George's advances seems cruel but not outlandish, given the culture of blame surrounding sexual abuse. What leaps out is her demand for exact dates, places, witnesses to child molestation, as if it were a road accident.

NOW THAT OUR vision of Virginia Woolf is supplemented by her published diaries, letters, and memoirs, let alone a mountain of secondary material, we can better appreciate the breadth and sensitivity of the Quentin Bell biography. Many of the objections to his book have been met, in any case, by the choice of Hermione Lee as his successor. In her book, readers have an authorized life of Virginia Woolf penned by a woman, a university-trained critic, a feminist, neither indebted to Leonard nor enthralled by Vanessa. The Quentin Bell biography will remain in print and, I predict, settle back on its fundamental richness as the nephew's biography, a work that illumines Virginia and her milieu not in spite of Quentin, with his "family bias" and Bloomsbury turn of mind, but because of him. Virginia Woolf wrote in her diary that "the one thing needful in criticism, or writing of any sort" was to be—as Quentin was—a personage: "for we're all as wrong as wrong can be. But character is the thing."

---

83. "22 Hyde Park Gate" was published posthumously in *Moments of Being* (1976), edited by Jeanne Schulkind. Later editions include "A Sketch of the Past," with its description of Gerald Duckworth examining Virginia's private parts when she was five or six. This essay came to light some days after the Bell biography was published, and it corrects Quentin on a point of detail. He was not able to attribute the early groping incident to Gerald, rather than George, until the seventh English printing. American editions retain the error.

PART TWO

We shall read her life; we shall read her letters; we shall study her portraits, speculate about her diseases—of which she had a great variety; and rattle the drawers of her writing table, which are for the most part empty. Let us begin with the biography— for what could be more amusing?

—VIRGINIA WOOLF,
"I AM CHRISTINA ROSSETTI"

THE MOST DIFFICULT part of a modern history is deciding what to omit, and I am not speaking only of the partial truth that each writer necessarily extracts from the exercise of her mind upon her material. I am speaking of the mind-numbing surpluses of latter-day Blooms-bury: the tireless offerings of emotion, of time, of intellect, like vo-tive objects—a foot, a face, a uterus—transforming a blessed surface into tin. There is no measuring the flood of ephemera that was, and still is, vital to the Bloomsbury boom: broadcasts, exhibitions, jour-nalism, symposia, postcards, scholarly essays, sharp exchanges in "Letters" sections, midnight readings of *The Waves*, the first Virginia Woolf teacup, the first exhibition of Carrington's art. What, then, to make of the second and third Virginia Woolf teacups, the rebuke of the scholarly essay, the next midnight reading of *The Waves*?

Repetition is an engine of culture but also, and more obviously, of destruction. In 1961 a writer for the *Guardian* newspaper first remarked on the growing fascination with Bloomsbury; twelve years later, Elizabeth Hardwick, surveying a confusion of books and stale anecdotes in the wake of the Holroyd biography and the Quentin Bell biography, produced what deserves to be a canonical statement of exhaustion:

> Bloomsbury is, just now, like one of those ponds on a private estate from which all of the trout have been scooped out for the season. It is not a natural place for fish, but rather a water stocked for the fisherman so that he may not cast his line in vain. . . . The period, the letters, the houses, the love affairs, the blood lines: these are private anecdotes one is happy enough to meet once or twice but not again and again.[1]

And this was written over twenty years ago.

Very little original material of earthshaking newness emerged after the Quentin Bell biography. The mid-1970s and 1980s were instead years of expansion, of an astonishingly thorough dispersal of information and goods. Enthusiasts were offered access to previously unpublished documents, like the Virginia Woolf letters, diaries, and reading notebooks. Major new biographies of almost every Bloomsberry appeared, along with exhibitions of Bloomsbury art, numerous plays and broadcasts, and eventually the opening to the public of Monk's House and Charleston Farmhouse, symbolic evidence that there were no more closed doors and, by implication, nothing left to

---

1. Elizabeth Hardwick, "Bloomsbury and Virginia Woolf," *Seduction and Betrayal: Women and Literature* (New York: Random House, 1974), 125.

hide. Having disgorged their secrets, down to the minutiae of their daily lives, the mythic Bloomsberries gave up their fabled exclusivity. Now all were welcome on the Monk's House bowling green and in the Charleston studio, where a grimy paint rag and a carelessly placed hat suggested that the occupants had only just stepped out.

Opportunities to buy Bloomsbury art, books, papers, and artifacts had been increasing since the early 1960s as dealers approached heirs and the elderly. Much material escaped to America before the English understood its value. David Garnett and Gerald Brenan are said to have kept up their correspondence in these years knowing that the Harry Ransome Humanities Research Center at the University of Texas would snap it up, like pieces of the True Cross. But some devotees required a fuller possession than that accorded by mere ownership of a signed copy of *Orlando* or a Duncan Grant nude. The Quentin Bell biography—a glimpse, however mediated, into that glittering archive—sparked a struggle for meaning that escalated in following years as the bulk of Virginia Woolf's private papers were published. Ownership of the truth was at stake. This involved a challenge to Quentin and Olivier Bell's authority and vision and hence, at one remove, to Leonard Woolf's. Those who had known Virginia Woolf in life were judged less and less able to appraise her as a writer, a woman, a feminist—less able, in fact, to *know* her.

Certainly the publication of her letters, diaries, and other personal writings made possible uncannily intimate inquiries into Virginia Woolf's life and thought, especially in combination with the critical tendencies of the period. Having dominated the field for thirty years, the formalist doctrine of New Criticism was giving way to sociologically and biographically based approaches—feminist, historicist, psychoanalytic or more broadly psychological criticism—and the notion of the proper sphere of criticism was evolving. What, for instance, constituted a text? Leonard's stock portfolio? A snapshot of Carrington? The ascendance of biographically based criticism did not go unnoticed by Bloomsbury scholars, and there were many, even among the younger generation, who protested its effects, arguing that exhaustive scrutiny of the Bloomsberries' private lives sapped attention from their achievements and cheapened critical discourse. How many graduate students, they argued, do not know of Virginia Woolf's periods of madness or her affair with Vita Sackville-West? Yet how few have read her novels? Alongside the multiplying essays on Woolf's madness, suicide, sexuality, ran a cautionary gloss that this was not, perhaps, a dignifying end for a great writer.[2]

The explosion of interest in Virginia Woolf and Bloomsbury not only made for repetition of material—anecdotes, photographs, even journalistic tones of voice and critical barbs—but fed and grew large on those repetitions. Many readers will have noticed that reviews of Bloomsbury-related books have a stock opening: a wry little snort that we have heard too much about the Group. This is even more common in favourable reviews, where the writer feels defensive in promoting what is thought to be already overvalued. "This is fortunately not yet another Bloomsbury book," began Alan Bell's review of Richard Shone's *Bloomsbury Portraits* in the *Times Literary Supplement* in 1976. The next year, with George Spater and Ian Parsons's *A Marriage of True Minds* before him, Bell pronounced it too "not just another Bloomsbury book." In Platonic terms, how far removed from reality is a journalist's cliché?

---

2. Despite the adverse criticism the Bell biography received from Woolf scholars, P. N. Furbank also chose to exclude discussion of Forster's novels from his authorized life of 1977–78. "To omit any in-depth consideration of the writings, particularly the fiction," wrote Wilfred Stone in response, "*is* to diminish Forster—it is literally to cut him in two" (*Biography* 3.3 [1980]).

With the market expanding like a pair of lungs, innumerable small, obscure items flew from darkness into light and were sucked at once into a deeper darkness. Richard Kennedy's illustrated *A Boy at the Hogarth Press*, a charming but slight effort, remains some critics' perennial example of the epiphenomena of Bloomsbury. The housekeeper Louie Mayer's essay in *Recollections of Virginia Woolf* is another. Both appeared in 1972. My favourite example also comes from this year, from the first issue of the short-lived *Virginia Woolf Quarterly:* the photograph of a monstrous bust of Virginia Woolf, strongly resembling her husband, of unknown size and materials, available for a limited time only in the USA for $37.50. "Proceeds from the sale of these beautiful statues," we are told, "will be used to defray costs of publishing the *Quarterly*." A close second would be Harcourt Brace's 1982 Virginia Woolf diary-calendar, which marked the anniversaries of her suicide attempts.

In October 1973, the *Sunday Times* began to publish extracts from Nigel Nicolson's new book, the story of his parents' forty-nine-year marriage, including his mother's autobiographical account of her affair with Violet Trefusis, the eighty-page manuscript of which Nicolson had discovered locked in a Gladstone bag in her writing room at Sissinghurst soon after his mother's death. Not strictly speaking a Bloomsbury book, *Portrait of a Marriage* became, and remains, compulsory reading for Bloomsbury enthusiasts, central to an understanding of Vita Sackville-West and her relationship with Virginia Woolf.

While Harold Nicolson's same-sex affairs may have surprised some readers, Vita's were less than staggering, having recently figured in the Quentin Bell biography. Nigel Nicolson knew his book would be controversial, nevertheless, and on two counts: he had not only broadcast the intimate details of his parents' marriage but dared to suggest that a union such as theirs could be secure and happy. "It is the story," he insisted in his preface, "of two people who married for love and whose love deepened with each passing year, although each was constantly and by mutual consent unfaithful to the other." As for Vita's anguished narrative, he added, far from tarnishing her memory, "it burnished it." He believed that she wrote her story with eventual publication in mind, even with the hope of it helping and encouraging "those similarly placed today," and that this is one reason she did not destroy the manuscript before her death.

"Let not the reader condemn in ten minutes," he pleaded, "a decision which I have pondered for ten years." Some of his readers may have remembered Nigel Nicolson's concern, voiced in the *Spectator* in January 1968, that those likely to be written about might now, after the Holroyd biography, destroy their private papers. He had been mulling over these issues while editing his father's diaries. "The trend toward over-frankness in biography and over-suppression in autobiography is plain," he declared, and added:

> The sexual or medical aberrations of prominent men are now regarded as material without which their biographies would be incomplete, like Michael Holroyd's life of Lytton Strachey, which Malcolm Muggeridge has described in a capsule blurb as "a fine study of sodomy at King's."

Since there was no such material in the Harold Nicolson diaries (he had always intended them for publication, and thus restrained his pen), we can suppose that Nigel Nicolson was speaking generally— but thinking, perhaps, of the explosive contents of his mother's Gladstone bag. The passage is noticeably testy, although the source of irritation seems to waver between Holroyd's *Strachey* and Muggeridge's reductive "capsule blurb," as if Nicolson is not sure which writer he should identify with. This article now reads less as an attack on Holroyd's *Strachey* than as a covert expression of Nigel Nicolson's ambivalence in the period between his mother's death in 1962 and Violet Trefusis's death ten years later, when he became free to use her name without fear of libel. He had not even shown the manuscript to his father, who died in May 1968, afraid that it would only increase his misery after Vita's death, and that "he might destroy it—or it him."

Nigel Nicolson's eventual decision to publish *Portrait of a Marriage,* and the fanfare that greeted the book, tell us much about what Holroyd has called the "barometric change" in social and cultural attitudes in the five years after the Strachey biography. Most reviewers applauded Nicolson's candour. In the *Times Literary Supplement* his editing was regarded as "beyond praise. He passes no judgments, he faces, without ever losing his affection for both his parents, their interlocking quiddities." Gordon Haight, writing for the *Yale Review,* called the book "remarkable" and observed that Nicolson wrote "with such calm detachment of his mother's turbulent passions that one forgets to question the decency of such an exposure." And Brendan Gill, in the *New Yorker,* announced that Vita's narrative was "as close to a cry from the heart as anybody writing in English in our time has come, and it is a cry that, once heard, is not likely ever to be forgotten." Her editor, he noted shrewdly, "keeps at a distance from his radically scandalous revelations; when his guard drops . . . he betrays his uneasiness by becoming sentimental." In a 1980 interview, Nicolson disclosed that he still worried whether he had been right to publish his mother's manuscript.

But there were weeds among the laurels. Nora Sayles began her appraisal in the *New York Times Book Review* with an admission of reverse snobbery: "Some of us can't approach this book without prejudice: an instinctive recoil from what Harold Nicolson and Vita Sackville-West represented, both politically and socially." She listed their rebarbative qualities—notably, anti-Semitism and class bias—and, as evidence of Vita's snooty assumptions, quoted the opening of one of her gardening columns in the *Observer:* "If you have a moat around your garden. . . ." Yet, despite her unease, Sayles felt drawn to the vulnerability and courage of the Nicolsons, especially Harold, and ended up declaring *Portrait of a Marriage* "one of the more radical books to appear in recent years." A more resigned disgust issued from John Richardson, in the *New York Review of Books,* and it can hardly be incidental that this was almost the only review to associate the Nicolsons, however peripherally, with Bloomsbury. "There is some pleasure," Richardson began, "in watching those prissy mandarins, whose stock-in-trade was the exposure of Victorian humbug, being stripped in turn of their fig leaves, and at the hands of their own children too." First prissy mandarins, then "a coven of high-minded swingers" and "a precious coterie" and "a hot item"; it took thirty lines for Richardson to explain that the Nicolsons were not actually part of Bloomsbury. And then, after providing a long account of Vita's snobbery, ostensibly to dull our sympathies for her, Richardson settled to his real task: the reading of *Portrait of a Marriage* as a salacious tract, the story of Vita's "career as a besotted transvestite" and her "kink for male attire."

For many readers, of course, Bloomsbury was now synonymous with sexual deviance, that siren call to the bookish and diffident. This may explain why Peter Luke chose just the one word, imprecise but savoury, as the title for his 1973 play about Lytton and Carrington. Luke had been among those (Christopher Hampton, Ken Russell, John Osborne, and Gore Vidal, to name others) angling for stage and film rights to the Holroyd biography, and he was the first to put his effort before the public, at the Phoenix Theatre in London. But material that seems to drop ready-made into a writer's hands is not always to be trusted. *Bloomsbury*, complained a *Times Literary Supplement* critic, was "not a play which deals with people but a charade which deals in names." In the *Sunday Times*, Harold Hobson reiterated that its actors "more or less well impersonate phantoms to which names like Virginia Woolf, Dora Carrington, Lytton Strachey are attached in the programme." "See Virginia Woolf going mad. See Lytton Strachey in bed with two close friends," wrote Irving Wardle in *The Times*, under a publicity photo of the latter scene. "The play leaves one in no doubt that these people lived red-blooded lives even though they may have gone in for painting and writing now and then." *Bloomsbury* was pronounced distasteful, pretentious, and incompetent by critics, and so sensational, even "filthy," that it aroused sympathy for its actors—among them Penelope Wilton as Carrington, the first of several Bloomsbury women she would portray. Daniel Massey was praised as Strachey, and Yvonne Mitchell earned consoling mention in the *Times Literary Supplement* as Virginia Woolf, the narrator: "a haggard female Prospero who seems in some deeply improbable way to create the play before us until she is driven into madness by guilt and, in a dottily melodramatic coda complete with projections of foaming sea, she is overwhelmed by, yes, the waves."

Virginia Woolf as narrator is another device that seems to arrive gift-wrapped from the muse. Many playwrights have chosen her lyricism over their own, though it may seem, when all her books are splayed open on the desk beside the typewriter, less like a choice than a divine imperative. Out-writing Virginia Woolf must feel like trying to outwit Oscar Wilde. Plays about Virginia Woolf, which multiplied in the 1970s and 1980s, typically attempt to trace the origins of her madness, her "frigidity," her suicide. A surprising number rely on extended monologues modelled closely on her writings. When liberties are taken, these, too, recall her more experimental work: layering of voices, for example, and disdain for action-driven plots and linear time sequences. Maureen Duffy's *A Nightingale in Bloomsbury Square*, a small production at the Hampstead Theatre Club in September 1973, failed to appeal to the *Times* critic for reasons that will sound familiar to any reader of Virginia Woolf: "instead of dramatic conflict, we get something perilously close to an ego trip." Against a spare set of three enlarged book spines, Virginia delivered a lengthy monologue on her Stephen upbringing, her companionate marriage, and her childlessness for two guests, Vita Sackville-West and, oddly, Sigmund Freud (both in male evening dress), who were said to offer "ineffectual smiles and sympathy from the sidelines."

Fascination with Bloomsbury seemed to reach a frenzy in the early 1970s and was continually remarked on in the press. A *New Yorker* cartoon of 20 May 1974 by Everett Opie showed a solid gentleman relaxing with his pipe and book, his wife confiding to a guest: "It all started with that trial subscription to the *TLS*. Then came that Nigel Nicolson book, the smoking jacket and pipe, the pint of bitter, and, bingo, little West Tenth Street has become Bloomsbury." In England, critical opinion held that only Americans could fall for Bloomsbury. Yet the affliction had spread. An English article entitled "What's New in the Bloomsbury Industry?"[3] provided an illustrated chart of relationships among the principal members of the Group (the need for which remains a stock joke of journalists), with dotted lines to indicate "blood," double lines for "marriage," and straight lines for "ro-

---

3. *The Sunday Times Magazine* 3 Feb. 1974: 58–61.

mance." Straight lines flash from Lytton Strachey's head like solar rays. The writer, Jenny Rees, observed that nothing about Bloomsbury, however trivial, seemed without interest. "Bloomsbury definitely has magic these days," she wrote, "a star quality, growing stronger all the time as the dimmest, furthest corners of the cupboards are searched for new material." She described the ranks of addicts and the constant intake of new recruits and identified the "regulation handbooks" of the movement as the Bell and Holroyd biographies. "A curious recruit to the Industry," she added, "is Major-Gen. A. L. Gadd, now retired from Southern Command to the peaceful countryside of Somerset."

In the interview that followed, David Gadd explained that he wrote *The Loving Friends* (1974) because he thought the Bloomsberries were "splendid" people: "What interests me is that they were thinkers. I agree that society, and indeed the Army, could not exist if we were all thinkers, but it is essential to have a small number of people who do not conform." What he could do without, however, was the noisy "Youth Movement," with its "people marching up and down, waving banners and shouting."

The Loving Friends, published in England by the Hogarth Press, was less a study of the Bloomsbury Group than a reiteration of how splendid they were. Splendid in love! For Gadd, all those ideas and bits of work served as a blurred background to their more diverting adventures *à deux* and *à trois.* He devoted special attention to Carrington and her "frank bisexuality" and indeed seemed to prefer her to the standard members of the Group. In the *New York Review of Books,* Irvin Ehrenpreis wrote that those who were "fatigued by thoughtful recollections in excellent prose and prefer spicy reportage may try David Gadd's *The Loving Friends.*" Quentin Bell produced a characteristically gallant review in the *New Statesman,* but Bernard

Bergonzi, writing for the *New Review,* suggested that a properly pro-grammed computer might have done equally well—"might, indeed, have achieved a marginally less flat and platitudinous prose style."

As well as rushing books like Gadd's through the presses and hunting down memoirs like Vanessa Bell's *Notes on Virginia's Child-hood* (1974), publishers cast around for suitable reprints. Quentin Bell's *Bloomsbury* and Lytton Strachey's *Eminent Victorians* were ob-vious choices, the latter issued by its original publishers, Chatto & Windus. In 1973, the University of Chicago Press even reprinted Clive Bell's *Old Friends* and *Civilization* in one hardback volume, al-though the latter must be the most universally detested of all Blooms-bury books, a reckless distortion of the Group's shared ideals. (Before Clive Bell became the reactionary who wrote *Civilization,* he had been the libertarian who wrote *On British Freedom,* a pamphlet advocating tolerance for social and sexual nonconformity.)

One of the few illuminating uses of *Civilization* occurs in another 1973 publication, Carolyn Heilbrun's acclaimed *Toward a Recognition of Androgyny.* Heilbrun, a Columbia professor and distinguished Woolf scholar, began her career in 1961 with a history of the Garnett family, connected at many points with Bloomsbury. Like Michael Holroyd, Heilbrun felt drawn to biography at an early age; she has said that, as a child, she worked her way alphabetically through the bi-ography section of the St. Agnes branch of the New York Public Li-brary. She has also, since 1963, written mysteries as Amanda Cross, commenting in an interview that her one regret is that she made her heroine, Professor Kate Fansler, so very good-looking. "I always saw her as not so much beautiful," she explained, "as tall and thin and, I guess, sort of looking like Virginia Woolf."[4]

4. *Publishers Weekly* 14 April 1989: 48.

Toward a Recognition of Androgyny hinged on Heilbrun's conviction that "our future salvation lies in a movement away from sexual polarization and the prison of gender toward a world in which individual roles and the modes of personal behavior can be freely chosen."[5] Bloomsbury, she believed, represented the first example of such a way of life in practice, although "to admit admiration for the Bloomsbury group still requires one to assume a posture either defensive or apologetic." In a 1968 article, the basis for her later chapter on Bloomsbury, Heilbrun had described the "profound hostility" with which a seminar at Columbia had responded to discussion of the Group. "The spokesman for the general contempt," she recalled,

> was a very bright young Englishman who tried heroically to enunciate the reasons for his loathing. Having accused them all of being shrill, arty, escapist, aristocratic, and insufficiently talented (was *Mrs. Dalloway*, after all, as great a book as *Ulysses*?) he finally attacked them, and with passion, for being, many of them, homosexual. This truly astonished me, for he was at that time engaged in a study of another Englishman, greatly admired by both of us, who is also homosexual.[6]

When she mentioned this contradiction, her Englishman blurted out: "Oh well, the truth is I just can't bear them."

In her chapter on Bloomsbury, Heilbrun quoted a long passage from *Civilization* on the hetaerae, educated women whom Clive Bell believed Athenian men appreciated as "a means to civilization."

---

5. *Toward a Recognition of Androgyny* (New York: Knopf, 1973), ix–x.

6. *Midway*, Autumn 1968: 72.

While a contemporary reading of this passage suggests that Bell located the hetaera's value in her ability to enliven male conversation, somewhat like dancing girls who quote Socrates, it must, in the early 1970s, have seemed an unusually generous reflection on the historical status of women. It is easier to agree with Heilbrun that when Bell praised his friend Roger Fry as ardent, intelligent, sweet, sensitive, cultivated, erudite, "these are the adjectives of praise in an androgynous world" and that if one looks at Lytton Strachey's writing "in the light of androgyny, one begins to see in it revolutionary implications." Her analysis of the essay "Florence Nightingale" in *Eminent Victorians* beautifully highlighted the contradictions in Strachey's attitudes toward dominating women and pointed toward their partial resolution in *Queen Victoria* and *Elizabeth and Essex*. Heilbrun went on to note that the same understanding, "that of the androgynous mind," pervades Virginia Woolf's works, though it is often misunderstood by critics, and to identify *To the Lighthouse*, rather than *Orlando* or *A Room of One's Own*, as the best expression of Woolf's vision of androgyny in art and life.

My own copy of *Toward a Recognition of Androgyny*, purchased from a secondhand bookshop, came annotated with the phrase "har har," among others, and it is true that initial responses to the book varied wildly. Writing for the *New York Times Book Review*, Joyce Carol Oates asserted that Heilbrun had "done a fantastic amount of reading" and that while she could not agree with all of Heilbrun's conclusions, she found the section on Bloomsbury "most rewarding." A critic for the *Yale Review* complained that, far from showing wide reading, Heilbrun's book was "so poorly researched that it may disgrace the subject in the eyes of serious scholars." His underlying objection may be glimpsed in his aside that the intellectual level of the book was revealed "by its four flattering references to Kate Millett and fifteen glib jibes at Freud," although for our purposes it is worth noticing the glib jibe at Bloomsbury in the reviewer's argument that Heilbrun, in extending the Group as an androgynous model, failed "to weigh whether absolute fluidity of sexual identity might not be the prerogative of a moneyed elite, at the expense of a vast laboring middle class." Conservative writers have been the most reluctant to abandon the censure of Bloomsbury as wealthy and leisured, not middle but upper class: a piece of cultural currency worn smooth as a lucky penny.

Joyce Carol Oates's review also addressed Nancy Topping Bazin's *Virginia Woolf and the Androgynous Vision* (1973), a book that offered a sharp contrast to Heilbrun's view and proved even more controversial, especially within the burgeoning Woolf community. What Heilbrun regarded as a sane, forward-thinking attempt to harmonize male and female qualities in the mind, Bazin regarded as a psychic accommodation to mental imbalance. Her study is an interesting precursor to Louise DeSalvo's later book on Virginia Woolf's childhood sexual abuse, and indeed it provoked similar outrage from some readers, who were appalled to see Woolf and her writings pathologized. In Bazin's book, Woolf's life and works were read against, and through, the literature of manic-depression, so that the author offered a portrait of Virginia Woolf as a manic-depressive in the way that DeSalvo later offered a portrait of her as an incest survivor.

THE SCHOLARS WHO clustered in that New York hotel room in 1970 for the first MLA seminar on Virginia Woolf vowed not to squander their newfound sense of community. One result was *The Virginia Woolf Newsletter*, informal, mimeographed pages edited at Columbia by Carolyn Heilbrun with the help of a graduate student.

Only three issues appeared before the arrival of a sleek successor, the *Virginia Woolf Quarterly*, co-founded by Mitchell Leaska and Suzanne Henig, and edited by Henig at San Diego State University. With its violet cover and impressive list of contributors, the *Quarterly* seemed all that a Woolf enthusiast could desire. Henig had even convinced the Bells to allow her to edit some previously unpublished juvenilia, "A Cockney's Farming Experiences" (touted by Henig as "Virginia Woolf's first novel") and "Experiences of a Paterfamilias," both of which had originally appeared in the *Hyde Park Gate News*. But almost at once—in fact by the second issue, when Henig skewered the Bell biography—the *Quarterly* began to fall apart. It is difficult to say exactly what went wrong, but Woolf scholars felt increasingly uneasy with the journal and its vivacious, combative editor. The *Quarterly* went through the usual financial crises, ceasing publication for a while, and then emerged with a minor celebrity, Françoise Gilot, as its art director. From England in 1977, Henig addressed her readers in an expansive mood:

> At the moment, it is Christmas Day in Maidenhead, Berkshire, England as I sit before the fire, sherry in hand, in the Richard Kennedy household, proofing the last pages of the galleys for this issue which must be mailed off in the morning before I board Air India's magnificent jumbo jet, the Ashoka, for New Delhi. Maidenhead, you will recall, is where Leonard first proposed to Virginia and was finally accepted.

During her last visit to India, she mused, she had met Dr. Mulk Raj Anand, "the great novelist who was an early peripheral member of

Bloomsbury."[7] She went on to describe her Christmas dinner and the sprightly conversation of her friends, "recorded in Urdu in Iftikhar's detailed diary for posterity," and interrupted herself to add that "the telephone has just rung again with the familiar voices of English and French friends whom it is impossible to see during these three English days."[8]

But this was to be Henig's last "Editor's Page." A legal battle with her university had left Henig with ownership of the *Quarterly*. Soon after, she dropped out of the Woolf community and, some say, went to Mexico, and the journal has never resurfaced. "She was a fascinating character," J. J. Wilson recalls, but few other scholars have been willing to offer comments on the record.[9]

Dismay over the *Quarterly* seems to have brought Woolf scholars closer together, and a group based in northern California launched the *Virginia Woolf Miscellany* in 1973. Intentionally modest in appearance and tone, the *Miscellany* was designed to appeal to the common Woolfian as well as to academics. It is still in print. Editorship rotates; no one critical approach is allowed to dominate. Spats erupt, especially over provocative books like Roger Poole's *The Unknown Virginia Woolf*, but the emphasis is on nourishing the Woolf commu-

---

7. This is beyond overstatement. Anand came to London as a student in 1926—already too late for early Bloomsbury—and met the Woolfs and others through a fellow student. For a time, he corrected proofs at the Hogarth Press. He returned to India after the war and in 1981 published *Conversations in Bloomsbury*, an inaccurate but lively account of his meetings with the Group.

8. *Virginia Woolf Quarterly* 3.3–4 (Summer and Fall 1977).

9. In issue 14 of the *Charleston Magazine*, Olivier Bell describes Henig as "an imperious woman, a dedicated Woolf scholar; she demanded to be shown the exact spot in the River Ouse where Virginia's body was found; she demanded to be taken to see the (then ailing) Leonard Woolf at Monk's House."

nity, and this accounts for the journal's longevity. Some of the most enjoyable pieces are unashamedly giddy and reverential, including tales of pilgrimages to Bloomsbury-related sites: St. Ives, for instance, or 22 Hyde Park Gate. After her trip to Talland House, the Stephen family's summer home in Cornwall, Jane Lilienfeld described how she had paced the flagstone terrace, "on which Mr. Ramsay had walked," then moved toward the front of the house, where two bay windows faced the sea. "I knew that when I turned to face the lighthouse," she wrote, "I would have revealed to me a vision."

> I turned. A mist had come in, obscuring the sea, and the lighthouse existed now only as an eye. A red eye, small but strong away in the mist. James' last vision before Ellen carries him to bed "made him gaze and marvel." Years later he remembers to have seen "a yellow eye." I had seen what James and Virginia Stephen had seen.[10]

Well, not exactly. Five years later a curious *Miscellany* reader wrote to the Trinity House Lighthouse Service to ask if the present lens were the original lighting apparatus for Godrevy Lighthouse. The public relations officer answered that no, while the lighthouse was built in 1859, the present, nonrevolving lens was installed in 1934, at which time the keepers were dismissed and the lighthouse converted to automatic operation. The original lens had flashed a white light across the line of the viewer every ten seconds. Through the mist across the bay, this light would have appeared yellow to the inhabitants of Talland House. Lilienfeld had seen the soulless red eye of modernization.

The *Miscellany* was conceived in opposition to the *Quarterly*, and

---

10. *Virginia Woolf Miscellany* 7 (1977): 3.

soon a faction within that community would align in opposition to the Bell biography. The timely topic for the 1973 MLA seminar on Woolf was "The Work and the Biography." Discussion centred on Ellen Hawkes Rogat's ground-breaking paper "The Virgin in the Bell Biography," published the following year in *Twentieth Century Literature* and since referred to by Jane Marcus as "the first of the new feminist approaches to Woolf scholarship."

FROM PERHAPS 1972 to 1988, the course of the Bloomsbury revival was overshadowed by the more potent and arresting history of American feminist Woolf scholarship. This history intersects not only with the larger women's movement and the student movement but with a panoply of concurrent developments, such as the resurgence of biographically and historically based criticism and increasing access to Virginia Woolf material at the Berg Collection, the University of Sussex, and elsewhere. The movement has been characterized as antagonistic toward Quentin Bell and the English Woolf establishment, although this distorts what was in many ways a fruitful, if sometimes fierce, transatlantic exchange. Certainly the spirit of the age worked against the orthodoxies that informed the Bell biography. The struggle has been more usefully described as a rejection of the English Woolf, that wilting maiden, in favour of a taut, adaptable survivor: a sort of frontier Woolf, spurs ajingle. This Woolf could not have been pieced together from her novels alone but emerges from her diary, her letters, even the scraps of her unfinished essays. One of the first radical acts of feminist scholarship was the revaluation of *Night and Day, Three Guineas,* and *The Years,* works disliked and neglected by earlier scholars, who had felt Woolf's importance lay in her more patently modernist writings. Another pivotal factor was new textual scholarship, the painstaking reconstruction and comparison of drafts, which allowed insight into Virginia

Woolf's thought and artistry. "Very often the drafts and unpublished versions seemed 'truer' texts—spectacularly true in the case of *The Years,*" Jane Marcus has observed, quietly turning away from a long critical tradition of privileging the published text.[11] Louise DeSalvo, who worked for ten years with the many surviving drafts of Woolf's first novel, *The Voyage Out,* told a writer for the *New York Times* that all of the scholars who worked with earlier drafts of Woolf's novels have found that "they are much more radical, more left-wing, more egalitarian, more lesbian, and more feminist than the published texts themselves."[12] Woolf's revisions can be seen then as not only aesthetic but pragmatic, the paring away of objectionable matter to ensure that the novels could be published and taken seriously. Marcus has wondered if Woolf, leaving this confusion of drafts and fragments behind her, had ever imagined future readers reconstructing her discarded texts, "playing the part of the ancients in piecing together Echo's body."[13]

Now that we have the benefit of so many tenured women professors, so many women administrators, and so many women's studies departments (not to mention the new heresy, gender studies, and the occasional men's studies department), it is easy to forget that feminist scholars of the early 1970s faced profound hostility, rudeness, and obstruction. Jane Marcus tells the story of receiving as a rejection from a prestigious scholarly journal a torn scrap of paper with the scrawl "Another piece of feminist trash." The first anthology she edited,

---

11. *Virginia Woolf and the Languages of Patriarchy* (Bloomington: Indiana University Press, 1987), xii.

12. Quoted in Leslie Bennett, "Scholars Discovering Less Subtle Virginia Woolf," *New York Times* 1 Nov. 1982: C11.

13. Jane Marcus, *"The Years* as Götterdämmerung, Greek Play and Domestic Novel," *Virginia Woolf and the Languages of Patriarchy,* 53.

New Feminist Essays on Virginia Woolf (1981), took four years to find an American publisher. Feminists from working-class backgrounds felt especially isolated within academia and came to relish the solidarity they gained through Woolf. Some yanking and tugging was needed to get the old Woolf to fit a radical new readership, but ultimately, the energy of these struggles yielded one of the most lively and contentious bodies of scholarship in this century.[14]

THE STRENGTH OF Ellen Hawkes Rogat's "The Virgin in the Bell Biography" is that it is more than a protest, more than a statement of what readers no longer wished to hear about Virginia Woolf. Issues raised in this early essay are still fundamental to the Woolf debate. Rogat began by complaining that "something central did not permeate" in Quentin Bell's depiction of his aunt. Although she felt grateful for the new material he had presented, "and for his many engaging anecdotes," she could not find in his biography the bracing intellect that emerged from her own readings of Virginia Woolf's novels and essays, but "only the pale figure of a neurotic virgin cloistered from experience."

> This phantom has haunted Woolf for years. But just when many readers, most notably a number of women, were developing a more complex view, Bell called up the vanished ghost. His claim that "there was, both in her personality and in her art, a disconcertingly aetherial quality" resurrected the spectral clichés.[15]

---

14. For a more complete history of Woolf criticism, see John Mepham's *Virginia Woolf*, part of the series Criticism in Focus (Bristol: Bristol Classical Press, 1992).

15. Ellen Hawkes Rogat, "The Virgin in the Bell Biography," *Twentieth Century Literature* 20.2 (1974): 96.

The roots of the problem were twofold. In the first place, there were Quentin Bell's unconscious sexual attitudes, which Rogat demonstrated by, among other means, plucking his descriptions of talented women like Anne Thackeray Ritchie and Julia Margaret Cameron from their contexts and surveying the grim array of adjectives used to qualify their achievements: for example, vague, tenuous, charming, imbecile, erratic, sentimental. In the second place, there was his refusal to discuss Woolf's writing, a particular weakness given that Woolf's life and art were "inextricably intertwined" and that ignoring her intellectual development laid, in Rogat's view, an unwelcome stress on "the sexual theme." Reviewers, Rogat pointed out, had been all too eager to snap up sexual molestation as a crucial influence on Woolf's character and work. Rogat made a good case that the terms in which Woolf's writing were often described—cold, insubstantial, diaphanous, ethereal— emerged not from stylistic analysis but "from a deep sexual grammar" and that the Bell biography only reinforced this critical failing.

Perhaps the most damning element of Rogat's critique was her unravelling of the flirtation between Clive and Virginia, as recounted by Quentin Bell, and her observation that Bell assigned "different motives to similar actions, according to the sex of the actor." In the Bell biography, Virginia's behaviour was described as hurtful and irresponsible, Clive's as merely gallant, a natural outgrowth of what Quentin Bell called "his ardent and sanguine temperament." When Virginia managed to elude bed, her biographer described this as, in some ways, a neurotic flight from sexuality. Rogat proposed another version of these events, according to which Clive was as responsible for the flirtation as Virginia, and Virginia continued with it in part because it was flattering and encouraging, but also because she could not comfortably break it off without losing Clive's friendship.

In the following issue of this journal, Quentin Bell responded to

Rogat's "severely critical review" of his biography, but only to the extent of correcting a minor point she had made, based on Leonard Woolf's autobiography; Rogat had said that Clive Bell was not considered an intellectual at Cambridge, nor had he talked about painting. She had meant, of course, to imply that Quentin Bell may have exaggerated his father's role in Virginia Woolf's development as a novelist. We can wonder, as did Rogat in her reply on the next page, why Quentin elected not to address her more central arguments. "I should have liked him to acknowledge the validity of the issues I raise," Rogat remarked, "quite apart from acquiescence or disagreement. The fact that he concentrates on a point so peripheral to the major criticisms of the biography forces me to conclude that we actually agree on very little."[16] This was the first of many instances in which Quentin responded to criticism of his biography. As a rule, he stuck by this precedent in discussing only the facts, and not his interpretation of them. Many years later, a journalist observed that Quentin Bell could be rather defensive "in his witty, twinkling way."[17]

In 1974, Madeline Moore organized a Virginia Woolf conference at the University of California, Santa Cruz, drawing together for the first time many of those whose work would animate the new movement: Brenda Silver, Jane Marcus, Florence Howe, Lucio Ruotolo, Ellen Hawkes Rogat, Sara Ruddick, and Margaret Comstock, to name a few. Papers were circulated beforehand, so that discussion could be more fluid; and the conference demanded "real inquiries," as Moore later wrote, "rather than presentations of views already held." Tillie Olsen was the keynote speaker and J. J. Wilson led a dramatic reading of *The Waves*. Papers were later reprinted in a special Virginia Woolf issue of

---

16. *Twentieth Century Literature* 20.3 (1974): 241–42.

17. Alan Hamilton, "Who's Afraid for Virginia Woolf?" *The Times* 16 May 1983: 9.

Women's Studies, along with a small group of photographs from the conference, each speaker caught midsentence, openmouthed, above the startling collars of the period. The next month, at the MLA convention, Ellen Hawkes Rogat and John Hulcoop coordinated the Virginia Woolf seminar on the pointed topic "Another Version of Virginia Woolf: Political, Social, and Feminist Concerns." Most of the presentations either furthered or reassessed the discussions at the Santa Cruz conference.

Perhaps the crucial essay from this MLA seminar was Jane Marcus's " 'No More Horses': Woolf on Art and Propaganda," for here she established the tone and some of the themes of her later work. Fearless and emphatic, Marcus quickly became the most influential of the American feminist Woolf scholars, a dazzling critic and polemicist with a reputation for nurturing other feminists' work. Few Woolfians do not have a Marcus story up their sleeve, some tale of kindness or affront. The whirling centre of Woolf studies for over twenty years, she seems to exert both centrifugal and centripetal forces, drawing a number of scholars into a tight, supportive circle but thrusting away less progressive thinkers and alienating many whose loyalties lean toward Quentin and Olivier Bell.

Her arguments rest on a single, breathtaking assertion: that Virginia Woolf was not only a pacifist socialist feminist but "deeply committed to the revolution." This simple phrase articulates a fundamental shift in the interpretation of Virginia Woolf's life and work. Marcus identifies herself, with Woolf, as an "Outsider," a position Woolf arrived at only late in life, and as a result, Marcus tends to denigrate Bloomsbury and its early influence on Woolf. The bawdy banter of Gordon Square leaves Marcus cold. Her Virginia Woolf is more sober, more solid, than the Virginia Woolf of legend. Her emphasis is on the 1930s and her key texts are *Three Guineas, The Years,* "Professions for Women," and the introduction to Margaret Llewelyn-

Davies's *Life As We Have Known It, by Cooperative Working Women* (1931).

In her role as a propagandist for the new Woolf, repetition is essential to Marcus's purpose. She restates the themes of her previous essays, recaps the achievements of feminist scholars. Readers of her work can come to recognize when the Henry James anecdote will make its tattered appearance, or the story of Forster telling Virginia Woolf that the London Library had upheld its precedent, set by her own father, not to include women on their board, or the quotes from Forster's Rede lecture that there were distressing "spots" of feminism all over Woolf's work, that she had "no great cause at heart," that she deserved "a row of little silver cups" for her achievements. Against those "provincial" and "antifeminist" Bloomsberries, typified by Forster at his worst moments, Marcus diligently asserts the influence of strong women like Ethel Smyth, Margaret Llewelyn-Davies, Jane Harrison, and Elizabeth Robins, the writer and feminist on whom she wrote her dissertation.

But there is just as wide a selection of topics Marcus will not raise, books she will not bother with. Not for Marcus the descent into the Stephen underworld, the deaths, gropings, breakdowns. Nor the tragic visionary novels on which Woolf's reputation was based. These seem to remind her, with disgust, of the critical tradition that acclaimed them. "Have the critics' eyes been so riveted on the 'feminine sentence,' " she asked, "that their ears have not heard what it says?"[18] This comment is also a subtle restatement of another of Marcus's themes: her emphasis on music, rather than the visual arts (read: rather than Bloomsbury), as an influence on Woolf's work.

---

18. Jane Marcus, ed., *New Feminist Essays on Virginia Woolf* (London: Macmillan, 1981), xiv.

While Marcus's tenacity and stylistic brio have had a tremendous impact on Woolf scholarship, especially in the States, some have found her interpretations of Woolf's politics forced and anachronistic. Toril Moi, representing a younger generation of poststructuralist feminists in *Sexual/Textual Politics* (1985), called her work "emotionalist" and questioned her recourse to biographical evidence, suspecting an underlying and far from revolutionary sympathy with "the old-style historical-biographical criticism" that New Criticism had sought to overturn.[19] The critic Mark Spilka, referring to a bravura passage from Marcus's essay *"The Years* as Götterdämmerung, Greek Play and Domestic Novel,"* in which she took on Wagner, Greek history, and the Virginia Woolf record, may have spoken for many when he wrote, "I can only stand before it in unconverted awe."[20]

In "No More Horses," Marcus first presented her argument that Quentin Bell and Leonard Woolf, "the official guardians of her image," had wilfully portrayed Virginia Woolf as far less politically inclined and committed than works like *Three Guineas* and *The Years* attest. In Leonard Woolf's case, we have the odd, frequently quoted remark in his autobiography that Virginia was "the least political animal that has lived since Aristotle invented the description." Marcus did not quote it here, however, but accused Leonard Woolf of tampering with his dead wife's image in a more insidious manner. In his edition of Virginia Woolf's *Collected Essays*, she argued, Leonard had neglected to say that a certain article had appeared in the British Communist Party newspaper the *Daily Worker* (beside a notice from the

---

19. Marcus, for her part, referred to *Sexual/Textual Politics* as a "historically incorrect anti-American diatribe" ("Pathographies," *Signs*, Summer 1992, 815).

20. Mark Spilka, "New Life in the Works: Some Recent Woolf Studies," *Novel* 12.2 (Winter 1979): 181.

editors strenuously disavowing the writer's opinions) and had also selected a less volatile draft of "Professions for Women" for inclusion.
But these seem rather bland, perhaps even accidental, misdeeds com-
pared with that sweeping comment in Leonard's autobiography.
What could have inspired such a response to a writer who had shown
a continual preoccupation with the status of women, the problems
facing women artists, the role of propaganda in art? Later scholars
would pick up the twigs Marcus broke in passing and build dissertations from them.

In Quentin Bell's case, however, Marcus shot to the heart of the
matter. His disapproval of Virginia Woolf's pacifism in the face of
the fascist threat of the 1930s led him to depreciate not only Woolf's
arguments in *Three Guineas*, Marcus contended, but her ability to argue at all. Like many good controversialists, Marcus has a sharp eye
for a quote. Here is Quentin Bell, for example, on Virginia Woolf's
political inefficacy: "She belonged, inescapably, to the Victorian
world of Empire, Class and Privilege. Her gift was for the pursuit of
shadows, for the ghostly whispers of the mind and for Pythian in-
comprehensibility."[21] Not a woman you would hire to write your pamphlet. But Marcus also seems to know when to suppress the context of
a quote, the better to force her point, and when to indulge in casual insult. "Quentin Bell," she recounted, "asserts that Virginia Woolf was
'amazed' at his 'socialist' analysis of the world crisis as economic.
Now it is true that Virginia Woolf was not in the habit of using the
rhetoric of vulgar Marxists."[22] Quentin Bell's anecdote, however
"vulgar," was much less self-aggrandizing than Marcus's summary

---

21. *Virginia Woolf: A Biography*, vol. 2 (New York: Harcourt Brace Jovanovich, 1972),
186.

22. *Art and Anger*, 105.

suggested: "After one such meeting [of the Rodmell Labour Party] Virginia did ask me why, in my opinion, things had gone so very wrong with the world during the past few years. I replied with what I suppose was the stock answer of any young socialist: the world economic crisis. . . . She was frankly amazed, neither agreed nor disagreed, but thought it a very strange explanation."[23]

This discord over *Three Guineas* is of more consequence than it may appear, since it touches on those mechanisms by which the helpless dead are assigned places in history. We know that Virginia Woolf's status as a major novelist has been fiercely contested. In terms of her placement in the canon of English novelists, it matters enormously whether she also happened to compose a clumsy and self-interested tract on women's rights or a trenchant socialist feminist analysis of English society. The perceived importance of *Three Guineas* bears directly on scholarship, and eventually on the common reader's assessment of Woolf's abilities, beliefs, and intellectual merit. It takes a lot to make up for Empire, Class and Privilege.

Generally speaking, British readers have had the most difficulty accepting Virginia Woolf as a political thinker, primarily because of the legacy of F. R. and Queenie Leavis and other critics of the 1930s: the dismissal of the Bloomsbury Group as irresponsible aesthetes and of Woolf's novels in particular as idle experiments—small, atmospheric, exquisite—cut off from the concerns of ordinary life. Quentin Bell never understood *Three Guineas* as a complex, speculative argument on the roots of fascism in the patriarchal family but instead read the book as an "attempt to involve a discussion of women's rights with the far more agonising and immediate question of what we

---

23. *Virginia Woolf: A Biography*, 187.

were to do in order to meet the ever-growing menace of Fascism and war."[24] He could not see that when Woolf suggested that women should refuse to participate in social rituals founded on competition and blood lust, she meant to underscore their compliance in fostering attitudes that led to war. She may have failed in this, of course, and as far as Quentin was concerned, she did. But as the Stanford historian Susan Groag Bell has explained, "Woolf's sense of politics was not a matter of immediate practice but rather one of persuasion through the development of thought. She understood that politics is concerned with issues of power, and that power relationships are reproduced in our everyday lives."[25] Another critic, Naomi Black, has suggested that Woolf may be perceived as apolitical because she lacked enthusiasm for the few activities that men are willing to recognize as politics. In the light of his own, very different political activities and the fascist advances to which he lost his brother in 1937, Quentin found *Three Guineas* only "the product of a very odd mind, and, I think, of a very odd state of mind."[26]

Years later, troubled by the new feminist readings of *Three Guineas*, Quentin revisited the argument. His lecture "Bloomsbury and the 'Vulgar Passions,' " reprinted in the Winter 1979 issue of *Critical Inquiry*, began by summarizing Bloomsbury's political beliefs and actions, stressing the immense influence on public opinion and, eventually, on government policy, of Forster's final novel *A Passage to India* (1924) and of Keynes's *The Economic Consequences of the Peace* (1919). This led to his observation that in the 1940s or 1950s

---

24. Ibid., 205.

25. " 'I Am an Outsider': The Politics of Virginia Woolf," *Virginia Woolf Miscellany* 20.2–3 (Spring 1983): 3.

26. *Virginia Woolf: A Biography*, 205.

"no one would have seen Virginia Woolf as a maker of political ideologies comparable with the great anti-imperialist or the prophet of deficit budgeting." Although she was passionately feminist, her life was not devoted to the cause, Quentin insisted, and her specifically feminist writings form only a small part of her total oeuvre. In *A Room of One's Own*, he could discern "the Bloomsbury habit of rational thought combined with moral purpose" (and with humour), but while *Three Guineas* "contains much that is wise and true . . . in some ways it is a saddening and an exasperating production," by no means so beautifully convincing as its predecessor. Quentin maintained that in *Three Guineas* a perfectly good argument about the status of women was being hobbled to a remote and unwieldy theory concerning the causes of war, and he offered the suggestion that Virginia Woolf's anger and frustration in the 1930s had been intensified by the events of Julian Bell's short life. Here, close to her, was an example of masculine unreason, "the fever in the blood" that she must have supposed was typical of the younger generation. Her eldest nephew had begun as an ardent pacifist, but he took such delight in political conflict that he ended up declaring that the war-resistance movement would succeed "by force if necessary." By 1934, Julian was longing for war experience, and three years later he was killed in Spain.

In almost all her essays on Virginia Woolf and in countless book reviews, lectures, and tangentially related articles, Jane Marcus returns with vigour to the perfidy of Quentin Bell. She never tires of him. He is her constant irritant: the thorn in her side, the bee in her bonnet. She was not beguiled by the mildness of Quentin's essay, nor its rhetorical balance, and headed straight for what she perceived as an underlying hostility in his argument: "He is infuriated by her feminism and enraged by her pacifism, and he fights back like a man. It is dirty fighting to be sure. She is dead, and cannot respond."[27]

What Marcus seems most to resent is that Quentin Bell, in the English tradition, sought to domesticate his aunt and her talent, to make her personality and milieu accessible to the general reader. But as far as Marcus was concerned, Woolf had no sister, no husband (only a "keeper"), no male friends, and certainly no nephews. Her mind was occupied almost exclusively with revolutionary politics, and few of her aesthetic or personal decisions can be divorced from this concern. Quentin Bell, she contended, "shows her only from the neck down and in the bosom of her family."[28] Resenting his depiction of Woolf in the official biography, and alert to his defensive forays in lecture halls and journals, she came to believe that he also exercised a repressive influence as Virginia Woolf's literary executor. "Because we are dependent on the estate for permission to quote Virginia Woolf," she wrote, "it has been difficult for Woolf scholars to take issue with his analysis without jeopardizing their careers."[29]

It is not uncommon for literary estates to exert this sort of control over scholarship, and the Bells made themselves vulnerable to censure by their active involvement in perpetuating and promoting Virginia Woolf's work. Not many heirs or family members are able to write best-selling biographies or skilfully edit five volumes of a great writer's diaries. Most engage in a sort of wary entente with interested scholars, and some, like Roger Fry's daughter Pamela Diamand, must wait decades for those scholars to appear. But Marcus

---

27. "Storming the Toolshed," *Art and Anger*, 195.

28. "Tintinnabulations," *Art and Anger*, 162.

29. *Art and Anger*, 187.

made no attempt to substantiate her allegation until Quentin dared once again to challenge Marcus's vision of Woolf's politics and influences. He had not referred to her by name in "Bloomsbury and the 'Vulgar Passions.' " Now she became "Professor Jane Marcus, a person of great charm and ability, whose opinions are, I understand, accepted by a multitude of admirers."[30]

The gloves came off. In her rebuttal of his essay, Marcus sniped at the "unearned income" Quentin Bell and Angelica Garnett collected from Virginia Woolf's royalties and copyright fees. "Not only does he own and control the literary labor of his aunt," she asserted, "he also, to some extent, owns and controls the labor of literary critics, who must ask him for permission to quote from Woolf's works—and some, though not all, must pay for the use of those words."[31] As evidence that the estate's decisions shaped Woolf scholarship, she claimed that Sandra Gilbert and Susan Gubar had been denied permission to reprint *A Room of One's Own* in *The Norton Anthology of Literature by Women*, a text that would have offered many undergraduates their introduction to Virginia Woolf as a political thinker. In a tired rejoinder, Quentin reminded readers that requests to reprint material go to the publishers rather than the estate. He had heard nothing of Gilbert and Gubar but had contacted the Hogarth Press, who informed him that no request for *A Room of One's Own* had reached them. They had granted a request from the same scholars for other material.

In 1988, when Marcus reprinted her side of the *Critical Inquiry* debate, she quietly omitted the reference to Gilbert and Gubar, sub-

---

30. "A 'Radiant' Friendship," *Critical Inquiry* (June 1984): 558. In a brief essay, "Virginia Woolf, Her Politics," in the *Virginia Woolf Miscellany* 20.2 (Spring 1983), he had described her as "that learned and eloquent lady, Professor Marcus."

31. "Quentin's Bogey," *Critical Inquiry* (March 1985): 491.

stituting the case of Woolf's early journals, although she must have known that rather than being suppressed by the estate, they were at that moment being prepared for publication by Mitchell Leaska, from transcripts made in part by Louise DeSalvo. Scandal travels at the speed of light, however. The Bells have said that Germaine Greer once stopped by their home in Sussex to tell them that they were operating an illegal closed shop in the Virginia Woolf industry. Although Quentin felt strongly that the Marcus school was misreading Woolf's work and misinterpreting her life, I have not been able to confirm a single instance in which the Virginia Woolf estate denied permission to quote material on ideological grounds. For a short time after Leonard's death, access to the diaries was severely restricted because of a lawsuit against his heirs. Later, during the early stages of editing of the diaries and letters, note-taking from some unpublished Woolf material was prohibited. Since then, only rarely has the estate denied permission to quote from unpublished material. Louise DeSalvo might be considered to have a grievance against the Bells for holding up publication of her scholarly edition of *Melymbrosia*, an early version of *The Voyage Out*, and for disallowing a paperback edition, which the Bells felt would mislead the reading public. Woolf had, they argued, rejected this version for publication, whatever its interest to scholars. Yet DeSalvo has said, "I have no quarrel with the Bells. I have no problem with the literary estate." Angelica Garnett had been, she thought, especially supportive of her work. In DeSalvo's view, the literary estate is "an awesome responsibility thrust on them by an accident of birth. If it were me, I'd be extremely angry."[32]

---

32. Interview with the author, 6 April 1994.

Jane Marcus has maintained her attacks on the estate, and, until his death in December 1996, Quentin Bell continued to refer sadly in the press to what he called "Lupine critics." Even his last book, *Elders and Betters* (published in America as *Bloomsbury Recalled*), concluded with a reconsideration of the *Three Guineas* debate, this time distinguishing between the "total pacifism" Virginia Woolf seemed to espouse in *Three Guineas*, which he found so unreasonable, and the more "limited pacifism" evident in her diaries. Quentin could not make himself like *Three Guineas*, but he insisted on understanding why. In this, and many other ways, he gave Virginia Woolf and her later champions more intellectual credit than is generally acknowledged. As recently as March 1994, in the *Women's Review of Books*, in an article on new editions of Virginia Woolf springing up after the lapse of English copyright, Marcus tossed in this aside: "Let's face it. The author was never a heroine to her nephew and biographer. Stepping briskly out of copyright, the debutante writer returns to her native soil—this time, one hopes, not as a suicide or a Bloomsbury bubblehead with no social conscience, but as a writer."

In 1977, at the invitation of the Blake scholar David Erdman, editor of the *Bulletin of the New York Public Library*, Marcus guest-edited their Virginia Woolf issue, devoted to *The Years* and *Three Guineas* and including photographic reproduction of the "two enormous chunks" of galley proofs that Woolf deleted from *The Years* before it went to press. Marcus boldly declared this issue of the *Bulletin* "a landmark in Virginia Woolf studies," an example of the "cooperative ideal of contemporary Woolf scholars." The next year, in the pages of the *Times Literary Supplement*, she would single-handedly defend the American Woolf community from an insipid editorial called "Woolf Whistles," making good use of those

Forster anecdotes. She edited three important anthologies in the 1980s. The introduction to the first of these collections, *New Feminist Essays on Virginia Woolf*, served as a manifesto for the new movement. Here Marcus proclaimed that, among other tenets, "we do not consider 'Bloomsbury' as an important influence on Virginia Woolf."[33]

The feeling among many scholars was that Virginia Woolf had been too long entangled with Bloomsbury, an association that seemed not only a crude simplification of her interests and influences but a public relations nightmare, calling to mind Henry Lamb's portrait of the drooping Strachey and that immortal semen anecdote.[34] While Woolf and Bloomsbury had been virtually synonymous in the popular press for decades, one began to find reviewers of her diaries referring to her as the "sacrificial victim" of a pretentious and insensitive milieu. Elaine Showalter was especially hard on the Group:

> When we think about the joy, the generosity, and the absence
> of jealousy and domination attributed to Bloomsbury, we
> should also remember the victims of this emotional utopia:
> Mark Gertler, Dora Carrington, Virginia Woolf. They are

---

33. *New Feminist Essays on Virginia Woolf* (Lincoln: University of Nebraska Press, 1981), xvii.

34. "Vanessa and I were sitting in the drawing room [at 46 Gordon Square]. . . . Suddenly the door opened and the long and sinister figure of Mr. Lytton Strachey stood on the threshold. He pointed his finger at a stain on Vanessa's dress.

" 'Semen?' he said.

"Can one really say it? I thought and we burst out laughing. With that one word all barriers of reticence and reserve went down." From Virginia Woolf, "Old Bloomsbury," in *Moments of Being* (New York: Harcourt Brace Jovanovich, 1985).

the failures of androgyny; their suicides are one of Bloomsbury's representative art forms.[35]

For many feminist scholars, "Bloomsbury" had come to signify only
a group of Cambridge homosexuals, hostile to the advances of
women. Ellen Moer had delighted in "the new Virginia Woolf" revealed by her letters, the Woolf "without Bloomsbury." She saw no
evidence for that prewar immersion in the Group described by
Quentin Bell and others, except that after meeting Lytton Strachey,
Virginia's letters grew shrill and lifeless, "filled with nasty and sometimes lewd gossip . . . all very old-maidish. Is this perhaps the
Bloomsbury tone?"[36] To put this in Forster's terms, there were distressing spots of Bloomsbury all over her work.

Yet was she not, more than ever, the Queen of Bloomsbury? To
Cynthia Ozick, as to many less articulate admirers, "Bloomsbury"
meant simply "Virginia Woolf and her satellites. The men and
women she breathed on shine with her gold. She did not know she was
their sun; they did not know they were her satellites; but it is easy now,
seventy years after they all seemed to glitter together, to tell the radi-
ance from the penumbra."[37] Virginia Woolf's ascent in the 1970s,
while drawing attention to her milieu, can also be seen to have left that
constellation permanently dulled.

At the 1975 MLA convention, when Madeline Moore, Morris
Beja, and James Naremore first proposed a society devoted to Vir-

---

35. Showalter, *A Literature of Their Own* (Princeton, N.J.: Princeton University Press, 1977), 265.

36. *New York Times Book Review* 23 Nov. 1975.

37. Cynthia Ozick, "Diary Keeping," *New York Times Book Review* 2 Oct. 1977, reprinted in *Art and Ardor*, 56.

ginia Woolf, or perhaps to the Bloomsbury Group as a whole, almost no one raised a hand for Bloomsbury. At the next year's MLA convention, 27 December 1976 was dubbed "Woolf Day" and featured three sessions in a row, the third on Leonard Woolf. The first official meeting of the Virginia Woolf Society followed.[38] Officers were selected (including a nod to the English contingent: Quentin Bell, John Lehmann, and Nigel Nicolson were named honorary trustees), Lucio Ruotolo presented a slide show of photographs from his stay at Monk's House, and Carolyn Heilbrun delivered her inaugural speech as president. "I expect there are two questions in all our minds," she began.

> Why a Virginia Woolf Society? Why Heilbrun as President? The second question is the more readily answered. The Founders of the Society determined that its first President should have three qualifications: She should be female; she should have been a full Professor teaching Woolf at a prestigious university; she should be aging. A moment's thought will indicate to you the scarcity of such creatures.[39]

Concurrent developments sometimes mirrored what was happening in American universities and sometimes contradicted it, or altered it, or seemed to reflect another impulse altogether. Some months after the 1974 Santa Cruz conference on Woolf, for instance, a very different gathering took place at Cerisy-la-Salle, France, the "Colloque de Cerisy: Virginia Woolf et la Groupe de Bloomsbury." The aim of the

---

38. In its first year the society attracted 175 members. Current estimates hover between 350 and 400. About 100 Woolfians attended the first meeting.

39. *Virginia Woolf Miscellany* 7 (1977): 1.

conference, explained its organizer, Jean Guiguet, was to debate the existence of Bloomsbury and to determine whether it could be placed on any map—critical, intellectual, geographical, political, psychological. The speakers were distinguished, often famous, and distinctly male. David Daiches, David Garnett, Quentin Bell, and the Strachey scholar Gabriel Merle were among the participants, and their uncontroversial agenda, with topics like "Virginia Woolf and Water" and "Maynard Keynes, Biographer," seems now like a map of the world before Columbus, with only sea monsters and blue expanses where America should be.

The English continued to react against new American readings of Woolf, trying to wrench her from the compromising embrace of feminists and "cultists." Hermione Lee began her 1977 study *The Novels of Virginia Woolf* with an assertion that she now says makes her cringe: "This is not a book about Bloomsbury, lesbianism, madness or suicide. It does not deal with Woolf as a feminist." In a sense, Nigel Nicolson's introductions to the Virginia Woolf letters can be read as position papers for the English Woolf establishment; each year, he elaborated one or two points of contention —Woolf's verbal malice, for instance, or her feminism. He could be counted upon to concur with the official biography in most respects, although he was less timorous regarding her sexuality. The great English contributions to Virginia Woolf and Bloomsbury studies in this period were not critical or theoretical but textual and historical.

In fact, the most widely agreed upon basis of the Bloomsbury revival is the mammoth amount of original material made available in these years, most of it edited by British scholars. "It was as if the reading public were witnessing a long and complex archeological excavation," wrote Michael Holroyd recently, "at which a lost way of life

was gradually being revealed."[40] Many expected that the Lytton Strachey letters would surface first, or something from the voluminous
Forster archive at King's College, but the first important work to appear was *The Letters of Virginia Woolf*. With the encouragement of
Quentin Bell, Norah Smallwood had asked Nigel Nicolson to edit
Woolf's correspondence for the Hogarth Press. Nicolson decided to
bring aboard a collaborator for help with the many letters in American collections. He had met Joanne Trautmann two years before,
when she came to interview him for her thesis *The Jessamy Brides*, on
the relationship of Vita Sackville-West and Virginia Woolf. He cabled
her, outlining the task, and she fired back: "Let's do it. Jo."

By the end of summer 1973, when Trautmann and Nicolson had
written to the curators of public collections across England and
America, as well as to everyone who might have ever bought or inherited or received in the post a letter from Virginia Woolf, they knew
that some 3,800 letters survived. Since so few of those written about
remained alive, and in the light of increasing interest in Virginia
Woolf, they decided to publish everything, with the exception of a
few social-arrangement notes. Six volumes would be filled, appearing
annually from 1975 to 1980.

Trautmann recalls a moment of panic when she first looked as an
editor at a Virginia Woolf letter and realized she could not read it.[41]
Nigel Nicolson had tricks, she remembered, for deciphering Virginia's
"cramped and constipated" hand. He would hold the letter at an angle
and take an oblique look at the script. Trautmann's method was to put
difficult letters aside, pace or stretch for a moment, and pick them up

---

40. *The Sunday Times* 17 Sept. 1995.

41. *Miscellany* 3 (1975): 1. See also Joanne Trautmann's "The Editor as Detective,"
Charleston Magazine 13 (1996): 5–13.

again "with deliberate casualness." Typists, guests, the Sissinghurst cook, and the National Trust secretary were all enlisted in the cause of word identification. Having decided, too, that the annotation should insult neither English nor American readers, the editors sometimes battled over what should be explained. The Adirondacks, for instance, were judged too basic. But what about "pumping ship," or as Virginia used the phrase, in reference to T. S. Eliot's extreme reserve: "It's on a par with not pump shipping in front of your wife." "What's that?" Trautmann asked, certain they would have to annotate it. "Pumping ship means urinating," Nicolson told her. "Every Englishman knows that." Trautmann decided to test his assumption.

So the typists, the cook, and the nanny were asked. Nigel's children were asked, as was every guest at Nigel's next dinner party. . . . Only one man knew, a physician, as it happens. I say "as it happens," because Nigel determined that it was not the doctor's profession that led to this particular genito-urinary information, but his age and schooling. "Only Old Etonians over 50 know about pumping ship," Nigel announced. We annotated it.[42]

Some letters were impossible to trace, like those to Adrian Stephen, who seems not to have kept any family letters. Trautmann has written amusingly of their hunt for Virginia's letters to Lytton, which turned out to have been sold by Leonard Woolf to a Miss Frances Hooper through the enterprising Chicago dealers Hamill and Barker. Miss Hooper failed to respond to a letter from Nigel Nicolson. When Joanne Trautmann rang her, she explained that the letters were piled

---

42. *Charleston Magazine* 13 (1996): 12.

somewhere in her attic. She had once been intrigued by Bloomsbury but now longed to write a book on Sweden and had hired a Swedish gardener for this purpose. Sadly, the man was illiterate. Short of becoming Swedish, there was little Trautmann could do to arouse Miss Hooper's interest in digging out those Woolf letters. Finally she secured the woman's grudging consent for a research assistant to find and photocopy the letters. Before the appointment, however, Miss Hooper phoned Trautmann in horror. Friends had told her exactly who this Nigel Nicolson was, and she refused to have anything to do with the man who had written that appalling book about his own mother. Meanwhile, in England, a microfilm of the Lytton-Virginia correspondence had fortunately turned up in the files of the Strachey Trust. Only a four-page letter to Katherine Mansfield remained unread in Miss Hooper's attic, beyond the reach of Trautmann and Nicolson.[43]

Most of the editing took place in concentrated sessions each June and July at Sissinghurst, with the help of a different American research assistant every summer. Trautmann and Nicolson set up in the book-lined "Virginia Room," where they received a series of visitors, whom they grilled on obscure details from the correspondence. "And we always had a lot of Bloomsbury people to stay," Nicolson told a reporter, "First, second or third generation, people who knew Virginia well. It was great fun."[44]

Virginia Woolf's fame had swelled so dramatically in the preceding few years that the publication of the first volume of letters was a literary event almost rivalling the appearance of the Bell biography. Even popular magazines like *Time* and *Newsweek* took notice. For

---

43. Miss Hooper bequeathed her letters to Smith College, and Trautmann was able to include the letter to Katherine Mansfield in her 1989 selection *Congenial Spirits*.

44. Pauline Peters, "Lunching with the Bloomsbury Industry," *The Sunday Times* 21 Sept. 1980.

Leon Edel, acutely aware of what makes a literary reputation, the letters reinforced a conviction that in the coming decades Virginia Woolf would emerge "as a George Eliot of our time, but a finer artist and perhaps a towering figure in the imaginative writing of England's twentieth century."[45]

Remarking on the founding of the Virginia Woolf Society, Sonya Rudikoff observed that the formal establishment of a society devoted to a literary figure was "a kind of predictive index to that figure's scholarly weight."[46] This can also be said of Virginia Woolf's letters and diaries in their complete and unexpurgated editions. Once a case can be made for publishing six volumes of a writer's letters, it is harder to dismiss her out of hand. The 1974 edition of *The Norton Anthology of English Literature*, for instance, represented Woolf with only "The Mark on the Wall," part of the editors' effort to include more work by women. But by 1979, "as befits a major writer," two more stories and three essays had been added, including a long extract from *A Room of One's Own*.

One or two reviewers took against the self-consciousness of Virginia's letters or focused, as of old, on their snobbery or malice. John Bayley, in a general reaction against the Bloomsbury industry, with its "endless detritus of memoir, gossip, and recollection," argued in the *New York Review of Books* that the letters had a "lowering effect" and seemed disattached from her genius. (Years later he would argue the same of her diaries.) Those letters in which the young writer seemed to be honing her skills he found "anxious and narcissistic." Bayley also thought the "Bloomsburian gaiety" was inimical to Virginia

---

45. Leon Edel, "The Group and the Salon," *American Scholar* 46 (Winter 1976–77): 116–24.

46. Sonya Rudikoff, "Afraid of Virginia Woolf?" *American Scholar* 47 (Spring 1978): 245–71.

Woolf's art and that humour was not her strong suit. No wonder the letters did not appeal to him, for they very often intend to make the recipient laugh. "I discovered a letter written to you," she told Violet Dickinson in 1904, "but not sent. It was in my pocket all the time when it should have been sending shocks and thrills through a maiden bosom in Hertfordshire."[47] Amazingly, the letters do seem to have helped dispel the impression of Virginia Woolf as cold, aloof, ethereal, at least for many readers. It is one of the few chestnuts that have faded over the years, and we should mark its passing. "The temperament reflected in these letters," wrote James Atlas in the *New York Times Book Review* after the last volume appeared, "was anything but rarified."

While it was fashionable to disparage Virginia Woolf, reviewers did so with delight and ingenuity. Most seem to have sensed, by the mid-1970s, that disparagement was out of date, and yet the new fashion had not declared itself. In this limbo between derogation and canonization, they took their lead from Nigel Nicolson's introductions to the letters. In volume one, for example, he had described her early letters to Violet Dickinson as "embarrassing," and reviewers followed suit. Virginia's "repellent pet-names and quasi-erotic baby talk" were deplored in *Time* (in a paragraph reassuringly titled "Platonic Passions"), while the reviewer for the *Christian Science Monitor* referred with distaste to her "cutesy animal nicknames and embarrassing baby-talk pledges of friendship to women-friends." In the *Yale Review*, Gordon Haight also found her letters to Violet Dickinson "embarrassingly frank." While many reviewers alluded to Virginia's feelings for women, usually at a fast trot on their way toward Leonard, Haight

---

47. Nigel Nicolson and Joanne Trautmann, eds., *The Letters of Virginia Woolf*, vol. 1 (New York: Harcourt Brace, 1975), 139.

devoted his opening paragraphs to this topic, speculating that her intense early passion for Madge Vaughan "may have fixed for life the pattern of her sexual inclinations."[48] This was just one of the lines of inquiry that the letters made possible. Most reviewers also looked for evidence of madness but were disappointed.

In the "Editors' Note," Trautmann and Nicolson had assured readers that the Bell biography formed the basis of their chronology and of their interpretation of Virginia's character. In fact, in the first volume, Nicolson found only one area of disagreement with the mother text. Virginia's affectionate letters to George Duckworth, written after his alleged molestation of her, seemed to belie Quentin Bell's version of events at Hyde Park Gate, and Nicolson suggested that had her biographer known of these letters, he would not have written so harshly of Virginia's half brother. What Nicolson did not explain at the time is that Henry Duckworth, George's son, had at first refused to show him and Trautmann these letters. Considering the ill-treatment of his father in the Bell biography, why should he now assist the Virginia Woolf estate? In 1993, Nicolson gave his Bloomsbury-related correspondence from this period to the University of Sussex Library, and a series of letters is preserved there in which he attempted to mollify the younger Duckworth. In the end, Nigel Nicolson was able to convince Henry Duckworth to let them publish the Woolf letters because, in demonstrating the fondness between Virginia and George, they would help to contradict Quentin Bell's allegations of abuse.

Nicolson made good on this assurance by casting the letters in this light in his introduction and by walking readers through an alternate scenario, in which Virginia misinterpreted and then exaggerated the

---

48. "Letters Schooled Her Style," *Yale Review* 65 (Spring 1976): 419–25.

harmless caresses of her fond half brothers. Reviewers picked up the cue. Gordon Haight announced that the letters made Quentin Bell's tale of sexual abuse untenable: "It is inconceivable that after the trauma of his 'mawkish incestuous sexuality' Virginia could have written so affectionately to 'My dearest Georgie.' " Perhaps George's malefactions were no more real, Haight contended, than Virginia's 1904 hallucination of King Edward VII lurking in the azaleas and swearing violently. Ellen Moers, writing for the *New York Times Book Review,* went much further, blasting the Bell biography for the "family gossip" that made it a best-seller. "The letters in this volume should, but do not," she continued, "provide evidence for the scandals Bell put forth so sanctimoniously about his near-relations." In her 1976 study *Literary Women* Moers returned to the fray, arguing that Quentin Bell had only demonstrated "the reality of a sister's incest fantasy." In this early response to the Virginia Woolf letters, only Alan Bell countered Nicolson's argument, insisting in the *Times Literary Supplement* that "convention, innocence and reticence were all too strong" to allow an immediate response to George's behaviour.

Phyllis Grosskurth, in an accusatory review of the final volume of the letters, announced that the whole enterprise of Virginia Woolf's posthumous publications was part of "the mausoleum erected to her memory by vigilant relatives, who have presided over the Family Romance through the ownership of the copyright of her letters, the publication of her biography, and through successive editions of her writings."[49] It is hard to tell whether Grosskurth disapproved of the Woolf estate in particular or simply of the immortality machine—there is, of course, no other way to perpetuate a dead

---

49. Phyllis Grosskurth, "Between Eros and Thanatos," *Times Literary Supplement* 31 Oct. 1980: 1225–26.

writer's work than by "successive editions," and so on—but this is the sort of harsh analysis that Quentin Bell and Angelica Garnett, having brought copyright on themselves, learned to expect. It explains, perhaps, why Olivier Bell has been at such pains to justify her appointment as editor of Virginia Woolf's diary, a choice that she thought "seemed, and seems, to many people a typical example of Bloomsbury nepotism."[50] But no one who has read these diaries can possibly question the estate's decision. They are gorgeously edited and annotated. It is odd, perhaps, but not unfitting, that Virginia Woolf's royalties (taxed for many years at 85 per cent) financed the editing of her own diaries. Olivier has written that she could never quite reconcile her dependence on Virginia's posthumous earnings with their shared attitude "to the dignity and rights of women."

Nevertheless, Quentin's half of the royalties supported both Olivier and her assistant Andrew McNeillie for several years, leaving them, as she put it, "free to pursue the aim of excellence without subjection to external pressures." In contrast to the spare annotation of the Virginia Woolf letters, the diaries are supported with lush, meticulous notes, evidence not only of Olivier Bell's scholarly zeal but of her sensitivity to detail. "I never spoke to Virginia in my life," Olivier told a journalist.

> I saw her only once, across a room, at a party. It was a wonderful image of a beautiful, distinguished and riveting figure, in a long red dress. A vision. But an impression? No. I go with my nose through the text of her diaries. I am not good at taking a long term view.[51]

---

50. Anne Olivier Bell, *Editing Virginia Woolf's Diaries* (London: Perpetua Press, 1989), 16.

51. Quoted in Alan Hamilton, "Who's Afraid for Virginia Woolf?" *The Times* 16 May 1983.

Her later remark on the process of annotation conveys something of her exacting nature: "I pinned up before my desk a notice with the words: ACCURACY/RELEVANCE/CONCISION/INTEREST, and these were my objectives."[52]

Another significant difference between the editing of the letters and of the diaries is that Olivier chose to exclude the earliest, irregular volumes, later transcribed by Louise DeSalvo and edited by Mitchell Leaska, and instead took up the record in 1915, when Virginia Woolf began in earnest the diary that she would maintain, with few interruptions, until her death. Thus Virginia appears on page 3 with an adult voice and manner, instead of the unguarded exuberance of the early letters, a strategy that invited less speculation and dissent. The critical response to the first volume of the diary in 1977 was markedly more respectful than that accorded to the letters. Only one reviewer, for the *New Yorker,* taking against Quentin Bell's claim that this was among the great diaries of the world, retorted that it was "no such thing," partly because one already knew the friends and acquaintances Virginia Woolf describes "as well as, if not better than" one wanted to. More readers agreed with Claire Tomalin, writing for the *New Statesman,* who expressed surprise that the diary brimmed with happiness and saw that "beneath it all there is a woman of force and self-confidence at work in these notebooks."

It is rare for the principal source materials of a major biography to be published so soon after the biography itself, and some of the ensuing challenges to the authorized version of Virginia Woolf's life were simply excited attempts to revisit the controversies that the bi-

---

52. Ibid., 22. Incidentally, Jane Marcus found these notes hostile to Woolf and wrote that "the only way to read volume 1 of the Diary is to cover up the footnotes," which "betray an uncommon case of editorial antagonism" ("Tintinnabulations," *Art and Anger,* 161).

ography had so recently made public. They do suggest, however, increasing awareness of the ways in which biographical truth is determined and propagated. The publication of the letters and diaries invited even casual readers into an ongoing interpretation of the historical record, with special attention, as always, to madness and sexuality—or more saliently, to those aspects of Virginia Woolf's life that remain just beyond our grasp. No amount of documentary evidence can fully explain Virginia Woolf's suicide. No history of Hyde Park Gate can account for her mental instability or her genius. Our attention remains riveted on what we cannot know; but this is in the nature of attraction. One of her biographers, Jean Love, tried to explain her fascination with Woolf: "Why did I write about Virginia Woolf? Why did she interest me? It began years ago, because she was doing something in the novels that I knew was beautiful and extraordinary. I loved it, and I could not understand it. . . . I don't think Virginia Woolf and I have very much in common. I wish I could write as she does. I would even take on a few of her other attributes, a few, if I could write as she does."[53] As another observer put it, "She has become the Marilyn Monroe of American academia, genius transformed into icon and industry through the special circumstances of her life and work."[54]

One of my private theories on the burgeoning Woolf cult is that the love letters of so seductive a writer constitute a public health hazard. Few who have read volume three of her letters can remain indifferent, and we can date the collective swoon from the publication of this dangerous volume in September 1977. But the compulsion to

---

53. Jean Love, "Portraying and Explaining Lives: The Case of Virginia Woolf," *Michigan Quarterly Review* 23.4 (Fall 1984): 539.

54. Helen Dudar, "The Virginia Woolf Cult," *Saturday Review* Feb. 1982: 32.

know more—to immerse ourselves in another's life—also has something to do with the order in which material is made public. In most cases, only after a writer's death, and then only gradually and in part, can readers come to understand her as a private person. I find it suggestive that Virginia Woolf's complete letters, written so much with their recipients in mind, began to appear before the complete diaries, the most private of documents, which register only occasional awareness of future readers. Layers of persona seemed to strip away sequentially. Between the diaries and letters, in 1976, Woolf's autobiographical sketches were edited by Jeanne Schulkind and published as *Moments of Being*, including "A Sketch of the Past," discovered after the publication of the Bell biography. Had a new novel been found among the Monk's House papers, instead of these tantalizing, half-revised pages of memoir, the critical focus in the later 1970s might have been less personal. Or might not. One aspect of Woolf criticism in this period is an increasingly unabashed use of the novels to illuminate her life.

Perhaps because they threaten our private feelings for a cherished figure, attempts to explain the few veiled elements of Virginia Woolf's character arouse frenzied opposition. Armed with Freud or Laing or Husserl or Lacan and the immense written record of Virginia Woolf's life, numberless critics and biographers have tried their hand at the puzzle only to be judged, at best, plausible and sensitive or, at worst, hostile, fanciful, unreflective, biased, arrogant, self-serving, and violently appropriative. Even the official biographer was attacked for broaching the possibility of sexual molestation: those who came after were torn by jackals. Some observers, like Leon Edel, blamed Michael Holroyd for establishing a prurient interest in the Bloomsberries and setting the tone for subsequent journalism and scholarship. This overlooks not only the growing candour of the period, however, but the perennial appeal of other people's private lives. "Let me confess," wrote Quentin Bell, "horrible though it may be to do so, that I would rather read almost any frivolous and salacious journalism than almost any literary criticism."[55]

Most of the new books on Virginia Woolf have made a point of diverging from the Bell biography, or what some have called "the Bloomsbury party line" (an epithet over seventy years old but springing anew to each generation), though rarely seeking to discredit Quentin's work. Carolyn Heilbrun, in a note to her essay "Virginia Woolf in Her Fifties," may have put the case most succinctly: "Here, and at certain other points, I take issue with Quentin Bell in his interpretation of the facts of Woolf's life. It is important, therefore, to state my belief that he has given the facts fairly and that, where he has prejudices, he has stated them. He has given us materials no one else could give, or give as gracefully, and if we reinterpret them . . . we can do so only because of his enabling work."[56] The shift from "I" to "we" shows the extent to which Heilbrun hoped to mediate between the Woolf establishment and the young bloods of new American scholarship, and how obvious the gap was becoming.

Although a surprising number of critical trends, disputes, and controversies in the Woolf world were reported in the mass media, they typically made their way to general readers through literary biography—also a boom industry in this period—and it is here that we can best trace the evolving image of Virginia Woolf and Bloomsbury in the later 1970s and 1980s. Since these works so closely succeeded a massive, best-selling authorized life of Woolf, they can be read (and

---

55. Introduction to George Spater and Ian Parsons's *A Marriage of True Minds* (London: Cape and Hogarth, 1977).

56. *Hamlet's Mother and Other Women* (New York: Columbia University Press, 1990), 96.

were sometimes intended) as glosses on the Bell biography. Together with their reviews, they highlight points of contention within the expanding Woolf readership and show the almost infinite malleability of documentary evidence.

Jean Love's psychological study *Virginia Woolf: Sources of Madness and Art* (1977) was announced as the first of two volumes exploring topics in Woolf's life that had remained enigmatic, among them her "so-called madness, her physical health difficulties, her atypical sexuality, and her preoccupation with death which led finally to her suicide."[57] In an earlier book Love had explored Woolf's mythopoetic thought. In time, she hoped to elucidate the connections between Woolf's madness and her writing. Only the first twenty-five years of Woolf's life were addressed in *Sources of Madness and Art,* and even so, she remained in the margins for 150 pages while Love conducted a lengthy and absorbing analysis of the relationship between Woolf's parents, based on their five hundred newly found letters. Love, a professor of psychology, tried to correct the sentimental distortions of Julia's character in Leslie Stephen's *Mausoleum Book,* then being edited for publication by Alan Bell. Like most of the new biographers, she relied heavily on Virginia Woolf's 1939–40 memoir "A Sketch of the Past," another source discovered after the Bell biography.

Sources of Madness and Art was not rapturously received by the Woolf community, perhaps because it appeared so soon before Phyllis Rose's elegant *Woman of Letters: A Life of Virginia Woolf* (1978) and held up poorly in comparison. The search for nursery traumas and proofs of anomalous emotional development wearied. Love seemed unnecessarily timid, too, with regard to the molestation

---

57. Jean Love, *Virginia Woolf: Sources of Madness and Art* (Berkeley: University of California Press, 1977), 1.

charge, subjecting Woolf's statements on this matter to a degree of scrutiny that none of her other autobiographical remarks have invited. She gave an impression of nervous agreement with both sides of the argument.

Phyllis Rose contributed perhaps the mildest feminist critique of the Bell biography in supplying the literary criticism, the blend of life and work, that Quentin had abjured. She hoped to establish Virginia Woolf's "personal mythology, the set of stories she made up about herself," and which informed all Woolf's writing, and to shift attention away from illness and suicide. Rose proved a thoughtful biographer, indebted but not enslaved to psychoanalytic theory, and there is only one grating, injudicious sentence in the book, when she complained that Virginia could "hardly have been helped in her sexual adjustment by Bloomsbuggery."[58] Leaving aside its larger implications, the remark seems condescending toward Virginia, who was in her mid-twenties by the time Lytton Strachey made his sexual orientation clear to his friends and by the time he foolishly proposed. Wounded feelings are one thing, sexual adjustment another. But this comment was part of Rose's displacement of Bloomsbury as a viable influence or support for the young writer. Where Bell recounted the delights and freedoms of early Bloomsbury, Rose focused on the resentment Virginia still felt, and would feel all her life, at having been denied a university education. Instead of the friskiness, the bravado, the gaiety, Rose emphasized the silence and boredom of the Gordon Square and Fitzroy Square gatherings, and Virginia's alternating relief and affront at attracting so little sexual attention.

The positioning of *Woman of Letters* as a companion volume to

---

58. Phyllis Rose, *Woman of Letters: A Life of Virginia Woolf* (New York: Oxford University Press, 1978), 79.

the Bell biography may explain its popularity with all but the most radical of American readers and its nomination for a National Book Award. On the hot spots of the Woolf legend—madness, sexuality, marriage, suicide—Rose adopted a position midway between Quentin Bell and his detractors. She adored Leonard, for instance, and saw the marriage as fruitful and supportive, as did Jean Love, but took issue with (and slightly misread) Leonard's romantic vision of Virginia Woolf's mental illness as allied with her genius, as seeming to come, as he put it, from the same part of the brain. For Rose, madness was not the source of Virginia Woolf's creativity but something that set her apart, like Dostoevsky's epilepsy: "in madness she found her own unique adventure."[59] As for the fabled frigidity, Rose used the term unquestioningly. In *Mrs. Dalloway*, moreover, she discerned an argument about the "strategic value of frigidity, its use in preserving a woman's sense of autonomy and selfhood."[60] She concluded that Woolf had been sane at the time of her suicide, although severely depressed by the war and her usual misgivings on finishing a book. Fearing madness, she had courageously chosen to direct her own fate.

Trautmann and Nicolson, in their final volume of the letters in 1980, reached a similar conclusion. From dating and internal evidence in the three suicide notes Virginia left, Nicolson speculated that they had not been written on the same day, 28 March 1941, as Leonard Woolf and Quentin Bell had assumed, but perhaps over the course of ten days. This suggested a level of premeditation that, to the editors' minds, argued against her "final madness."

In the course of his argument, Nicolson referred admiringly to Susan Kenney's "Two Endings: Virginia Woolf's Suicide and *Between*

59. Ibid., 72.

60. Ibid., 144.

the Acts," an influential 1975 article that examined the tangled relationship between Virginia's writing and her breakdowns. After some jabs at Leonard for his apparent lack of insight into his wife's character, Kenney tried to reconstruct the crosscurrents of Virginia Woolf's emotional life after 1939. She concentrated on the draft endings of *Between the Acts,* one of which is as bleak and despairing as readers might expect from a suicidally depressed writer. But this was not the ending Virginia chose to publish. She decided to strike a more affirmative note, at least in fiction. Kenney concluded that in the spring of 1941 Virginia Woolf realized that, given the war, her isolation in Rodmell, and the threat of another rest cure, she could no longer "be free to choose her own terms for existence" and thus her suicide "can be seen less as a denial of life, or even the meaningless irrational act of a madwoman, than as a denial of the terms on which she was going to have to live to preserve whatever fragments of identity she might be left with."[61]

Kenney's article bore strange fruit in the form of Phyllis Grosskurth's *Times Literary Supplement* review-essay of the final volume of the Virginia Woolf letters in 1980. Her opening is quoted earlier as an example of attacks on the Virginia Woolf estate. The review, titled "Between Eros and Thanatos," promised much in its early, acerbic comment that the cult that had grown up around Virginia Woolf had transformed her from a fallible woman to "a complex image constructed of woman, writer, suicide—an objectified symbol of our death instinct."[62] Oddly, Grosskurth dropped this intriguing assertion and chose instead to deliver a sensational and loosely rea-

---

61. Susan Kenney, "Two Endings: Virginia Woolf's Suicide and *Between the Acts,*" *University of Toronto Quarterly,* Summer 1975.

62. Grosskurth, 1225.

soned account of Virginia Woolf's suicide, peppered with rhetorical questions that implied that Quentin Bell, Nigel Nicolson, and Leonard Woolf had all suppressed vital information about the act. Why had Quentin Bell not quoted both suicide letters to Leonard in his biography? Why had Nigel Nicolson tantalized readers by referring to a gay and hilarious 1933 letter to Vanessa that he then said he could not yet publish? "Once started," Grosskurth interjected, "the process of suspicion accelerates." She upheld the Kenney article as brilliant and courageous, then scavenged it for passages that seemed to implicate Leonard in Virginia's death. That readers had not been given every detail of the search also aroused Grosskurth's suspicions. How thoroughly was the river dragged, she demanded to know, and commencing from where, and at whose direction? She then devoted a few paragraphs to anti-Semitism in *The Years*—an interesting lead, again, that sputtered out—and ended hastily, with a long quote from *Between the Acts*. Whatever happened to Eros and Thanatos?

The key to Grosskurth's uncharitable attitude toward Leonard Woolf may lie in her mention of Nicolson's "startling oversight" in not referring to Roger Poole's "important book" *The Unknown Virginia Woolf* (1978). It is Poole's book, much abused and much reprinted, that firmly established the anti-Leonard school of Woolf criticism. Five years earlier, Cynthia Ozick had first pointed out Leonard's streak of anti-Semitism and the mixed motives for his ambitious marriage. Poole took the argument much further, portraying the Woolf marriage as doomed from the start, since the wedded pair had "quite different kinds of intelligence, quite different kinds of perceptions, quite different kinds of thought-process." As Poole saw it, Leonard's reductive rationalism and intellectual arrogance prevented sympathetic accord with his wife. Not only did these qualities spoil Leonard's marriage, they prevented him from recognizing that Virginia Woolf was never mad, and that he and the official biographer were cruel and irresponsible to perpetuate this error. Surely a woman who had experienced so many family deaths at such a young age, Poole reasoned, and who was sexually abused by her half brother had more than enough excuse for "a temporary loss of control of some kind."

"Loss of control" is a typical euphemism, for Poole could not claim that the breakdowns did not take place at all. What he objected to was Leonard's "primitive, witch-doctor attitude" toward mental health, which led him to consult doctors when Virginia seemed unwell, sometimes without telling her. "Surely a subtler way would have been to fall in with his wife's hypothesis that she was not 'ill,' " Poole argued, "and to have tried to work it out together? But no."[63] Her symptoms undoubtedly pointed to something, he continued, and were not there "merely to be pointed at, as further examples of a traditional 'madness.' "[64] He assumed that Leonard never asked Virginia what was bothering her and never learned about the sexual molestation. Poole quoted almost none of Virginia's letters and diary entries after marriage, perhaps because they fail to support this picture of unbreachable silence and entrenched antagonism between her and Leonard.

It must be said that for many of the rash judgments and breezy imprecisions in his book, Poole offered compensating passages. But his version of the Woolfs' marriage required a blinkered reading of a complex body of material. To argue in good faith, for example, that Virginia's suicide notes confessing the onset of madness were nothing

---

63. Roger Poole, *The Unknown Virginia Woolf* (Cambridge: Cambridge University Press, 1978), 138.

64. Ibid., 130.

but gallant lies, since "it is surely impossible to believe that everything she had ever said to Leonard (and to the world) about her alleged madness had been untrue," Poole had to shut his eyes to Virginia's numerous references to her madness in her letters, diaries, and conversation and concentrate exclusively on those protests she voiced when her headaches and other recurrent symptoms were flaring up and she was in danger of collapse.

With a few exceptions, reviewers took against *The Unknown Virginia Woolf*. Most objected to Poole's treatment of Leonard Woolf, and many to his use of the novels to shore up what seemed a specious argument about the life. Mark Spilka pointed out that Poole's moral outrage demanded "a flawless female martyr and her obtusely 'rational' and chiefly male oppressors."[65] He complained, too, that Poole judged Leonard and the doctors he consulted by "Freudian assumptions which then had little currency and by Laingian assumptions which would not be conceptualized for some fifty years to come."[66] Jane Marcus explained that American feminist critics had long since given up blaming Leonard, despite his shortcomings as a lover and caretaker. A row flared up in the *Virginia Woolf Miscellany* over Poole's alleged cavalier use of evidence and his rancour toward Leonard. This eventually subsided with Poole's complaint, seconded by his colleague Mark Hussey, that his book had been given a grossly literal reading—he had "hoped that some general discussion (along the lines of Michel Foucault's 'discourse of power') might be forthcoming"—and Olivier Bell's retort that Poole had contrived portraits of Leonard and Virginia Woolf that neither they nor their friends

---

65. Mark Spilka, "New Life in the Works: Some Recent Woolf Studies," *Novel* 12.2 (Winter 1979): 177.

66. Ibid., 176.

would recognize, and that this fundamental flaw derived "from his over-addiction to theory, and a consequent misuse of evidence."

In the Poole book, we can see the genesis of three important strains in recent biography of Virginia Woolf. In the first place, the adherence to a theoretical framework, to which documentary evidence is largely subordinated. This makes for a tight, persuasive argument, except perhaps for those few readers, like subscribers to the *Miscellany*, who are deeply familiar with the source material. Contradictory evidence is rarely cited, let alone allowed to modify the thesis. In fact, contradiction of one or another piece of evidence scarcely affects the argument, since the work at hand seems to be based on the ingenious application of a theory or theories to a carefully selected body of evidence, a stacked deck that will turn up an ace for Poole every time.

Poole's reading of the novels as autobiography was another of the controversial new approaches that would inspire the work of his immediate followers, such as Stephen Trombley, and culminate in studies like Louise DeSalvo's *Virginia Woolf: The Impact of Childhood Sexual Abuse on Her Life and Work* (1989). While admitting that novels are not transcripts from life, Poole argued that in struggling not to be transcripts, they become perilously like them. This is one way of justifying what in practice were often crudely literal readings of the novels, including a fraught identification of fictional characters with real people. Poole thought it "inevitable," for instance, that we should read the encounters between Septimus Smith and Sir William Bradshaw in *Mrs. Dalloway* "as a direct reconstruction of certain passages of the conversation which took place [between Dr. Head and Virginia Woolf] on the afternoon of the 9 September 1913."[67] Interpreting the

---

67. Poole, 138–39.

novels as a superior form of autobiography calls to mind Jane Marcus's remark that the rejected drafts of Woolf's novels seemed "truer" than the published texts. In both instances, critical boundaries are dissolved and hierarchies subverted. It is a wonder that Olivier Bell's four-by-six-inch card indexes, those monuments to empirical truth, have not spontaneously combusted.

Some reviewers referred to Poole's "passion," others to the book's "self-evident 'need to be written.'" What is certain is that Poole, and others to follow, rejected the conventions of critical detachment. Mary Ann Caws would finally embrace and put a name to this approach, "personal criticism," in her 1990 book *Women of Bloomsbury,* defining it as "a willing, knowledgeable, outspoken involvement on the part of the critic with the subject matter, and an invitation extended to the potential reader to participate in the interweaving and construction of the ongoing conversation this criticism can be."[68] Strictly speaking, this critical stance and its definition required a poststructural perspective that Roger Poole could not have attained by the mid-1970s. He could only commit himself to the first step of such a project—an outspoken involvement with his subject matter—for part of him clung to the old absolutes. Hence his incredulity and sarcasm, his outrage at Leonard's obtuseness, alternating with a strange confidence in his own analysis of Virginia's needs, ideas that he regarded as "doubtless," "obvious," even "glaringly obvious." He made it clear that he, Roger Poole, would have known how to handle Virginia. "That would have been the time," he insisted, referring to her misery in March 1941, "to enter into a subjective dialogue with Virginia, wheedling her little by little towards an assurance that these things could be understood." It is hard to say which would

---

68. Mary Ann Caws, *Women of Bloomsbury* (New York: Routledge, 1990), 2.

unhinge a woman sooner: Leonard Woolf's ubiquitous milk glass or
Roger Poole's "wheedling."

As Paul Levy saw it, the worst aspect of Poole's book, "and one
which deserves the attention of both the producers and the consumers
involved in the Virginia Woolf industry, is the fact that it was published at all."[69] Not only was *The Unknown Virginia Woolf* published,
it is now in its fourth edition, and sporting a long, self-congratulatory
preface. But Poole may have earned his flourish. The book floats,
where many have sunk without trace.

At the time his work appeared, Roger Poole's colleagues at the
University of Nottingham included two other Woolfians, Mark
Hussey and Stephen Trombley. Trombley's 1981 study of Virginia
Woolf's doctors drew directly on Poole's work and was received with
similar elation by the Woolf community. *All That Summer She Was
Mad: Virginia Woolf, Female Victim of Male Medicine* reads like a revised and expanded edition of *The Unknown Virginia Woolf*. The thesis was nearly identical: Virginia Woolf was not "mad," and neither
her doctors nor Leonard tried to understand what has happening from
her point of view. Poole had acknowledged the usefulness of Laing
and Merleau-Ponty; Trombley provided page-long quotes from their
work. Poole mumbled something about embodiment; Trombley devoted a whole chapter to the concept. One of Trombley's chapter titles even referred to "the discourse of power," the sort of discussion
Poole had hoped his own book would inspire among critics. And
when his work appeared, Trombley came in for many of the complaints lodged against Poole. In the *Times Literary Supplement* Galen
Strawson spoke out against Trombley's hostility toward Leonard
Woolf and Quentin Bell, declaring the book not so much an intellec-

---

69. *Miscellany* 16 (Spring 1981): 5.

tual failure as a failure of sensibility. (A Bloomsbury biographer who had lost track of the controversy remembers haplessly introducing Poole and Trombley to Quentin and Olivier Bell at a conference and registering a sudden chill.) The Trombley book was not without advocates, however, even in the pages of the *Virginia Woolf Miscellany*. In one respect, he may have done his job too well. So horrific were his accounts of Virginia Woolf's doctors, based on their published writings—bumbling, eugenic, reactionary—that the treatments Woolf actually received seemed a miracle of gentleness and compassion.

Trombley's critique of the medical establishment was cited in Elaine Showalter's later, more comprehensive study *The Female Malady: Women, Madness and English Culture* (1985). Showalter did not address Woolf's situation in any detail in *The Female Malady*, however, perhaps because she had dealt so decisively with Woolf in her 1977 book *A Literature of Their Own*. Like Poole and Trombley, Showalter put little faith in the official versions of what Virginia Woolf thought and experienced, since these came "from those most concerned to deny or repress their own complicity in her sickness." Yet she felt none of the protective zeal of Poole and Trombley. In fact, it appears that Showalter toiled through seventeen pages of the awful details of Virginia Woolf's madness only so that she could better illustrate the dangers of Woolf's androgynous ideal, as espoused in *A Room of One's Own*, and her worthlessness as a feminist role model. According to Showalter, androgyny was no paradise, no "natural fusion" in the mind, but a myth that helped Virginia Woolf "evade confrontation with her own painful femaleness and enable her to choke and repress her anger and ambition."[70]

As Woolf critics, Elaine Showalter and Jane Marcus have much in

---

70. Elaine Showalter, *A Literature of Their Own*, 264.

common—more, perhaps, than they would like to hear—and one is not surprised to see Showalter moving from a stunning thesis to an increasingly dour and reductive argument. She began by asserting that each of Woolf's major breakdowns was associated with a crisis in female identity. Her breakdown after her mother's death, for instance, must have coincided with the onset of menstruation. Her worst breakdown followed Leonard's decision that they would not have children. Her suicide followed menopause. But what seemed an empathetic reconstruction of events on Showalter's part gave way to a stern critique, in which she arranged female rites of passage like a series of gymnastic ordeals. Woolf had shied at the vault, slipped from the uneven bars, pitched off the balance beam. And then finally, in 1941, "her feelings of female inadequacy and her immense internalized anger against [Leonard] and against Vanessa became so overwhelming . . . that only self-destruction seemed commensurate with her despair."[71]

Virginia Woolf had failed as a woman. Showalter's strictures remind one of Queenie Leavis's famous review of *Three Guineas*, with its gibe that Woolf could have no insight into women's lives, since she scarcely knew which end of the cradle to stir. Showalter even quoted Leavis approvingly at the close of her argument. Since we have touched on the maternal metaphors, however, it is difficult not to feel that Showalter threw out the baby with the bathwater. Her disenchantment with Woolf and her writings is not at issue. Other feminists, like Adrienne Rich, have complained that *A Room of One's Own* is a mousy piece of work, too intent on placating male readers. But in her desire to expose Woolf as a weakling, undeserving of our adulation, Showalter seemed to prescribe a sort of muscular femininity,

---

71. Ibid., 280.

with requirements as rigid as those of the Victorian tea table, and it is hard to interpret this as a feminist act.

It should be remembered, perhaps, that the relationship between the Bloomsberries' androgynous ideal and their sexual radicalism had been largely unexplored at the time Showalter wrote.[72] Carolyn Heilbrun had mentioned the connection but left it for others to pursue. Readers were barely accustomed to the idea of a sexed Woolf, let alone a woman capable of spiking her fiction with subversive messages or seducing a tall lesbian. In Alan Bennett's 1978 television play *Me, I'm Afraid of Virginia Woolf,* directed for the BBC by Stephen Frears, both images of Virginia Woolf—sexed and unsexed—complicate the present-day action. Ultimately, the Bloomsbury writers serve as a bridge between an English instructor's dull life and the relative glamour promised by a homosexual affair with his best student, Skinner, who dares to wear an earring. One night at the Polytechnic, Hopkins, the instructor, discovers that someone has defaced council property: two posters of the Bloomsbury novelists. E. M. Forster has been provided with facial hair and a fat cigar; Virginia Woolf has been given large breasts. Skinner suggests that the vandal has been "indulging in a crude form of literary criticism" by indicating the "vital particulars" in which these authors are deficient. Class is interrupted before the teacher can turn this remark into a viable discussion.

Some critics have felt that Bennett's play only recasts Forster and Woolf as objects of ridicule, but this overlooks the erotic subtext of Skinner's remark, the come-on implied in his having sexualized, or homosexualized, a bland classroom discussion. Forster and Woolf are

---

72. See Barbara Fassler's thought-provoking article on the possible sources of Bloomsbury's androgynous ideal, "Theories of Homosexuality as a Source of Bloomsbury's Androgyny," *Signs* 5.2 (Winter 1979).

only ridiculous here to the extent that Skinner and Hopkins are ridiculous, with their nervous advances, missed cues, and comic indirection. Skinner's initial sally precedes a very funny scene in which Hopkins's students reiterate all the conventional comments on the Bloomsbury Group and obsessively return to Woolf's sex life, in particular, while Hopkins struggles to redirect discussion to her work. As Hopkins is tidying up after class, Skinner regards the altered image of Virginia Woolf and asks her, "Well, love. Was it worth it?"

> Look at the figures. Ten novels, five nervous breakdowns, no kids, one suicide. And this is where it landed you, sweetheart: a further education class in the Mechanics' Institute, Halifax, on a wet Tuesday night in 1978. Let me introduce you, Virginia, old love. Here it is. Posterity.[73]

The best-received of the new biographies was Lyndall Gordon's *Virginia Woolf: A Writer's Life* (1984), which aimed, like Phyllis Rose's *Woman of Letters*, to complement the official biography with a serious consideration of Woolf's creative life. Gordon followed Poole—though more cautiously—in regarding every scrap of Woolf's published and unpublished writings as potentially autobiographical. In an argument resting in part on Mark Spilka's *Virginia Woolf's Quarrel with Grieving* (1980), she addressed the Stephen children's post-Victorian reticence about death and declared that memory and the perpetuation of the dead would become the motivating forces behind Woolf's writings. She downplayed Woolf's modernism

---

73. Alan Bennett, *Me, I'm Afraid of Virginia Woolf* in *The Writer in Disguise* (London: Faber and Faber, 1985), 32–72. Brenda Silver offers a less sympathetic critique of this play in her essay "What's Woolf Got to Do with It? Or, The Perils of Popularity," *Modern Fiction Studies*, Spring 1992.

as a result, arguing that her principal allegiance was to the past.

More than most biographers, Gordon shuttled sentence to sentence between the life and the work. Although this made for some awkward prose, she did manage to suggest the incontinuities and divagations of a writing life: how the unpromising residue of a Monday or Tuesday could ignite in the "particular, rare mind" of Virginia Woolf. At its best, *A Writer's Life* reads like an intellectual adventure story. But troubling charges were made by American scholars after the book's publication. Writing for the *New York Times Book Review*, Carolyn Heilbrun noted that Gordon, an Oxford professor of South African birth, seemed to respect only British writers on Woolf and had implied "that one can read a huge body of material, mainly by Americans, only to scorn and dismiss it. I should think that she has inevitably learned much from what she has read. It simply will not do to claim all this as virgin territory."

Gordon had made it clear that she disdained previous Woolf criticism, pronouncing the work of feminist scholars, in particular, "predictable rather than subtle." She added, somewhat eccentrically, that the best Woolf criticism to date had appeared in two recent book reviews in England. But it was one thing to disregard the work of other scholars, quite another to be suspected of lifting it wholesale. In the *Miscellany*, Jane Novak pointed out that a witty description of Leonard from Richard Kennedy's *A Boy at the Hogarth Press* appeared verbatim in *A Writer's Life* seemingly as Gordon's own work. Jane Marcus, too, thought she discerned one of her own sentences embedded in Gordon's text, and remarked that Gordon had assimilated more of Louise DeSalvo's published arguments on the young Virginia and *The Voyage Out* than she seemed willing to acknowledge. It is hard to know whether these are examples of bad proofreading or scholarly sleight of hand.

The singular aspect of *A Writer's Life* is Lyndall Gordon's conviction that the Woolf marriage was a thing of unparalleled beauty. Her Leonard was cast in a heroic, rather than a saintly mould, and she situated his early appeal for Virginia in his willingness to take on the animal names and personae that Virginia seemed to require of those she loved. Among Woolf scholars, Gordon was almost alone in speculating that Leonard and Virginia maintained some form of sexual relationship after Virginia's 1913–15 breakdown. This view, however refreshing, led to what Heilbrun called a "surprisingly tasteless abuse of Vita Sackville-West and a gross underestimation of Woolf's love of women." Indeed, Gordon can be seen to extend the subtle bias of Love, Rose, and others against Woolf's lesbian leanings—a tendency to interpret her feelings for women as "immature" (Gordon's term) or more often "infantile," an adjective not correspondingly applied to her relations with Leonard, despite the milk feedings and baby talk. These commentators found the affair with Vita more than slightly embarrassing. Gordon thought that Virginia "gushed and postured" with Vita and that her amorous letters rang false. "Gush" and the more compromising verb "pump" recur in proximity to Vita's name, Gordon reiterating that Virginia's letters to Vita were "pumped with manufactured excitement" and "pumped with a monotonous gush." Against Gordon's will— against even her cherished thesis—those letters brought a blush to her prose.

I have wondered if a single issue better illustrates the volcano depths of Virginia Woolf partisanship than the treatment of Woolf's sexuality, and especially what Olivier Bell has called the "delicate sentimental transaction" between her and Vita Sackville-West. There is a world of difference, for example, between Mark Spilka's description of that relationship as "a flighty adolescent love without much passional depth or sexual richness which soon—and not surprisingly—fizzled out"[74] and Jane Marcus's rumination that "it seems perfectly natural that she should fall in love with Vita, and just as natural that she should fall out again."[75]

Although Hermione Lee's new authorized biography of Virginia Woolf contains one of the most sprightly discussions of this affair, Lee has not always been among the pro-Vitas. She has more than once winced in print at *Orlando* and, in the *Times Literary Supplement*, applauded Gordon's dismissal of the relationship with Vita in favour of Virginia's friendship with Katherine Mansfield—a much slighter though more intellectually challenging attachment. Resistance to Vita takes many forms, the most prominent of which is a sort of incredulity that Virginia Woolf could really have cared passionately for a woman like Vita, with her retrograde social attitudes, her commonplace novels, and that high-voltage sexuality that jolted her from one "muddle" into another. Among English critics, reverse snobbery comes into play. In a 1991 television programme on Woolf, for example, Angela Carter dismissed *Orlando* as "a slobbering valentine to an aristocrat." Carter fastened here on the properties of *Orlando* that repelled her, concealing how far the dart had sunk into her own flesh. (Isobel Armstrong and Hermione Lee have explored Carter's troubled relationship to Virginia Woolf, and *Orlando* as the antecedent to Carter's magical realist novels like *Nights at the Circus*.[76] At her death,

---

74. Mark Spilka, "New Life in the Works," 174.

75. Jane Marcus, "Tintinnabulations," *Art and Anger*, 169.

76. See Isobel Armstrong's "Woolf by the Lake, Woolf at the Circus" and Hermione Lee's "A Room of One's Own, or a Bloody Chamber?" in Lorna Sage's *Flesh and the Mirror: Essays on the Art of Angela Carter* (London: Virago, 1994).

Carter left a partial draft for the libretto of an operatic version of *Orlando*.)

What is more disturbing is that biographers and critics of biographizing tendencies have felt a need to explain Woolf's attraction to women in the same terms, and with the same methods, that they have ferreted out the supposed causes of her mental breakdowns. Occasionally scholars will admit defeat with regard to the breakdowns. We have so little information, after all. They seem convinced that lesbian feelings, on the other hand, will quite naturally unfold on the death of a mother and a stepsister, or as a result of irritation at a tyrannical old father, like a pearl forming in the frontal lobe. Such events, of course, no more explain a preference for one's own sex than they explain a love of opera. There is little question that Virginia Woolf's "sapphism," like Lytton Strachey's more manifest homosexuality, has functioned as a wild card in an otherwise orderly revival, and that tracing this tendency to a string of childhood disasters is a defensive gesture. It also suggests bewilderment, intolerance, anger on the part of critics. The first hint of censure in Lyndall Gordon's biography occurs at the mention of Woolf's feelings for women. But just as it is impossible to establish, for instance, the source of her genius, it is impossible to assign Virginia Woolf a slot on the Kinsey scale or fit the unruly evidence into a pat theory of pre-Oedipal longing. "All such attachments," as Sonya Rudikoff wrote, "defy text-book designation. . . . If the sexual lives of any modernist writers are offered for comparison—Lawrence, Woolf's close contemporary, Colette, Proust, Mann, Joyce—a similarly labile emotional disposition is evident in all of them."[77] Our exertions only reveal our Inner Woolf:

---

77. Sonya Rudikoff, "How Many Lovers Had Virginia Woolf?" *Hudson Review* 32.4 (Winter 1979–80): 562.

what we need from her, what we would deny her, how we would protect her from others.

There is reason, however, to think that many common readers welcomed further knowledge of Vita Sackville-West and her relationship with Virginia. Victoria Glendinning's 1983 biography *Vita* was favourably received, and a 1984 edition of Vita's letters to Virginia, edited by Mitchell Leaska and Louise DeSalvo, did well despite Leaska's cloying introduction, in which he registered the consummation of the women's love with an appearance of the Goddess Astarte at their bedside. In 1993, when Suzanne Raitt's critical study of their relationship appeared, publication coincided with the release of Sally Potter's film *Orlando*. The book was reprinted within weeks, perhaps because it supplied the illicit kisses so notably absent in the film. The relationship between the women had long since passed into lesbian legend and now generates opaque post-structuralist essays with titles like "When Virginia Looked at Vita, What Did She See; Or, Lesbian: Feminist: Woman—What's the Differ(e/a)nce?"

Veneration for Woolf easily spills over to include Vita Sackville-West. The Woolf scholar Madeline Moore spent the summer of 1979 at Sissinghurst as the guest of Nigel Nicolson while she worked nearby at Knole on the manuscript of *Orlando*. She remembers it as an idyllic interlude. Each morning, Nicolson's cook would make her a sandwich, which she ate under the trees at Knole. In the afternoons, a member of the Sackville family would bring her a cup of tea, and she would glance up from her work to watch tour groups pass through the rooms. One day Nicolson told her of the arrival of a group of American enthusiasts from some extension programme on Bloomsbury and asked if she would show them the *Orlando* manuscript, which she did. They crushed forward to touch the pages. But where, they asked her, was the oak tree that Virginia Woolf and Vita Sackville-West had sat under? "Well, you know," she recalls, "there must be four hundred oak trees. And I said, 'Come on, I'm going to walk out of this room and take you to that oak tree.' So I took them to the oak tree and said 'This is it!' and they touched it, and Nigel loved it. Nigel told the story forever and ever."[78]

ONE OF THE useful features of Edna O'Brien's play *Virginia* is that it crystallizes so many of the attitudes of the moment and embodies so much of what intelligent nonspecialist readers were thinking of Virginia Woolf in the early 1980s, after ten years of conflicting scholarship and hype. Had the Woolfs been happily married? Was Virginia's affair with Vita a delusion, a mistake, an enrichment, a pity? And was she really mad? How mad? Why mad?

At the end of January 1981, *Virginia* opened at the Theatre Royal in the Haymarket, following a solid run at Stratford, Ontario. The show drew considerable press attention because it offered the first new role Maggie Smith had created in a decade and marked her return to London after four years in Stratford. "I've wanted to play her for about ten years," she told an interviewer, "ever since I began reading the Quentin Bell biography while I was on location for *Travels with My Aunt*. The director of that film, George Cukor, thought we should do it as a movie but somehow there never seemed to be a script until last year."[79] In some ways it had been easier opening the play in a venue so far from London, she added, although some of the Stratford

---

78. Interview with the author, Feb. 1996.

79. Quoted in Sheridan Morley, "Maggie Smith: Moving Closer to Bloomsbury," *The Times* 27 Jan. 1981: 9.

audiences seemed to expect "an episode of *The Virginian*, and others thought they were getting Edward Albee."

In taking on a life so minutely documented and disputed, the playwright must have known she risked offending a good portion of her audience. Even Woolf's inner life had been, as we know, the subject of intense scrutiny. O'Brien could probably have anticipated Hermione Lee's complaint that she had played up "all the more modish areas of interest," like Woolf's madness and childlessness and jealousy of Vanessa, and confirmed the popular prejudice against Bloomsbury as "an idle, elitist bunch of coffee-swilling, bun-munching buggers."[80] But *Virginia* did not aim to reinvent its subject. O'Brien's Virginia was largely the Quentin Bell Virginia, with adjustment for the recent investigations into the sources of her mental instability. Indeed, the extent to which this new Virginia adhered to her previous incarnations showed the durability and charm of the existing image. What O'Brien attempted was not so much a reinterpretation of Woolf's life as a lyrical compression of its main events and emotional currents, through dialogue composed almost entirely of judicious extracts from Woolf's novels, diaries, and letters. Issuing from any of the three characters in the play, Virginia, Vita, or Leonard, who doubled as Leslie Stephen for a few pivotal lines, these quotes and near quotes gave the play a stylized, disjointed quality. Sometimes a string of non sequiturs yielded to a pithy exchange—for example, Virginia: "You do, I suppose, disapprove of my dress, my apparel?" Vita: "It's dreadful"—but otherwise one could imagine the actors successfully delivering their lines into microphones from distant corners of the theatre.

Once Edna O'Brien had fixed on this lush, logocentric approach,

---

80. Hermione Lee, "Author? Author?" *Times Literary Supplement* 6 Feb. 1981: 139.

she could settle into devising patterns, like a quilt maker, with material from disparate times and sources. In act 2, scene 3, for instance, Vita and Leonard discussed her affair with Virginia in phrases lifted from the letters between Vita and Harold Nicolson, Leonard Woolf's autobiography, Virginia Woolf's diary, and Virginia's letters to Vita. Stir these fragments and they might settle into a very different scene. O'Brien knew that her Virginia Woolf was not definitive. "You could write her," she told a reporter. "Anybody could. There could be fifty plays about her."

She had spent many days at Sissinghurst during her work on *Virginia*, walking in the garden and eliciting stories from her friend Nigel Nicolson. These talks must have contributed not only to her portrayal of her characters but to her overall conception of the play—the centrality of Vita, most obviously—and O'Brien eventually dedicated her work to Nicolson. Unfortunately, as he reported to the *Virginia Woolf Miscellany*, "when Patricia Conolly finally made her appearance as Vita, it was so ludicrously unlike her that I laughed." Where was his shy, restrained mother? The stage Vita, this "cross between Eva Perón and Mae West," had none of the qualities that could have attracted a woman like Virginia. Nicolson could not understand how his long conversations with O'Brien had yielded these puzzling results. "One is left," he remarked, "with the impression of an adventuress who found it amusing to toy for a year or two with a woman of genius, recklessly indifferent to the harm it might do to her." In another letter to the *Miscellany*, Frances Spalding wrote that Conolly's Vita looked "like a discarded *Vogue* model, scheming and hard as nails," and that Maggie Smith's intelligence and humour could not disguise her basic lack of sympathy with Virginia Woolf.

Drama critics, however, were inclined to feel generous toward Maggie Smith after her long absence from the London stage, although the role she had chosen did not excite them. Something about Virginia Woolf made phrases like "bloodless lethargy" spring from their pens. Irving Wardle of *The Times* took against what he described as a "central mood of unexplained anguish" and considered the play "not much of a homecoming for our best comic actress." Hermione Lee thought that Maggie Smith's elegant nervous gestures and versatile expressions worked wonders with the "profoundly undramatic material" of O'Brien's play, although both she and the *Sunday Times* critic James Fenton noticed Smith's odd, mannered reworking of Woolf's punctuation, her pauses midphrase, midbreath—part of an attempt, perhaps, to wrench a little verbal authority from Woolf and O'Brien. After the four-month London run of *Virginia,* there was talk of a transfer to Broadway, but Smith was committed to an Agatha Christie film, *Evil Under the Sun,* and nothing came of the plan.

MICHAEL HOLROYD IS fond of quoting Johnson's quip that fame is a shuttlecock that needs determined opposition from enemies to keep it in lively contention. By this definition, Bloomsbury should flourish for another half century. Following a decade of heated discussion of Virginia Woolf, culminating in a major new play on her life, the centennial of her birth came and went in England with just one hastily assembled conference to mark the occasion. Some of the writers chosen to participate announced that, in preparation, they had troubled themselves to read Woolf's novels for the first time. Just two years before, in 1980, Bernard Levin had pledged in *The Times* that he would never, to his dying day, read another word about Somerset Maugham or Bloomsbury, especially Virginia Woolf, "a figure in whom I had—and have—no interest at all."

> In my opinion, all Virginia Woolf's novels are unreadable,
> and none of them would be worth reading even if they
> weren't. . . . With the obvious exception of Forster, the
> whole of Bloomsbury and everyone who passed through it
> amounts to no more than a footnote.[81]

Nigel Nicolson fired off a protest to *The Times*, which was rejected.
Some sort of market correction was clearly under way: an aspect, per-
haps, of the English reaction against American appropriation of
Woolf. The next year, Nicolson told an American journalist that in
welcome contrast to those Americans, who had elevated Woolf to
"Joan of Arc status," no special notice was taken of Virginia Woolf in
England. His son, he added, who was reading English literature at
Cambridge, had assured him that no one taught or studied her there.
Even the Bells, smarting from their clashes with American feminists,
expressed relief that her centennial passed unmarked. English disdain
for the Woolf centenary was more than compensated for in France
and the United States. At one of these events, Nicolson offered an expanded, reconsidered version of his earlier comment, warning that
"American and British scholarship could grow apart, the British resenting that 'our' Bloomsbury has been collared by America, that
'our' Virginia has become your Woolf."[82]

Journalists on both sides of the Atlantic had seized on the
Bloomsbury boom, although American articles appeared under head-
lines like "Bloomsbury: History, Myth, and Metaphor," while their

---

81. Bernard Levin, "Cry Woolf, but I Won't Be Listening," *The Times* 8 May 1980. This
conviction did not prevent Levin from speaking at the Charleston Festival years later.

82. Nigel Nicolson, "Bloomsbury: The Myth and the Reality," in Jane Marcus, ed.,
Virginia Woolf and Bloomsbury (Bloomington: Indiana University Press, 1987).

English counterparts preferred titles like "The Bloomsberries: Snobbish, Sniping and Self-Absorbed." Explaining the continuing appeal of Bloomsbury had become almost a journalistic subgenre, with prurience yielding to nostalgia as the most frequently given cause. In an English radio broadcast of 1982, Frances Donnelly said that she suspected that her own attitude toward the Bloomsberries, "compounded equally of dislike, envy and fascination," was fairly typical. Nostalgia was at the heart of it. She had pored for hours over those sepia photographs of early Bloomsbury. Not only the time and leisure the Group had for cultivating friendships but even the mention of the three o'clock post could send her into a reverie: "Remarks about the meaning of life require an instant response if they are not to fall rather flat."[83] Or as Bernard Bergonzi chose to put it, "Reliving in imagination the kind of life favoured by Bloomsbury offers a momentary escape from the pressures of social-democratic orthodoxy."[84]

Writers, especially, cherish a fantasy of community—the antithesis of the isolation of their daily lives. For Anatole Broyard, therein lay the charm of Bloomsbury. "I too have longed for a Bloomsbury life," he confessed, adding that one of his most persistent daydreams was of ten neighbouring country houses inhabited by his favourite writers, or a building in New York that they occupied exclusively. He felt that an American writer reading today about Bloomsbury

> may well feel a sense of having been born in the decline of
> the world, too late for happiness, for Paris in the '20s or

---

83. Frances Donnelly, "The Bloomsberries: Snobbish, Sniping and Self-Absorbed," *Listener* 5 Aug. 1982: 7.

84. Bernard Bergonzi, "Who Are You?" *New Review*, November 1974, reprinted in *The Myth of Modernism and Twentieth Century Literature* (New York: St. Martin's Press, 1986).

Greenwich Village in its best days. The yearning for such a literary community may be responsible for the irony, the sadness and irascibility we find in much of our fiction. Because our writers have been left to do their difficult work alone, their books sigh with unshared emotions.[85]

This quality of longing suffuses Cynthia Ozick's essays on Forster and Woolf. In her review of the Bell biography, she acknowledged Elizabeth Hardwick's weariness of the topic but argued that for most American writers, the legend of Bloomsbury retained its allure. "Like any Golden Age," she reflected, "it promises a mimetic future: some day again, says Bloomsbury of 1905, there will be friends, there will be conversation, there will be moods, and they will all again really matter, and fall naturally, in the way of things that matter, into history."

Hence the mesmeric power of those Bloomsbury snapshots, in which Ozick discerned "so much tension, so much ambition . . . so much heartbreaking attention to the momentariness of the moment." The nostalgia argument gained credence in the later 1970s and 1980s as an iconographic feast arrived in bookshops and was speedily consumed—not only heavily illustrated books like Spater and Parsons's *A Marriage of True Minds* but selections from the sources themselves: *Lady Ottoline's Album* (1976), edited by Carolyn Heilbrun; *Vanessa Bell's Family Album* (1981), edited by Angelica Garnett and Quentin Bell; and Frances Partridge's *Friends in Focus* (1987), which also included photographs from Lytton's and Carrington's albums. Had they not been mercilessly scavenged, the Monk's House albums, now at Harvard, would no doubt have been published as well. In the

---

85. Anatole Broyard, "Perennial Bloom," *New York Times Book Review* 18 Oct. 1981.

making of idols, what can be more intoxicating than the visual image—literally iconic—a god we can rest our eyes on? Writers on Virginia Woolf, in particular, like to meditate on those dreamy country-house snapshots. The *Virginia Woolf Day Book*, an illustrated calendar first published in 1986, includes two such sequences taken by Ottoline Morrell, one in the war years and one in the 1920s: Virginia in and out of focus, smoking, reading, listening, smoking, laughing, standing, sitting, smoking. Among the many familiar Bloomsbury photographs, the most famous by far was taken before the Stephens moved to Gordon Square, before the agreed-upon beginnings of Bloomsbury. Beresford's 1902 profile of Virginia, abstracted gaze and pendant lower lip, has been for many years the best-selling postcard at the National Portrait Gallery shop, the image most often seen on T-shirts, posters, advertisements: the corporate logo of Bloomsbury.

When *Lady Ottoline's Album* appeared, with its affectionate reminiscences by Lord David Cecil, Alan Bennett brilliantly lampooned those who would rush to buy the book. "Dilys and I," he wrote in character,

> have been dedicated Bloomsbury fans ever since Dilys's dandruff and my appliance finally put paid to the ballroom dancing. Together we travel the length and breadth of the country, spending a fortune on fares simply for the thrill of meeting other Bloomsbury groupies.
>
> Billingham, Prestatyn, Loughborough—scarcely a town of any size but does not boast one, sometimes two, Woolf Clubs. This last Tuesday, for instance, saw us both at Garstang, a fork supper prior to Kevin Glusburn's thought-provoking paper "Lytton Strachey: An Hitherto Unrecorded

Incident in the Slipper Baths at Poulton-le-Fylde." Need I
add that Carrington fans were out in force?[86]

Dilys and Duggie are so "genned up on Bloomsbury" that Leonard and
Virginia Woolf seem like family friends to them: " 'I don't think Virginia would like that,' says Dilys,—'sitting in front of the fire cutting
your toenails.' 'Toenails nothing,' I retort. 'If we had Morgan Forster
coming round to his tea, you might invest in a new brassiere.' "

ABOUT THIS TIME, Quentin Bell opened a catalogue essay with the
query, "Dear Reader, Haven't you had enough yet?"

IN DECEMBER 1974, reacting against the sensationalism of David
Gadd's *The Loving Friends,* Leon Edel had announced his own forthcoming book on the Bloomsbury Group, complaining in the *New York
Times* that "everybody's been concerned with their going to bed. Nobody seems to bother with their achievements." The best correction
to this error in emphasis proved not to be the popular biography Edel
eventually produced, *Bloomsbury: A House of Lions* (1979), but S. P.
Rosenbaum's anthology *The Bloomsbury Group: A Collection of Memoirs, Commentary, Criticism* (1975), which remains an essential selection and perhaps the best one-volume introduction to the Group. It
even includes the most influential of the anti-Bloomsbury writings,
excerpts from D. H. Lawrence's "black beetles" letter to Ottoline
Morrell, Wyndham Lewis's Round Robin letter protesting his treatment at the Omega Workshops, and F. R. Leavis's acerbic essays on
Keynes. A professor at the University of Toronto, Rosenbaum came

---

86. Alan Bennett, "Say Cheese, Virginia!" reprinted in *Writing Home* (London: Faber and
Faber, 1994), 387.

to the Group through an interest in the interconnections of modern English literature and British philosophy. "My main professional interest," he stresses, "is in Bloomsbury works, not their lives. . . . I think people too often forget that it was the remarkable creative achievement of these people that makes us interested in their lives, not the other way around."[87] *The Bloomsbury Group* was a preliminary step toward Rosenbaum's mammoth literary history of Bloomsbury. *Victorian Bloomsbury,* his exhaustive exploration of the Group's intellectual origins, appeared in 1987. *Edwardian Bloomsbury* followed in 1995, and a third volume is under way. While lengthy discussion of the Group's undergraduate writings and philosophical influences may fail to entice the general reader, the Rosenbaum volumes do effectively counter the charges of frivolity and dilettantism that have dogged Bloomsbury since the late 1920s. There is not a glass of wine or a discarded undergarment in the entire series. Reviewing *The Bloomsbury Group* in the *New York Times Book Review,* Peter Stansky applauded the rigour of Rosenbaum's critical enterprise, agreeing that in Bloomsbury studies, the achievements of the Group "must be kept continually in mind. They should eclipse the lives."

Eclipse the lives, the friendships, the affairs, another might argue, and the Bloomsbury Group dissolves like smoke. Perhaps this is what Leon Edel discovered when he began to write his account of the Group, an endeavour he'd first planned in the 1950s, when the coterie looked much less confusingly interwoven. Despite its initial strong reception, *Bloomsbury: A House of Lions* has not worn well. The book may still hold up as an experiment in group biography, but it cannot stand beside Edel's magisterial five-volume life of Henry James, nor contribute much to our knowledge of Bloomsbury. What once struck

---

87. Letter to the author, 14 Feb. 1996.

reviewers as deft, artful observations now seem muted, like piano chords played with the damper pedal down. And peculiarly, considering his announced intentions, Edel stopped his narrative in 1920, thereby excluding Bloomsbury's mature achievements and concentrating instead, as had so many before him, on those legendary Gordon Square days. To simplify his task, Edel assigned each member of the Group an attribute, like the saints—Clive had his hunting, Leonard his Hebraism (his "ancestral hurt"), Lytton his homosexuality—and interpreted their characters through that shaping quality or preoccupation. Whether it was these schematized portrayals that weakened the book is unclear, but Edel's arguments were not helped by his jaunty aphorisms along the lines of "Minds that soar, art that transcends the commonplace—for when was art common?—can never be egalitarian." This warm and reverential work would have made a great difference to the perception of Bloomsbury had it been published in 1954, in place of J. K. Johnstone's tentative appraisal of the Bloomsbury writers. Twenty-five years later, it could make little impact.

PART THREE

There is mystery in the word, and money too perhaps.

—CLIVE BELL, "WHAT WAS 'BLOOMSBURY'?"

IF OPPOSITION IS essential to fame, so is the ability to mutate, to present a shimmering new facet at just the moment that the previous image wins public acceptance. Both give the glorious dead the illusion of life, as if they could still flash us a profile or leave the room and return wearing a scarf. There is a sense in which those postcards of the adolescent Virginia Woolf, pinned to the wall of every literary undergraduate, fix her like a fly in amber: wistful, virginal, indirect. To codify an image is, at least partly, to arrest it, often to the detriment of an artist's reputation. While the image of Virginia Woolf has been almost eerily alive to change since the appearance of the Bell biography, enabling us to read her as everything from a pacifist socialist feminist to a lesbian avenger to the snobbish highbrow of legend (the adult form of the wistful pupa on the postcard), the image of Bloomsbury as a whole can be seen to have evolved in similar, though less dramatic ways. Most notably, in the late 1970s, the long-neglected Bloomsbury artists began to emerge from the shadows cast by their writer friends, and two women—Vanessa and Carrington—leapt ahead of the pack, a development that few could have foreseen a decade earlier.

But a larger and less-definable movement can be discerned behind the strategies of the moment. Somewhere between the first indignant responses to the Virginia Woolf revival and the writing of this book, the Bloomsbury boom itself began to vie in interest with the original Group. This shift reflects both a hunger for fresh material and the postmodern enchantment with the making of culture. Bloomsbury's rising and falling fortunes have been evaluated by countless commentators since the mid-1970s; some hope to explain its attractions; others enlighten readers with first-person articles on their feelings about the Group, or how its continuing appeal is carefully engineered, or a fluke, or only natural. Published complaints about the commodification or exploitation of Bloomsbury proliferate—a critique from which no one in the chain of consumption fully escapes, and which flows as easily from the New Left and Right as from the traditional enemies and defenders of Bloomsbury. As we know, this impulse often manifests itself as a reaction against the biographical thrust of much writing on the Group, with all that it suggests of low tastes and waning critical standards. Even writers who are fond of Bloomsbury point out that most of its members are famous only by association, and that "association" has swelled to include many people who never met the Bloomsberries but now profit from them or in some way bear their marks: distant relations, grandchildren, scholars, heirs, dealers, biographers. Others are busy compiling profiles and interviews of these tangential figures, aware that while they cannot tell us much about the hallowed Group, they are primary sources for our current absorption with idol making and the function of Bloomsbury in the present day.

THE EXTENT TO which the Bloomsbury artists benefited from the Virginia Woolf boom and the larger Bloomsbury revival is open to debate. Clearly the proliferation of visual images kept their work and their faces before the public. Their auction prices show a perceptible link with the fortunes of the Group as a whole, with significant rises after the Bell biography and again about 1981, when the publicity for the Charleston Appeal began to take effect. Like many Woolf scholars, though, art historians specializing in these artists have tended to disdain the help offered by the Bloomsbury boom, stressing instead the renewed interest in British modern painting and the efforts of Anthony d'Offay. Simon Watney and Richard Shone have both argued that the connection with Bloomsbury has been damaging for Vanessa and Duncan. "Art critics in England," wrote Shone, "have seemed incapable almost of divorcing their Bloomsbury prejudices from any objective appreciation of Vanessa Bell's actual achievement as an artist. . . . Are the private lives of Mo and Peter and Celia and Ossie particularly relevant to a review of David Hockney's drawings or Winifred Nicholson's marriages to an estimate of her joyous still lifes?"[1] Although the persistent twitters about the Group are a factor here, the implicit argument is that a celebrity based on anything but the excellence of an artist's work is demeaning—more demeaning, even, than oblivion, or at least the sort of comfortable Thieme-Becker oblivion that awaits almost every worthy artist, and from which a few might conceivably be rescued. Artists survive for a myriad of reasons, but "good" fame, these critics would argue, rests on the work and its influence: a theme that

1. Richard Shone, "Portsmouth," *Burlington* 121 (Oct. 1979).

surfaces again and again in writings on the Bloomsbury revival. Simon Watney will not even countenance the pro-B forces and their elevation of these artists, arguing that while Duncan Grant "indeed shared much of the general outlook of his friends, his work should not be made to shoulder the heavy load of illustrating a later generation's fantasy of wish-fulfilment projected onto the Bloomsbury Group, understood as a rare idyll of civilized social relations and values."[2]

Among early advocates for the Bloomsbury artists, there may be irritation, as well, that their own quirky enthusiasms now appeal to the masses. Some allies clearly fell away as the Group's popularity increased. The editor of *Apollo*, Denys Sutton, for instance, withdrew his support around the mid-1970s, observing that the Bloomsberries' lives attracted keener interest than their works, and understandably, "for their achievement is on the meagre side."[3] It is also possible that the term "Bloomsbury" is so rife with competing connotations that it confuses the appraisal of individual merit. With the exception of the generous response to the shows celebrating Duncan Grant's ninetieth birthday, Bloomsbury exhibitions continued to receive a mixed press, with an emphasis on the Group or its aesthetic theories rather than the art. Not until 1976, with the publication of Richard Shone's *Bloomsbury Portraits*, was there a full and sympathetic account of Vanessa and Duncan's careers, and not until Simon Watney's *English Post-Impressionism* in 1980 were they granted a dignified place among their peers in the English response to French modernism.

In the early 1970s, however, as we know, Anthony d'Offay had begun quietly conducting important exhibitions of Vanessa and Duncan's paintings, selling their work to the Tate and other major

---

2. Simon Watney, *The Art of Duncan Grant* (London: John Murray, 1990), 77.

3. Denys Sutton, "And Is There Honey Still . . . ?" *Apollo* 105 (Jan. 1977): 77–78.

museums, as well as to prominent collectors. His gallery also represented Roger Fry's estate, although d'Offay was never able to assemble enough good work for a show. Since Fry had died forty years
earlier, his paintings were scattered widely, some pieces having
changed hands several times. Fry's daughter Pamela Diamand was
eager to promote her father's art but did not want to sell the works
she owned, and d'Offay felt unable to invest a great deal of money
over a long period of time to collect pieces for a show that would
not, in any case, have drawn a large crowd. Caroline Cuthbert, now a
curator at the Tate, worked for Anthony d'Offay from 1973 to 1984,
the years in which he most actively promoted the Bloomsbury artists,
and recalls it as an intense and exciting period. D'Offay's exhibitions
had a refreshing, collaborative quality, with various art historians,
like Richard Shone or Richard Morphet, brought in to help date
works and write the catalogues.[4] Cuthbert remembers that one small
exhibition of Vanessa's works on paper was conceived and executed
within three weeks. She and Richard Shone stayed up one night until
four in the morning selecting images, which then went off to be restored and framed while the catalogue and press releases were hastily
compiled. In general, however, shows were planned months in advance and the gallery's contacts with critics and reviewers were carefully thought out. Indeed, d'Offay's relations with the press seem
unusually close and efficient. He kept track of reviewers' special interests, made certain they received advance notice (sometimes three
months in advance) of every opening or event, and gave them plenty
of photographs and supporting material. For each exhibition, d'Offay planned a special party, usually at a restaurant—a private room at

---

4. Dating of the pre-1914 art is "still dodgy and questionable," Frances Spalding writes,
and "not helped by Duncan's later habit of dating his early pictures inaccurately with a
biro" (letter to the author, 30 Oct. 1996).

the White Tower, for instance, dinner for twelve—and writers were often invited, so that they eventually became, as Cuthbert puts it, "friends of the gallery." "They weren't bribed, it is clear, 'but they had everything they needed to write about these artists.'"

Cuthbert and many others have argued that without d'Offay, there would have been no significant revival of the Bloomsbury artists. It was not just a question of business acumen on d'Offay's part, or even of clever timing, but of his willingness to pay vast sums of money to have crumbling, mildewed, bruised canvases painstakingly restored and framed. Many of Vanessa and Duncan's early works had been quickly, clumsily executed with makeshift materials, and the conditions in which they had been stored did not foster their finer qualities. In his book *With Duncan Grant in Southern Turkey*, Paul Roche tells of confronting Duncan with his unworldliness in these matters. "All your pictures at Charleston are carelessly stacked," he complained. "They're scratched with nail marks because you refuse to hammer the nails into the stretchers properly, and for years you used a lovely flower piece to keep out the rain. Once I found a little sketch used as an oil rag. I straightened it out, found a frame for it, and sold it for good honest cash at Heal's."[5] Oddly, the commercial indifference Vanessa and Duncan faced at various points—in their early, most experimental period, for instance—may have helped their eventual revival, in that so many of these paintings and works on paper were preserved (just barely) in the two studios at Charleston, awaiting the Prince's kiss.

D'Offay was an early subscriber to the *Virginia Woolf Quarterly*

---

5. Paul Roche, *With Duncan Grant in Southern Turkey* (London: Honeyglen Publishing, 1982), 81.

and in other ways made his presence known to American Woolf scholars, who soon provided a steady stream of summer visitors to the gallery. "Anthony got the bit between his teeth regarding Bloomsbury," Angelica Garnett recalls, "and did his damndest to make them into a huge success and put the prices up."[6] An arrangement was made with the Davis and Long Gallery (now Davis and Langdale) in New York, where the first American exhibition of Vanessa Bell's work appeared in 1980. D'Offay also lent the bulk of the paintings for the large Vanessa Bell show at the Vassar Art Gallery three years later. His gallery had become "a centre for all the people interested in Bloomsbury," Cuthbert remembers. It seemed to her that no sooner did she hang a Vanessa Bell or Duncan Grant painting than it sold. The pop singer Bryan Ferry snared five Bloomsbury paintings on his first visit to the gallery, including Vanessa Bell's portrait of Aldous Huxley and her painting of the Memoir Club. The Queen Mother bought her fourth Duncan Grant, *Still Life with Matisse,* for four hundred pounds from a small 1973 exhibition at King's Lynn, by arrangement with d'Offay. Other major collectors included the Reader's Digest Association, whose twenty or so Bloomsbury works, selected by Barney McHenry, were eventually exhibited in a show that travelled to three American cities in the late 1980s. The co-founder of *Reader's Digest,* Lila Acheson Wallace, donated the funds to restore the Charleston garden.

Without question, Anthony d'Offay's efforts kept Duncan Grant afloat financially in the 1970s. He still showed tremendous vitality as an artist, painting or sketching nearly every day. The critic Marina Vaizey, not always a friend to Bloomsbury art, found the 1975 d'Of-

---

6. Letter to the author, 13 Sept. 1995.

fay show of his recent paintings "wonderfully heartening" and "among the finest of Grant's work."[7]

Which is not to say that his powers were undimmed. In 1982, Duncan's companion of many years, the poet and translator Paul Roche, published *With Duncan Grant in Southern Turkey*, the story of their first long trip abroad together in 1973. The book might as accurately have been titled *With a Very Old Man in Southern Turkey*, for much of its disquieting humour derives from Roche's descriptions of Duncan's physical debility and occasional mental lapses—often followed by adroit and puckish sallies. Roche sometimes assumed the character of "Nanny," for instance, in ironic acknowledgment of his caretaking role. "Nanny" would concoct medicines for Duncan or wedge his frail body upright between rocks so that he could sketch while Roche bathed in the sea. During one such transaction, Duncan muttered, "I hope Nanny knows what she's doing." Roche also recounted the story of an ill-fated portrait of an earl, which Duncan had first undertaken in the late 1960s. The countess demanded an exact replica of her husband, and even rang Duncan two years after the earl's death, insisting that he alter the eyes and lips. The portrait was brought back to Duncan's flat off Regent's Park. "That was when I first caught sight of his portrait of the Earl," Roche recalled, which struck him as "a good solid piece of work: the colours muted, almost sombre, but alive and warm. We propped the picture up on a chair in our one big studio room and Duncan got his brushes out. The tinkering began. After each onslaught I noticed he quickly turned the picture to the wall."[8] Weeks passed, and Duncan confessed his despair. Eventually Angelica came to visit and carried the painting off,

---

7. Marina Vaizey, "London," *Artnews* 74 (March 1975): 86.

8. Roche, *With Duncan Grant in Southern Turkey*, 113–15.

promising to finish it. From Angelica, the canvas passed to her daughter Frances Garnett, and from Frances back to Duncan. All were defeated. About a month later Duncan arrived at the studio with the dread portrait under his arm. Roche unwrapped it.

> What I beheld filled me with hilarious dismay. The torso remained untouched, but the process of shrinking the head had been pushed to an extreme. And the neck had grown. The expression on the Earl's features at the end of it hardly mattered because the whole cephalogical landscape had become reduced to a cellar-pale Chinesey face arching out of a body and shoulders much too big for it.

Eventually the piece had to be returned to the countess, who offered them sherry and waited with touching eagerness for Duncan's work to be unveiled. Finally the men could stall no longer, and Roche swung the earl into view.

> The Countess reeled and, before she could stop herself, the words were out.
> "Ohhhh! It's horrible! Quite horrible!"
> . . . Appalled at what she had just uttered to the Master himself, she tried to cover it with: "Oh, no no no! I didn't mean that. I'm sure in its own way it's a masterpiece," but each time her eyes fell upon Loch Ness Monster, the words burst out: "Horrible! Quite horrible!"

Many years later, Paul Roche published a sequel to this book, an essay about his 1976 trip to Tangier with Duncan, who was by then over ninety years old. In fact, soon after arrival, Duncan collapsed at a luncheon, having first outlined a figure on the tablecloth with the tip of his fork and asked his hostess, "Do you think I should offer this to the Tate?" Roche's memoir plunged into Duncan's long illness and recovery, detailing his own role in these events, and culminating in an excited description of how he saved Duncan's life by giving him an enema in front of the enormous tiled hearth of their borrowed villa. It cannot be nostalgia alone that led Roche to divulge so much of what was clearly a harrowing private ordeal, many years past, and the reader veers uncomfortably between a less than commendable interest in Duncan Grant's bowel activity and impertinent speculations on Paul Roche's motives and his present life.[9] Still, there was something wonderfully characteristic in the invalid's dementia. One day, Roche found him crouched over the velvet seat of a fine Regency chair with a felt-tip pen in his hand: " 'This expanse of grey needs breaking up,' he said with enthusiasm, 'I have given it a geometric design.' "[10]

Surviving his enema by two years, Duncan died on 9 May 1978 at Paul and Clarissa Roche's house at Aldermaston. His estate was divided equally between Paul Roche and Angelica Garnett. Many paintings that went to Angelica remain at Charleston, on view for visitors. She passed control of Duncan's artistic estate to her daughter Henrietta Garnett, who had already been appointed his literary executor.[11] Rumour has it that when Charleston first opened to the public, Henrietta was liable to burst into rooms full of tourists and declare that

---

9. A 1987 biography of Duncan Grant by Douglas Blair Turnbaugh also qualifies as a Roche memoir, since he was Turnbaugh's principal source, to the extent that chapter 9 opened with "Paul's life at Taviton Street continued to include posing for Duncan."

10. Paul Roche, "With Duncan Grant in Tangiers," *Charleston Magazine* 8 (Winter-Spring 1993–94).

11. Any profits go to all three of Angelica's daughters.

she was Duncan Grant's granddaughter, much as Nigel Nicolson is said to smuggle himself into tour groups at Knole and await strategic moments to announce, "This should have been *my* house." At Duncan's memorial service at St. Paul's Cathedral, Paul Roche read his poem "The Artist" and Kenneth Clark delivered a eulogy in which he professed to find Duncan "completely outside the Bloomsbury ethos. He was sweet, gay, uncritical and charming."

THE LANDMARK BOOK *Bloomsbury Portraits: Vanessa Bell, Duncan Grant and Their Circle* originated with Anthony d'Offay, who brought together John Calmann, commissioning editor at Phaidon, and Richard Shone, then a Cambridge undergraduate and a longtime friend of Duncan's. He had recently organized an Arts Council exhibition of Duncan's portraits. Work began in 1971, when Shone left Cambridge, and came to an abrupt stop four years later. "The last chapter was completed with Phaidon's gun to my head," Shone recalls. This was pioneer research, especially where Vanessa was concerned. "Of books, there was none," Shone has written, "I virtually had *carte blanche* and no one outside the family had read the extensive Charleston papers."[12]

Although his book ended in 1937, with the death of Vanessa's son Julian and her entry into permanent semiseclusion, Shone's principal focus was Duncan, in part because he was alive and able to help but also, one feels, because no one at the time questioned that he was the stronger artist. In 1975, Duncan's ninetieth birthday celebrations had included a show at the Tate, a New York show of works on paper, and back-to-back exhibitions of early and new work at Anthony d'Offay

12. Richard Shone, exhibition notice for *Bloomsbury Portraits*, 8 Feb.–3 Mar. 1994 at the Bloomsbury Workshop, London, on the occasion of the new edition of Shone's book.

Gallery. Reviewing the Tate show, Shone argued that Duncan's association with Bloomsbury had "been more hindrance than help." By the following year, when *Bloomsbury Portraits* appeared, Shone felt that "Sunday Paper sensationalism and the gathering Bloomsbury industry had done its work" and that his book was unfairly neglected. It cannot have helped that it was published only a few months after Richard Cork's celebrated two-volume history of Vorticism, which did so much to convince critics and readers that the most vital and aggressively modern art in England had sprung from the enemies of Roger Fry. Bloomsbury art enthusiasts, however, greeted Shone's book like a long-awaited firstborn, and good copies of the first edition are said to have fetched as much as one hundred pounds in the dry years before its revision and republication in 1993.

Although Roger Fry's painting received much less attention in *Bloomsbury Portraits* than Vanessa's or Duncan's and remains much less appreciated, this was to some extent offset by a show of his portraits at the Courtauld Institute galleries in 1976, organized by a young art historian, Frances Spalding, then writing her thesis at Sheffield on the relation between Roger Fry's painting and criticism. As well as bringing together the three remarkable portraits of Lytton Strachey that Vanessa, Duncan, and Roger painted one day at Asheham (Roger's went to the University of Texas), the show managed to represent the full range of Roger's career, beginning with his early Whistlerian portrait of Edward Carpenter, now at the National Portrait Gallery. The opening night of the exhibition was a Bloomsbury event, crowded with secondary and second-generation members, among them Angelica Garnett, Igor and Anabel Anrep, Alison Waley (Arthur Waley's widow), and Roger's daughter Pamela Diamand. Duncan came in a wheelchair, wearing a large straw hat, and spent the evening surrounded by younger friends like Paul Roche and Lindy Dufferin.

Fry's letters had appeared in 1972, edited by Denys Sutton, joining a number of dissertations on his formalist aesthetics, their relation to Clive Bell's theories, and, increasingly, their possible influence on Virginia Woolf's fiction. About the time Frances Spalding completed her thesis, Richard Shone was approached by a publisher to write a new biography of Fry. Weary of the subject in the wake of *Bloomsbury Portraits*, he recommended Spalding for the job. In fact, 1980 would mark the peak of interest in Fry, with the appearance of the Spalding biography, Jacqueline Falkenheim's critical study *Roger Fry and the Beginnings of Formalism*, and the reissue in England of Virginia Woolf's official life of Fry (Woolf's American publishers, Harcourt Brace, had republished the book in the mid-1970s). Donald Laing's annotated bibliography of Fry's writings (essays numbering close to a thousand) had been published the year before. Evaluating Fry's art and writings in the light of this overdue attention, Richard Morphet returned to a favourite theme of his, arguing that "appreciation of Roger Fry's calm and thoughtful paintings has long been impeded by a general restlessness in the art community."

> Its hunger for the striking expression, the bold innovation, has led to a relative imperviousness—now happily showing signs of breaking down—to the qualities of quiet painting. . . . It is ironic that the misunderstanding and neglect of Fry's paintings should have been compounded by his own writings on art. The stress he laid on the importance of formal qualities unintentionally aroused false expectations that the formal language in his own paintings would be consistently emphatic.[13]

---

13. Richard Morphet, "Roger Fry: The Nature of His Painting," *Burlington* 122 (July 1980): 482.

Although the Spalding biography was not scorned as "yet another Bloomsbury book," reviews were typically ambivalent. In the *Times Literary Supplement*, Quentin Bell pointed out the improvements it offered over Virginia Woolf's official life, but other reviews reflected the aura of disappointment that clung to Fry's name and work. In England, Michael Holroyd described Fry's art as "painted with the dead hand of intellectuality." Hilton Kramer, writing for the *New York Times Book Review*, praised Spalding for so clearly explaining Fry's intellectual history and his relations with Bloomsbury but wished she had not lavished so much attention on his "failed career" as a painter and on paintings that "belonged unmistakably to the very conventions that his criticism was designed to subvert."

Looking back on the Fry biography, Spalding stresses its importance in her development as a writer: "Fry made me read and look at a great range of art, opened my mind to new things, made me go to France in search of the places and people he'd known and was a major part of my general education. I learnt far more from him than is apparent in that book."[14] She also remembers with pleasure her long hours with Roger's daughter Pamela Diamand and the curious sensation, new to her, of working within the history of living memory. As a girl, Pamela had lived with Roger's sisters, deriving from these women a Quaker directness and simplicity and an unwavering egalitarianism. "At the time of my first visit," Spalding has written, "I mistook the absense of undue social charm for a reproving austerity and felt chastened by it." Pamela answered her questions willingly, however, and then wanted Spalding to see every Roger Fry painting in the house. "This involved a visit to the upstairs flat," Spalding recalled,

---

14. Letter to the author, 30 Oct. 1996.

"blindingly furnished and littered with underwear, all of which dwindled from view as we looked at Roger's sober and slowly rewarding canvases."[15]

At the time Spalding knew her, Pamela was deeply involved with something called the Aetherius Society, a religious group that believed it possible to store prayer power in black boxes and then redirect it to some person or country in need. (Roger had gone through a strangely similar episode, to his friends' delight, in which he insisted on the curative powers of a certain black box.) There was a tallboy in the corner of Pamela's living room from which she would fish out papers and memorabilia. One day, the conversation turned to Victorian domestic life. They were talking about how the Victorians coped with such frequent childbirth, and Pamela Fry told Frances Spalding about an especially ingenious Quaker clothing design of the period, a dress that could be expanded for the various stages of pregnancy. She then produced one of these black dresses from the tallboy.

The moment Spalding knew that she wanted to write biographies came during a visit in the mid-1970s to a woman named Margery Rackstraw, a friend of Roger and Margery Fry's, who had a number of Roger Fry paintings. Over tea, the woman casually recalled that during the war she had worked for the Quaker War Victims' Relief Fund. After a moment, Spalding realized that "the war,"

in her terms, was the First World War. . . . To be sitting in the company of this rather distinguished elderly lady who was talking about "the war," and it was the First World War, gave

15. Frances Spalding, "Pamela Diamand, 1902–1985: A Personal Appreciation," *Charleston Newsletter* 12 (Sept. 1985).

me this wonderful sense of a ribbon of time that my questions had touched or caused to vibrate that went back to the trenches and the hideousness of the Marne and the Meuse.[16]

A further aspect of the genre that intrigued Spalding was that it could not be done well—in fact, hardly at all—without the writer pouring an immense amount of time and emotional energy into it: "Although you spend a period of time negating your own life in order to acquire someone else's life, it does somehow feed back into your own life, and in some peculiar way time is redeemed."

In "The Silent Woman," her long *New Yorker* essay (later a book) on Sylvia Plath biography and the problems of modern biography in general, Janet Malcolm has described Frances Spalding, whom she met by chance at Clarissa Roche's home, as the exemplar of the "good" biographer: "one who doesn't overstep, who is respectful of the given, who is unintrusive, judicious, who evaluates wisely and evenly."[17] Though these virtues inform all of Spalding's professional writing, they are most obviously apparent in the Vanessa Bell biography, perhaps because they approach some of Vanessa's own traits—her austerity, for example, her sense of irony, and the innate authority with which she presided for forty years over the dining-room table at Charleston: "It was round," Angelica has written, "but where she sat was the indubitable head of it."[18] These qualities also emerged in Spalding's writing as a result, to a great ex-

---

16. Interview with the author, 20 Feb. 1995.

17. Janet Malcolm, "The Silent Woman," *The New Yorker* 23 and 30 Aug. 1993: 134.

18. Angelica Garnett, *Deceived with Kindness* (London: Chatto & Windus, 1984), 167. Compare Olivier Bell's remark that "the Charleston dining table being round, there was no head to it; but Vanessa *was* the head," from an essay for the June 1993 exhibition *Images of Vanessa* at the Bloomsbury Workshop, London.

tent, of her work on this biography. Although the published book bears little trace of struggle, the final months of its composition can be seen as a sort of crucible in which her biographical voice and technique were forged.

Spalding had seen and admired d'Offay's 1973 show of Vanessa Bell's painting, but it was while reading her letters to Roger Fry that she realized that, despite Holroyd's Strachey and Quentin Bell's *Virginia Woolf*, Vanessa's story had not been told: she had remained the silent, enigmatic figure of her sister's imagination. When she approached the Bells and Angelica Garnett, she learned that two Americans had also asked to write the official biography. A contest was arranged, for which each would produce a sample chapter. Spalding won, with the condition that Quentin Bell would have approval "not so much over what I said," she remembers, "but of how I said it." To this end, Quentin read and seemed to approve each chapter as it appeared, making very few comments. Eventually she sent off copies of the finished manuscript to Quentin, Angelica, and her publisher. "And a few days later my publisher rang up," she recalls, "and said, 'You've heard the news, have you?' and I said 'No,' and he said, 'They think you perhaps ought to abandon this book and maybe you could edit the letters.' "

Angelica Garnett had been writing *Deceived with Kindness* at the time, working through some of the same periods and materials that Spalding had covered (she had allowed Spalding to read an early draft, which differed considerably from the final, published version), and Spalding wonders whether this may have affected Angelica's reading of the Vanessa Bell biography. "I may be totally wrong or inaccurate in saying this," Spalding adds, "but I think that reading mine for the first time was a shock for her because it was a different interpretation, a different voice." It was decided she should entirely rewrite the book. She did so, and maintains that it only became good during this complete overhaul.

The critical and popular success of the Vanessa Bell biography is based in part on Spalding's mastery of the vast written record of Vanessa's life and in part on the measured, sympathetic approach to her subject that she developed during this revision. Timing also helped. The book appeared at the same moment as Victoria Glendinning's *Vita* and was frequently reviewed with it, setting up an opposition between Vita and Vanessa as personalities that tended to benefit Spalding's biography. In one such joint review, for the *New York Times Book Review*, Samuel Hynes observed that books about the lives of gifted women were "inevitably also books about the restraints in women's lives—society, conventions, manners, class, men—and about the desires of those women to free their gifts from such restraints and to live their lives on their own terms." Although he found Glendinning's *Vita* "continuously interesting," Vita herself was "a devourer" and Vanessa "a giver." For Hynes, the greatest difference between the women was that one of them "was at home in her life, and the other wasn't: Vanessa wanted to be an artist, and she was; Vita wanted to be the heir of Knole, and she wasn't."

The ground had also been prepared by a succession of excellent Vanessa Bell exhibitions at Anthony d'Offay Gallery and elsewhere. Spalding herself had organized a full-scale centenary exhibition, which opened in Sheffield in September 1979 and traveled to Portsmouth. A smaller show of late works appeared that summer at d'Offay. In April 1983, some months before her biography appeared, the Royal Museum at Canterbury mounted a loan exhibition of forty Vanessa Bell paintings from 1910 to 1920. That August, d'Offay presented a Bell exhibition to mark the publication of the Spalding biography. The most important of these shows was the large, well-selected

1980 retrospective at the Davis & Long Gallery in New York. Among the eighty-five works included were major paintings like *The Bedroom, Gordon Square* (1912) and *Studland Beach* (1911), as well as curiosities like Roger Fry's Omega pyjamas, sewn from the "Maud" fabric designed by Vanessa. Press response was unusually favourable, with several long reviews in leading journals. Writing for *Art International*, Nina French-Frazier admired the "Pascalian simplicity" of Vanessa's best work and concluded that although it was never quite possible to disentangle her from "the ubiquitous Bloomsbury Group," her "intense search for essence" drove her, in the crucial decade after 1910, "to paint pictures that have a really different look, and which for their time and place were uniquely personal and amazingly radical." The Davis & Long exhibition coincided with the beginning of the Charleston Appeal, and events were planned in New York to draw attention to the campaign.

As early as 1976, in the introduction to *Bloomsbury Portraits*, Shone had described Vanessa Bell as "the pivotal figure in Bloomsbury," though she was not, he implied, its major artist. Three years later he noted that her artistic reputation was undergoing an extraordinary transformation, the reasons for which were manifold: "First and foremost, there is the high quality of her work as an easel painter and designer in the period 1910–1920," much of which had only recently come to light.[19] In 1977, Keith Roberts offered the grudging concession that Vanessa Bell, no favourite of his, "survives a little better" than Duncan Grant. Isabelle Anscombe's *Omega and After* (1981) poured on praise for Vanessa Bell. To Hilton Kramer, in 1980, she remained "a very gifted minor painter," but a review of her 1983 Canterbury show referred to Vanessa as "the only major painter among the Bloomsbury

---

19. Richard Shone, "Portsmouth," 673.

Group." She could still sometimes face erasure. To *Arts* of May 1978, Jed Perl contributed a negative review of the small travelling show *Bloomsbury Painters and Their Circle,* organized by the Beaverbrook Art Gallery, in which, after listing Bell among the painters included, he dropped all mention of her and referred consistently to "Grant and Gertler"—four times—as if they were a team. This puts me in mind of a later *New Criterion* book review in which Perl dismissed Victoria Glendinning as "one of those women who writes about other women." For the most part, however, it was increasingly apparent that Vanessa Bell was "coming out of Grant's shadow now as perhaps the more powerful and inventive painter."[20] She had not only regained her reputation of the 1920s but surpassed it.

This impression was confirmed by two mammoth Omega shows that opened simultaneously in London on 18 January 1984, one at the Crafts Council, organized largely by Fiona MacCarthy, and the other at Anthony d'Offay. Both had taken years to assemble, and both relied on the research help of Judith Collins, now a curator at the Tate but then an independent art historian, who had just published her definitive study of the Omega Workshops in 1983, a work so dense with detail that Quentin Bell opened his foreword with the admission, "I was sick in the Omega. It must have happened sometime in January 1919 . . . and if I allude to it now it is only because it is, as far as I can tell, the only thing about the Omega that [Judith Collins] does not know." Two years before the Collins book, Isabelle Anscombe had published *Omega and After,* a lighter affair, with many photographs of prerestoration Charleston by Anscombe's husband, Howard Grey. The Crafts Council exhibition represented the full range of Omega products—screens and panels, ceramics, furniture, rugs, fabrics,

---

20. John Russell Taylor, "Roger Fry's Amazing Time-Capsule," *The Times* 24 Jan. 1984.

small wood items, including a toy theatre by Roger Fry with puppets by Winifred Gill, designs on paper, and related paintings and sculpture—with many works from Charleston, the Fry Collection at the Courtauld Institute galleries and the Victoria and Albert Museum, whose impressive Bloomsbury-related holdings had been somewhat neglected since their Omega exhibition twenty years earlier. At the Crafts Council, Omega wares were arranged in domestic tableaux, with Hogarth Press books and other likely clutter on the tables. The d'Offay show was much more formal and, as well as unveiling little-known abstract paintings by Vanessa and Duncan, included a good deal of work by Wyndham Lewis and his friends, in keeping with the show's subtitle, *Alliance and Enmity in English Art, 1911–1920*. Richard Cork had recently written an article for *Artforum* on Madame Strindberg's Cabaret Theatre Club (The Cave of the Golden Calf), which opened in June 1912 with decorations by Lewis, Epstein, and others, and in a smaller gallery d'Offay showed all the extant designs for the nightclub, inviting comparison with Omega schemes.

Although these shows were extremely well attended, press response was disappointing. Especially disturbing was an anti-B review in the *Financial Times* by Roy Strong, director of the Victoria and Albert Museum, which had lent many works to the Crafts Council show. Most reviewers recognized that the very aims of the Omega, "an organization which relied on spontaneity of expression rather than a theoretically-based house style,"[21] would result in uneven achievements, the worst of which could be enjoyed for their joie de vivre and the best of which wittily challenge the austere functionalism of later European design. In *Studio International*, however, Mario Amaya sought to correct these errors of taste, insisting that Bloomsbury art

---

21. Richard Shone, "London: The Omega Workshops," *Burlington* 126 (June 1984): 374.

"was nothing more than a local, actually a provincial, manifestation of continental post-impressionism and decorative Cubism, totally misunderstood, naively applied, poorly executed." He resented that Omega design was "not conceived in terms of the surface to which it would be applied" but was chosen at random, on the impulse of the moment, and he detected a pernicious social agenda in their clumsy little bead bags and blue sheep screens. Such a degree of artistic willfulness, he claimed, "reflects the selfish motivations that seem to have permeated the social and sexual life of the group."

Anthony d'Offay's involvement with Bloomsbury art reached its apex with his Omega show. The estates of most of his modern artists, like Gwen John, Robert Bevan, and the Bloomsbury artists, were running dry; the market was tightening; and his interest turned increasingly to contemporary art. In this arena, Gilbert and George were among his earliest finds. He even introduced the young men to Duncan, who painted a portrait of one of them. Quentin Bell remembered seeing a good deal of d'Offay and his first wife in the later 1970s and recalled that d'Offay once turned up "with those two absurd figures, Gilbert and George. I seem to recall a stormy night when our old car collapsed and I had to employ these two gentlemen to push the thing for some distance. Poor Anthony was in a great state seeing his 'property' used in this demeaning way."[22] Angelica Garnett thinks that even before the Omega shows in 1984 the market for Bloomsbury art had collapsed in England: "Duncan Grant was no longer in fashion or even given a posthumous retrospective at the Tate. . . . Anyhow Anthony gave up Bloomsbury, wisely enough I suppose, and went in for Gilbert and George."[23]

---

22. Letter to the author, 12 Sept. 1995.

23. Letter to the author, 13 Sept. 1995.

Technically speaking, Anthony d'Offay still represents Vanessa and Duncan's estates, but there is very little left. Three or four important pieces remain at his gallery, and he is said to be holding out for good prices.

AS EARLY AS 1975, Angelica had been looking for ways to "preserve and continue the existence of Charleston as a Bloomsbury house," but the outlook was bleak. Enormous sums of money would be needed to repair the building alone, let alone the restoration of the murals, textiles, and furniture. Angelica consulted Nigel Nicolson, who had dealt with the National Trust. She also took advantage of one of Duncan's visits to Paul Roche's home to tour the property with the landlord's agent and his assistant, hoping to convince them to help with repairs, and has described their grim passage through the near-derelict house in her prologue to *Deceived with Kindness*.

> They were visibly unmoved by the charm of the decorations, and indeed as we went round it the house seemed to shed all its qualities, like so many petals falling from a flower, to reveal the mark of damp on the walls, the holes in the roof, the plaster coming away from the wallpaper, the exposed laths filled with woodworm, etc. The imperceptible shrugs of the two men, their loaded silences, the way the agent said, "I'm no connoisseur, but . . . ," my feeling that I seemed to be doing the wrong thing in showing them round, added up to something unpleasant like a drop that gathers at the end of one's nose.[24]

---

24. Angelica Garnett, *Deceived with Kindness*, 4.

Her brother Quentin had also been worrying about Charleston and had conferred with a colleague who agreed that no one would want to save a monument to Bloomsbury, however charming, and that the best they could hope for was to remove some of the murals and give them to a museum. The heroic rescue of Charleston has been recounted elsewhere (there is an excellent guide to Charleston published by the Hogarth Press), but a bare outline would begin not long after Duncan's death, when Deborah (known as Debo) Gage, a cousin of Viscount Gage, who owned the property, rang Quentin Bell and exclaimed, "Charleston must be saved!" A committee was established, which met in the Bells' drawing room at Beddingham, not far from Firle. (As Quentin Bell recalled, "I, who had for many years been on the shelf, found myself in the chair.") The Charleston Appeal began in late 1979 with a press release, numerous articles by sympathetic writers, and the first of many fund-raising letters. In April 1980 the Charleston Trust was formed (along with its support organization, the Friends of Charleston, of which there were about two thousand by 1986; there are fewer now), a newsletter was founded, restorers were engaged, American tours for Angelica and the Bells were organized. Altogether some £800,000 was raised over the next six years. While English Heritage contributed funds for the repair of the building itself and Paul Mellon donated $100,000, the bulk of this money came in small cheques from Bloomsbury enthusiasts and well-wishers.

Some of the grander money-making schemes misfired, particularly one involving Texas oil magnates, but the Sotheby's benefit sale of the Charleston Papers in July 1980 was a complete success, earning over £100,000 toward the purchase of the house from the Gage family. Most items had been donated by Angelica Garnett and the Bells and had been housed at King's College, Cambridge, since 1965, soon after Clive Bell's death. It was at this sale that the Tate Gallery Archive acquired the core of its Bloomsbury manuscript collection, picking up some sixteen lots, including nearly seven hundred letters from Duncan to Vanessa for £2,600 and the correspondence between Roger and Vanessa, some nine hundred letters in all, for £8,500. Valerie Eliot bought the bankbook of the Eliot Fellowship Fund, the 1922 scheme by which Virginia Woolf and others hoped to free T. S. Eliot from the need for gainful employment. Clive Bell's rather chic collection of letters from Picasso, Matisse, Cocteau, and others was divided and sold piecemeal. As might be expected, Virginia Woolf material fetched the highest prices: twenty-two letters to her brother Thoby brought £4,500, while her 170 letters and cards to Clive Bell went for £13,000. By contrast, Vanessa's twenty letters to Thoby fetched only £350. More strikingly, Maria Jackson's nine hundred letters to her daughter Julia Stephen and her son-in-law Leslie were sold to Lady Bonham-Carter for just £100. Miscellaneous family items included five matching silver egg cups used at 22 Hyde Park Gate, sold for £400 to the Harvester Press (Olivier Bell says these were "useless," too small for modern eggs), a collection of Stephen family tableware later used at Monk's House, which fetched £300, and two pairs of Virginia Woolf's tortoiseshell spectacles, in their original cloth cases, which garnered £250 and £260 pounds each.

Although Vanessa Bell's star was already sharply ascendant by the end of the 1970s, the Charleston Appeal gave an incalculable boost to her fortunes. By its very nature, the appeal generated tremendous amounts of publicity, and whatever critics may say about her painting, very few have been able to resist Charleston—either the house itself (now restored to postwar grubbiness) or its legend. There may be a sad subtext here on the equation of women with houses, but it is hard to deny Vanessa's preeminence at Charleston. To Angelica, as a child, the world of Charleston seemed not only controlled but created by her mother, "in the same spirit attributed to God when He created the world. She had stretched out her hand and lo, Charleston, the Downs, the Weald and the watermeadows, even to a certain extent Lewes and Rodmell, Leonard and Virginia, came into existence full and complete."[25] With attention to Charleston came renewed respect for Vanessa's art and a resurgence of interest in Bloomsbury decoration, as evidenced by the Jocasta Innes books on decorative painting and Laura Ashley's 1987 line of Bloomsbury textiles, utilizing Vanessa and Duncan's fabric designs. Later, a book on Bloomsbury needlepoint would appear and kits for easy Bloomsbury needlepoint cushions would be sold at the Charleston giftshop.

Prior to the Spalding biography and the opening of Charleston, it may have been Angelica Garnett's 1981 American speaking tour for the Charleston Appeal that had the most immediate effect on educated opinion about her mother. Her talks on Vanessa's family relationships and life at Charleston did much to disrupt the myth of Vanessa's heartless and voracious sexuality, the sort of misconceptions of her life and character that had led Cynthia Ozick to write that "no marriage could survive Vanessa for long."[26] It also brought Angelica herself into the spotlight that her brother Quentin had once occupied alone. Diane Gillespie, who would later write the first book-length study of Virginia and Vanessa's relationship, *The Sisters' Arts* (1988), published an interview with Angelica Garnett in *Modernist Studies* in 1979. She and Jane Lilienfeld were instrumental in bringing Angelica to the States for a tour that began at the 1980 MLA convention in

25. Angelica Garnett, "Plums of Memory," essay accompanying exhibition invitation for *First of the Summer Plums* at the Bloomsbury Workshop, London, June 1995.

26. Cynthia Ozick, "Mrs. Virginia Woolf: A Madwoman and Her Nurse," *Art and Ardor* (New York: Dutton, 1984), 41.

Houston, where she spoke several times and made an appeal for Charleston to the Virginia Woolf Society, and went on to include eleven American cities.

In summer 1986, with its restoration nearly completed, Charleston opened to the public; it now attracts some fifteen thousand visitors annually, many of whom, to judge from comments during tours, know little about Bloomsbury and a few of whom have taken a wrong turn on their way to Firle Place, the sixteenth-century Gage family seat. Still, it is the major Bloomsbury shrine and compares well to Monk's House, which many enthusiasts see on the same day. Duncan Grant's big straw hat disappeared from the studio a few years ago, but otherwise visitors tend to be orderly and admiring, often announcing their compulsion to rush home and re-decorate. Behind the scenes are resident writers and artists, and there are exhibitions of congenial, though somewhat tame art in a small gallery adjoining the shop. The shop itself, specializing in Blooms-bury-related books and objects, like scarves by Vanessa's grand-daughter Cressida Bell and pottery by Sophie MacCarthy, a granddaughter of Desmond MacCarthy, has proved far more prof-itable than similar shops at National Trust properties. Artistic shrines are melancholy places, nonetheless—vacant rooms and pas-sages that offer everything but the object sought—and serious devo-tees find a way to attend the Charleston Summer School or the Charleston Festival each spring, which coincides with the Annual General Meeting of the Charleston Trust. Here Friends of Charleston can share a bottle of recent-vintage white wine with Olivier Bell, Nigel Nicolson, Michael Holroyd, and other luminar-ies; listen to famous and distinguished speakers; and hear the latest controversies threshed out under the roof of a large striped tent. In recent years the festival organizer, Diana Reich, has planned spectacular finales. Eileen Atkins and Harriet Walter performed *Vita and Virginia* in 1992, a dramatization of the women's correspondence, which would open as a play at the Ambassadors Theatre in London that October and later travel to Broadway, with Vanessa Redgrave playing Vita. In 1996, Patricia Hodge and Sam West (who played Gerald Brenan in Christopher Hampton's film *Carrington*) read *Letters to Julian*, adapted by Patrick Garland from Vanessa and Julian's correspondence in 1935–37. In a recent issue of the *Charleston Magazine*, Virginia Nicholson described the unsettling experience of hearing these family letters read aloud. Not even her father, Quentin, had read the correspondence. "He awaited its impact in a state almost of innocence," she wrote, "nearly sixty years after his brother's death." When she asked Quentin why he never read Julian's letters from China, he answered simply, "They were illegible." Praising Patrick Garland's adaptation, which ended with an account of Julian's death in Spain, Nicholson added that Garland had created something that went much deeper for her than an amusing evocation of Charleston life.

> He has resurrected a relationship and exorcised grief over long-ago losses with sensitivity and wisdom. I think many members of the audience who came for another snippet of Bloomsbury gossip came away having experienced a catharsis. "It brought everything back to me with extraordinary vividness; for a moment one thought one was living in the past," Quentin said later. For me, having never known my uncle, all I can say is, I know him a little better now.[27]

---

27. Virginia Nicholson, "Letters to Julian," *Charleston Magazine* 14 (Autumn-Winter 1996): 53.

Charleston is kept precariously alive by corporate grants and gifts from the Friends of Charleston. The Lewes District Council gives very little each year, despite the considerable hotel and restaurant revenues that Bloomsbury pilgrims must provide to the area. The East Sussex County Council also contributes a small sum. Perhaps the best ambassador for Charleston is the twice-yearly *Charleston Magazine*, now expertly edited by Frances Spalding, who has an eye for luscious cover designs, some using the repeating patterns of Bloomsbury textiles, such as Vanessa Bell's "White" fabric, designed for the Omega, or a modern copy of Duncan Grant's Ideal Home Exhibition rug. Charleston also relies on illustrious visitors to rouse an indifferent press, the most notable thus far being the Prince of Wales, who came by helicopter on 8 March 1994 and presented a donation of a thousand pounds. Official accounts of the visit are exactly what one would expect, but Olivier Bell can sometimes be led to recount her private conversation with the prince, who had just made a royal visit to the Body Shop, where employees had shown him a mysterious banana paste and left him to speculate on its uses. According to another unofficial account, the prince's visit actually cost Charleston money, since one of the local worthies knocked over and crushed a Quentin Bell ceramic.

The Queen also visited Charleston, in about 1980, while staying with friends nearby. She is said to have displayed only perfunctory interest in the house and gardens until she came across a plate of Duncan Grant's depicting her ancestor Queen Victoria.

In 1965, an American enthusiast wrote to Leonard, offering to buy Monk's House and maintain it as a "literary shrine." "I am afraid there is no question of Monk's House being made into a literary shrine," replied Leonard, "as I shall leave it to someone else after my death." The atmosphere and recent history of Monk's House are worlds apart from those of Charleston. In one sense, it has been more accessible to scholars, since the University of Sussex rented the house to a succession of Woolf-minded tenants in the years after they bought it for a very low price from Leonard's heir Trekkie Parsons in 1972. At least three of these occupants have written about their stay at Monk's House, and countless Woolfians have visited the house and garden, especially since 1979, when it was turned over to the National Trust. In 1982, the first year the house was open to the public, over five thousand people visited. Yet, however many Omega plates remain, whatever scraps of Leonard's mail have been left about, and however authentic the heavy black telephone, the interior of Monk's House has all the emotional resonance of a shop-bought dried flower arrangement. It is a disappointing pilgrimage. The house and garden possess an undeniable mystique, nevertheless, connected, for many, with Virginia Woolf's suicide. There is, of course, a Virginia Woolf death cult—if this is how one best describes a preoccupation with her last hours. Dozens of tourists each year make the ritual walk, originating at the back gate of Monk's House garden, skirting the water meadows, and ending on the muddy clay banks of the River Ouse. Here Virginia Woolf put down her walking stick, forced a stone into her coat pocket, and dot dot dot. Something in these intimate, orderly actions, pieced together from the scant evidence at the scene, is more affecting than a room full of Leonard's scattered papers.

Virginia Woolf's last walk has been made one of the crucial stages of her journey, though how the walk functions for those who follow her footsteps to the Ouse is a complicated matter, a re-enactment composed, to differing degrees, of spiritualism, empathy, catharsis, self-indulgence, and hero worship. Perhaps if Woolf had a marked grave somewhere, the walk would be unnecessary. Or it may be that these moments engage us as art. Death by drowning has, in

Woolf's case, a predestined quality, seeming the ultimate direction of the metaphoric drift of her novels. (A critic once determined that as many as half of Woolf's figures of speech relate to water.) "To reach [the Ouse] from Monk's House," wrote Lucio Ruotolo in the *Miscellany*, "takes about fifteen minutes. Virginia clearly had some time to speculate about the final decision of her life." A student of psychoanalysis, Alma Bond, chose to illustrate "the walk" with a series of photographs, like the Stations of the Cross, in her 1989 psychobiography *Who Killed Virginia Woolf?* In an article for the *Virginia Woolf Quarterly* on his stay at Monk's House, George Spater began by describing war-time conditions in Rodmell, the context to Virginia's "last walk down to the Ouse." He rented the house from April to October 1970, one of the earliest tenancies. One of the last tenants before the National Trust took over was Sarah Bird Wright, who recently republished her 1984 article on Monk's House as a pamphlet in Cecil Woolf's series Bloomsbury Heritage.

> Near St. Peter's, the church at Rodmell, the elm the Woolfs named "Leonard" can be discerned, a lonely sentinel between the canal-laced marshes and the garden of Monk's House. The elm they named "Virginia" was blown over in a gale in 1943. It was across these meadows that Virginia walked to drown herself in March 1941; it is beneath these trees that their ashes were buried.[28]

"Leonard," too, is gone now, the victim of Dutch elm disease, which also took the elms at Charleston.

---

28. Sarah Bird Wright, "Staying at Monk's House: Echoes of the Woolfs," *Journal of Modern Literature* 11. 1 (March 1984): 126.

Frank Dean, who still lives in the village, recently published an account of his life as a blacksmith and farrier in Rodmell, with some recollections—perhaps prompted by his publisher—of Virginia Woolf and the search for her body. Although locals do not generally regard Monk's House as haunted, the house takes on a palpable aura at times, seen from the street or the path beside it, with its high garden walls, tangled shrubbery, and dark windows. There are no street lights in Rodmell, and Monk's House is especially forbidding at dusk, with the church steeple outlined behind it. A Rodmell girl told me that in the period after Leonard's death, when the house was often vacant and unkempt, schoolchildren used to dare each other to dart through the bushes into the haunted garden. When it was her turn, she pushed her way frantically through some brambles and came upon a calm stretch of overgrown grass. There, on a bench, a woman in a large-brimmed hat sat reading.

Tenants of Monk's House find themselves barraged with visitors. Lucio Ruotolo, who took the house in 1975, has said that he "learned early to ration hospitality." That summer, he counted 150 visitors, not including those he'd invited. Ruotolo had learned of the house through a classified advertisement in the *New York Review of Books*. One appearing in 1973 began: "SUSSEX, ENGLAND. To let. The last home of Virginia and Leonard Woolf, maintained substantially unchanged." Rent was equivalent to about one hundred dollars per week, minimum let six months. It is said that Saul Bellow, responding to one of these ads for the "delightful cottage," was appalled to find the house damp, low-ceilinged, frigid and depressing.

A car park has been installed at the end of The Street, near Monk's House, to accommodate tourists, but the village would still be recognizable to Virginia or Leonard. The small school remains, and a working farm, and the Norman church (though it shares a rector with other villages), the annual fête, and the Horticultural Society that Leonard helped found. The Bells' son Julian and his family lived in the village for several years, dodging Bloomsbury enthusiasts. There is a single bed-and-breakfast, run by Bernadette Fraser, whose leaflets are craftily worded: "Barn House, Rodmell, Home of Virginia Woolf."

Leonard and Virginia bought Monk's House in 1919, after being forced to leave their charming, isolated summer house, Asheham, because the owner wished to reoccupy it. The garden at Monk's House affords a view of the Downs across the Ouse valley, and from here, in the 1930s, the Woolfs grimly watched the excavation of the hillside surrounding Asheham by the Blue Circle Cement Company, which had bought the land. The house was divided into two and let to tenants. In front, where a pasture field had once plunged away, offering an open view of the undulating landscape, trucks began to deposit the slag from their chalk-mining operation. This mound of soil sprouted a small wood, obscuring the original view and conveniently concealing the house from all but the most diligent Woolf-hunters. The hole dug from the hillside became a landfill. Loud machinery, often audible from Rodmell, operated day and night. In 1990, methane gas was detected at Asheham and the last tenant, Blue Circle's site manager, moved out. The Welsh roof slates and other valuable materials gradually disappeared from the house. Doors and windows were boarded over to dissuade local teenagers and middle-aged Americans from trespassing, and the Blue Circle Cement Company decided to enlarge the landfill.

In August 1975, Nigel Nicolson had written to Angelica Garnett to tell her that he and his children had camped out at Monk's House, "as the guests of that charming man Ruotolo and his family," and on the way there had crept by Charleston, seeing it for the first time. At the approach to Asheham, however, they had been repulsed by "a foul and disfiguring notice."

> I thought it so sad that these quarrymen, having destroyed the Down, should abuse Virginia's lovely little house in this way. After all, why shouldn't people walk past it, and climb to the Down beyond? I want to write them an angry letter. It left a sour taste in my mouth for hours afterward.[29]

It is difficult to say what part ignorance of the Bloomsbury Group or perhaps prejudice against it played in a decision that seemed, at first glance, purely practical, a matter of increasing the landfill so that it could accept seven or eight more years' rubbish from Brighton and Lewes. If the East Sussex County Council or Lewes District Council had been in the practice of supporting Charleston or Monk's House with substantial grants, it might be easier to acquit them in the demolition of Asheham, an act that Quentin Bell had advised them would be "tantamount to destroying Tom Paine's house in Lewes or Kipling's house at Burwash." On the other hand, when Blue Circle became aware of the outcry over their plans, they drafted a plucky proposal to move Asheham one hundred yards nearer the Newhaven road, tear down the intervening woods, and re-create the original setting in foreshortened form, even to the extent of remodelling the contours of the Downs behind the house when the landfill reached its capacity. Sadly, the plan fell apart when English Heritage explained

---

29. Nigel Nicolson to Angelica Garnett, 28 Aug. 1975, unpublished letter in Sussex University Library.

that the house was built of rubble between two skins of plaster, and would not survive an attempt to move it.

The *Sussex Express* of 3 July 1992 reported that "an American devotee of Virginia Woolf sobbed on Wednesday as county councillors voted in favour of the demolition of her former home, Asheham House. 'I am heartbroken,' said Dr. Carol Hansen of San Francisco. 'The spirit of Virginia Woolf is there—I have experienced it. It is a monument to a genius.' " Tears and petitions notwithstanding, the county development control committee of the county council had voted unanimously in favour of Blue Circle's original plans for the house and woodlands, stipulating that Blue Circle would have to compensate local arts organizations for the loss of this historically and architecturally significant building. Negotiations over the compensation agreement, which included the possibility of as much as £150,000 going to Charleston, continued for the next two years, with Woolf enthusiasts frantically trying to stall the project. Carol Hansen returned to the States and sent a packet of clippings, including the address of Blue Circle's Landfill Division, to every member of the Virginia Woolf Society. But in vain. After being carefully videotaped, Asheham was pulled down in May 1994.

AT THE TIME she was most actively involved with resuscitating Charleston, Angelica Garnett was completing the manuscript of *Deceived with Kindness* (1984), a troubling memoir that some feel powerfully challenges the Bloomsbury ethos. At the very least, the book forces a reassessment of Vanessa Bell's character and of her famed maternal instincts. When I was travelling around California promoting the *Selected Letters of Vanessa Bell*, I found that readers in my audiences had typically read three books on Bloomsbury: the Bell biography of Virginia Woolf, Louise DeSalvo's book on Woolf's childhood sexual abuse, and *Deceived with Kindness*.

"Bloomsbury believed in and largely practised intellectual tolerance," wrote Angelica Garnett in a preface to the new 1994 Pimlico edition of her book, "but often failed to recognise the power of the emotions or the reasoning of the heart. Fascinating and vital, they hid their feelings behind an apparent detachment that I found at that time repressive and confusing." She began her story in 1975, when acute loneliness and a sense of disorientation had led her to begin to trace the sources of her unhappiness. As her father, Duncan, aged and became more dependent on Paul Roche—and more clearly a part of Roche's family—Angelica had felt increasingly displaced at Charleston. Nor could she discuss her feelings with Duncan, who remained affectionate but undemonstrative, absorbed in his painting and his present life. A friend had suggested she write a short book about her childhood at Charleston, and while this seemed impossible to her at the time, she was becoming dimly aware of a need to come to terms with the unsettling emotions she felt for her parents. She began work on her memoir in 1977, at the age of fifty-nine. Soon after, when Duncan died, she fell into a severe depression, and it was only as she began to recover that she became able to write in earnest.

> As I thought about my childhood and adolescence I began to realise that the past may be either fruitful or a burden; that the present, if not lived to the full, may turn the past into a threatening serpent; and that relationships that were not fully explored at the time can become dark shapes, in the shadow of which we do not care to linger.[30]

---

30. *Deceived with Kindness*, 11.

"Writing it out, that is to say committing myself to a definite point of view," she explained later, "seemed to hold the promise of exorcism."[31]

On first reading, *Deceived with Kindness* appears to centre on Angelica's childhood, with emphasis on her fraught relations with Vanessa, an overly permissive mother who did Angelica no favours by removing her from difficult classes at her school or cancelling her violin lessons because the instructor had made Angelica cry. The deception of the title—the concealment of Angelica's true parentage until she was seventeen—seems to crown Vanessa's incompetence as a parent and to confirm Angelica's charge that she had been treated like an object, "the single unequivocally successful result of [Vanessa's] liaison with Duncan".[32] The reader is carried along not so much by the narrative, however, which is fragmentary and halting, often pausing to explain the lasting damage of this or that incident, but by Angelica's meticulously rendered sense-memories—the whisky-rich breath of Maynard's servant, carrying her on his shoulders, for example, or Vanessa's long, jewelled fingers cutting paper flowers. All betray a heartbreaking clarity of desire. For the paradox is that Angelica had, as she realizes, an idyllic childhood. Petted and adored by her mother and by the remarkable figures in her parents' circle, she grew into an insecure and resentful adult, unable to shake herself free of the past and determined to locate the source of her misery somewhere outside herself, where it could be dealt with.

Her principal grievance was not in fact her concealed parentage—although the novelty of the Charleston ménage during the First

---

31. Preface to Pimlico edition of *Deceived with Kindness* (1994), viii.

32. *Deceived with Kindness*, 156.

World War threw a good many reviewers off the scent—but that someone did not break through the inertia at Charleston, the silence and lack of direction engendered by Vanessa and Duncan's complex relationship (and compounded by their well-meaning tolerance), and rescue her from her misguided engagement to Bunny Garnett, twenty-six years her senior. Bunny seems to have been the only one of them with the energy to act, and Angelica's sleepwalking marriage to him is the coup de grâce of her unhappy tale. She summed up the twenty-five years of their marriage rather quickly as "the struggle on his side to maintain an unlooked-for realisation of a private dream, about which in spite of an almost wilful blindness, he must have had deep misgivings; and on mine the slow emancipation from a nightmare."[33]

Most critics responded sympathetically to *Deceived with Kindness* (it won the J. R. Ackerley prize for autobiography), accepting the book as both a therapeutic exercise and a startling glimpse of Bloomsbury family life. It offered, of course, the added allure of filial impiety, for although Angelica made weak hedging remarks, at one point admitting that she may have painted Vanessa "in darker colours than she merited," her unsparing portrait of her mother left a very different impression than Nigel Nicolson's anxious defence of Vita Sackville-West in his equally candid *Portrait of a Marriage*. Quentin Bell's published response was guarded but sufficiently clear: "To say that this is an honest narrative is not to say that it is accurate." The reviewer for the *Economist* offered a similar view: "It is an absorbing, though deliberately one-sided and somewhat hostile tale. One hopes that it serves its therapeutic purpose."

Angelica had written her book four times over, devoting seven

---

33. Ibid., 157.

years to what would finally appear as 181 printed pages. She told an interviewer that it had been a torturous process, "like a very hard session with a tough psychoanalyst. I think it was necessary to write it—but perhaps not to publish it. I have too much resentment."[34] Those who argued that she had good cause for resentment were often—no surprise—writers unsympathetic to Bloomsbury. Anthony Storr was quick to put Angelica's memoir to use against the Group, arguing in the *Times Literary Supplement* that Bloomsbury had often been "painted as a self-regarding, self-indulgent, intellectually snobbish society, but the damage which its artificiality and alienation from ordinary emotions could inflict upon a growing child has not before been portrayed with such perceptive accuracy." In the *London Review of Books,* John Bayley squeezed in a few lines on *Deceived with Kindness* in the midst of a severe thrashing of Virginia Woolf and Bloomsbury. Angelica's book, he claimed, "shows a quite exceptional understanding of the whole environment. Tolerantly and without malice she analyses the ways in which Bloomsbury licensed and indulged the grossest egoisms as if they were the finest flower of civilised and rational behaviour. Of these she was herself the victim." Bayley failed to specify which "egoisms" he was referring to, thus preventing an effective rejoinder. But if he meant Vanessa's failure to enlighten Angelica about her parentage, he must have known from the memoir that Vanessa's decision was hardly regarded by her as the finest flower of civilized behaviour. She knew it was a clumsy, temporary measure—socially expedient but potentially dangerous. Even Angelica suspects that Vanessa had planned to tell her the truth much sooner than she in fact felt able to. And far from rushing to correct her mother's mistake,

---

34. Quoted in Caroline Moorehead's "Exorcising the Ghosts of Bloomsbury," *The Times* 1 Aug. 1984: 8.

Angelica and Bunny did not tell their own four daughters that they were Duncan Grant's grandchildren until they, too, were teenagers, although one of them had apparently heard it from a school friend.[35]

There were those for whom Angelica Garnett's upbringing appeared far from crippling. In 1968, soon after Angelica's separation from Bunny, Frances Partridge invited her to dinner one night and afterward recorded in her diary: "The training given by a pure Bloomsbury background—a training I would say that ultimately conduces to honesty, directness and of course utter disregard to *idées reçues*—has stood her in good stead, even if it sent her blinkered into the sort of annexe to Bloomsbury that Hilton [Angelica and Bunny's home] was."[36] Although it is hard to imagine Virginia or Vanessa publishing their recollections of George Duckworth, the unpious memoir was also part of Angelica's Bloomsbury heritage.

Nevertheless, as Janet Malcolm recently observed, *Deceived with Kindness* introduced "into the Bloomsbury legend a most jarring shift in perspective."[37] When the American edition appeared in 1985, Malcolm had more or less trounced it in the *New York Review of Books*, contrasting it with Spalding's affectionate and empathetic biography of Vanessa Bell and aligning it with other books "by the children of the celebrated," whose authors, while insisting that they want to be free of their parents, "can think of no better way of achieving an

---

35. From Frances Partridge, *Hanging On: Diaries 1960–63* (London: Flamingo, 1995), 77. Henrietta Garnett told an interviewer: "I never knew [Duncan] was my grandfather until I was seventeen. It was when I was engaged to Burgo that my father told me, and he said that I would not be lucky. But it came as no surprise. I think I always knew. . . . My reaction when I found out was delight and pride, and gratitude to Clive. He couldn't have been a nicer pretence grandfather" (*Bloomsbury Reflections*, unpaginated).

36. Frances Partridge, *Good Company: Diaries 1967–70* (London: Flamingo, 1995), 132.

37. Janet Malcolm, "A House of One's Own," *New Yorker* 5 June 1995: 74.

identity than to retail to a callous and indifferent world the intimate secrets of their families." It was not the substance but the nature of Angelica's self-interested critique that irritated Malcolm, and she returned to the memoir in later essays with increasingly articulate distaste. In "The Silent Woman," for instance, she went out of her way to include discussion of *Deceived with Kindness*, describing the book as "full of aggrievement and complaint."

> We don't want to be told what vengeful memoirs like Angelica's . . . oblige us to consider: that our children and friends do not love us, that we are neurotic, blind, pathetic, that under the eye of God our life will be seen as a mistake, something botched and wasted.[38]

Angelica's memoir appeared in England just a year after the Spalding biography, only a few months after the closing of the two great Omega exhibitions of 1984, and in the midst of the restoration of Charleston. It has not turned out to be the mortal blow to Bloomsbury that some critics envisioned (and longed for), for when the shock of Angelica's narrative passes, what remains is a rich evocation of Charleston life, made the more poignant by the implicit rejection of all that Angelica so lovingly rendered. The walled garden, the studio, the morning routine: these were the pleasant outward aspects of her fumbled upbringing. Her censure of Vanessa had also, in some quarters, the unlooked-for effect of increasing sympathy for the woman. It took this small, bitter book to knock Demeter off her plinth. Somewhere among the pieces is a fallible and more affecting Vanessa Bell than readers had been led to expect. But whether or not they ac-

---

38. Janet Malcolm, "The Silent Woman," 134.

cept Angelica's version of the past, there are many who believe that the writing of her memoir showed, as Kennedy Fraser argued in the *New Yorker,* "real courage: this revelation of her truth, this determination of a middle-aged, underwater woman to break the surface of the myth and come up for air."[39]

Whether *Deceived with Kindness* worked as therapy is less clear, both to observers of the unfolding saga and to Angelica Garnett herself. A few months before the book was published, Angelica bought a farmhouse in Haute Provence and moved away from England, which suggests a grasp at the independence and self-assurance that she had hoped her long struggle with the memoir would enable. For a while, however, she thought she might rewrite the book as a novel, "with the same plot, feeling freer to say all the things I feel to be true but didn't dare say because they might not be."[40] This desire seems to have faded and may have been nothing more than the perennial wish of writers to write their books over again, better and truer. Angelica has often indicated that she would write her memoir differently now, although her ambivalence is hard to conceal. "In the ten years since it was published," she explained in the preface to the Pimlico edition, "I have had time to see things—above all myself—otherwise, even to grow up a little. I am also less obsessed by the personalities and relationships of my mother, father and husband, less desirous of apportioning the blame and less mesmerized by the idea of repeating or re-living my childhood." She then launched, however, into a recital of her injuries, drawn almost irresistibly by the earlier and more compelling narrative, and could only stop herself after two paragraphs,

---

39. Kennedy Fraser, "Ornament and Silence," *New Yorker* 6 Nov. 1989.

40. Quoted in Caroline Moorehead, "Exorcising the Ghosts of Bloomsbury."

reflecting that accusation and blame were, after all, "dreary props for the ego."

IF ANGELICA GARNETT'S memoir seemed to project a lifetime of discontent onto a single figure in her childhood, the other immensely influential book of this period laid waste to nearly everyone associated with Virginia Woolf, leaving even the heroine with scorched hair and a smell of smoke about her. Although Louise DeSalvo's *Virginia Woolf: The Impact of Childhood Sexual Abuse on Her Life and Work* (1989) is a milestone in Woolf studies, the first Woolf-related bestseller after the Quentin Bell biography, it is difficult to place within the larger Bloomsbury revival. It is even hard to decide where it falls in Woolf studies, for DeSalvo did not offer new information, or even radical reinterpretations of what we already know, so much as she made the familiar unfamiliar, in the way that Marjorie Strachey is said to have made fairy tales drip with obscenity by her manner of delivery. I have wondered if this book should even be discussed in detail here, since its apparent purpose and effect have been to comfort and inspire vast numbers of people hoping to recover from childhood abuse. Some sixty thousand paperback copies of DeSalvo's book were sold in America by early 1994. If this audience is served by DeSalvo's vision of Virginia Woolf, however it jars with conventional readings of the relevant documents, then it is possible that critical standards should be relaxed when discussing this book; it may take on the character of "applied" biography, like applied art. Yet, in the light of DeSalvo's considerable credentials as a Woolf scholar and her years of work in the Virginia Woolf archive at the Berg, hers is a voice we should be able to take seriously. Few scholars disagree with the premise of DeSalvo's book—that Virginia Woolf was sexually abused—but many have taken issue with her scholarly methods and with a host of provocative claims she made in her endeavour to portray the Stephens as a pathologically dysfunctional family "in which incest, sexual violence, and abusive behavior were a common, rather than a singular or rare occurrence, a family in which there is evidence that virtually all were involved in either incest or violence or both."[41]

From her first readings of *To the Lighthouse* in the early 1960s, DeSalvo was captivated by the children in Woolf's novels, especially Cam Ramsay.[42] Later, she studied under Mitchell Leaska, who was then editing *The Pargiters* (the novel-essay portion of *The Years*) and who brought a photocopy of the draft versions to class one day; she remembers being "absolutely transfixed" by these earlier versions of the published text. It was Leaska who suggested *The Voyage Out* for DeSalvo's dissertation, and from this work came her first book, *Virginia Woolf's First Novel: A Voyage in the Making* (1980), a biographically based interpretation of the nine surviving partial drafts of *The Voyage Out* that emerged from DeSalvo's close study of the thousand or so disordered, largely unnumbered manuscript pages at the Berg. Two years later, she edited and published the earliest recoverable version of this novel as *Melymbrosia,* a title Woolf had wisely cast aside. Jane Marcus had taken DeSalvo under her wing and they became extremely close friends in the late 1970s. She had also formed a friendship with Mitchell Leaska, and together they edited the correspondence between Woolf and Sackville-West and planned to edit Woolf's early journals. "At some point Nigel Nicolson came to New York and told me that it was his wish that Mitchell write the introduction [to the *Letters*]," DeSalvo recalls. "He said, 'You're in print regarding this re-

---

41. Louise DeSalvo, *Virginia Woolf: The Impact of Childhood Sexual Abuse on Her Life and Work* (Boston: Beacon, 1989), 1.

42. Interview with the author, 6 April 1994.

lationship in *Signs* and I'd like to give Mitchell a chance to have his say.' " Eventually she decided not to press the issue, but she withdrew from the early journals project, which meant that although she had completed a preliminary transcription of some sections of Woolf's notebooks, Leaska would get full credit for the finished book. This break with Leaska and the Woolf establishment she turned to her advantage, however. She had already roughed out some chapters on Woolf's childhood and soon approached a publisher. As the book began to take shape, DeSalvo realized she would be writing about incest (to the extent that, in conversation, she refers to this book on Woolf's childhood as "the incest book") and instinctively stopped sharing her work in progress with Jane Marcus and others. From this point on, she worked slowly and alone.

Nevertheless, DeSalvo's *Virginia Woolf* was not a book that could have been written without American feminist Woolf scholarship of the 1970s, and it represents an unexpected culmination of certain ways of thinking about Woolf and of reading her texts through her life. Kennedy Fraser, in a long, heartfelt review essay for the *New Yorker*, said she suspected that the world of Bloomsbury scholars was "a kind of magic circle, carrying an unspoken threat of punishment to any initiate who betrays it or launches out." Surveying the bilious replies to DeSalvo's book from the Woolf community, one might agree. More than anything, however, the divergent responses to this book may illustrate the gulf between academics, or others trained in rhetoric and critical methodologies, and mainstream readers, who could judge DeSalvo's work only by the strength of her convictions and by the wealth of sources she presented in support of her thesis, ranging from the Woolf archive to clinical studies of child abuse to Arthurian legend.

In essence, DeSalvo's book is a psychosocial study of the

Stephen family as abusive and incestuous, combined with an indictment of Victorian child-rearing practices and attitudes toward women. DeSalvo was trying to get at the emotional truths of Virginia Woolf's childhood, and she may have grasped some of them intuitively—her section on "Miss Jan," a reconsideration of an earlier essay, was especially suggestive. Yet she undermined her argument with an assortment of forced readings, misreadings, odd readings, and inflated language. Early in the book, for instance, DeSalvo declared that rape is defined as "violent seizure," a point Quentin Bell violently seized upon in the *New York Review of Books* and which had the effect of suggesting that if a crime could not be proven, DeSalvo would redefine it until it could. Later, in the same spirit, she described the unwanted affection Vanessa lavished on Angelica as a "violation of her body." She quoted a passage from *Deceived with Kindness* in which Angelica had described photographs of herself as a young child, held either by her nurse or by the "Madonna-like Vanessa, whose long straight fingers are too apt to find their way into every crevice of my body," and went on to claim that "that horrifying familial symmetry of Virginia's memory of Gerald's abuse and Angelica's memory of Vanessa suggests that Virginia and Vanessa, victimized by the Duckworths, themselves in turn victimized Angelica."[43] To many critics, DeSalvo appeared to have superimposed recently developed models of incestuous families on the Stephen-Duckworth household and then snipped, stretched, or omitted the evidence, as it has come down to us, whenever it failed to match this grim template.

DeSalvo's use of supporting documents was also severely ques-

---

43. DeSalvo, 93.

tioned. One of her techniques was to blur primary and secondary evidence by interleaving her argument with many quotes from unnamed sources, as in the sentence "Julia believed that the family was 'the smallest unit of the patriarchal state'; she had the right of 'physical and moral rule' over the lives of the family members and servants."[44] Readers have to consult the endnotes at the back of the book to learn that these are quotes from an essay by an American feminist scholar, Martine Stemerick, rather than Julia's own words or a contemporary report of her character. Another technique was to load plausible and often quite powerful arguments with increasingly sinister and far-fetched purport. In one instance, having devoted twelve pages to Leslie Stephen's abysmal treatment of Laura, his troubled daughter from his first marriage, and her eventual relegation to an asylum, De-Salvo moved on to claim it was "no wonder then that Stella became 'the Old Cow,' the family helper, and that Vanessa became 'the Saint.'"

> They were purchasing their right to stay within the family by their exemplary behavior. One of the effects of scape-goating one child within a family is to exact seemingly impossible standards of behavior from the other children. Seen in the light of Laura's treatment, Virginia Woolf's childhood and adolescent habit of reading voraciously—"Gracious, child, how you gobble," her father would say—becomes terrifyingly comprehensible. Laura had been locked away, it must have seemed, for not having read well enough, for having stumbled over her words. Every time

---

44. Ibid., 45.

that Virginia knocked on the door of her father's study, and asked him to hand down yet another volume, she was proving that she was not Laura: she was keeping herself from being called perverse; she was buying the right to live a life within the family; she was keeping herself from being locked up, from being locked away, from being sent to an asylum.[45]

Let alone the collapsing of Laura's many signs of emotional disturbance into this one innocuous symptom, Virginia's intellectual precocity was reduced here to a performance for her father's benefit, a survival strategy. What had seemed, to earlier readers, the stirrings of literary genius became only the frantic gestures of a frightened girl.

"The danger in analyzing lives and literature according to selective evidence or a single set of experiences," wrote a reviewer for the *New York Times Book Review*, "is that the essential spirit of people and their creative products can suffer severe misinterpretation if tucked neatly into Procrustean beds." Although the reductivism at the heart of DeSalvo's project was a source of complaint for many critics, the greatest objections were to DeSalvo's stubbornly literal readings of Woolf's supple, playful prose (DeSalvo was especially appalled by the flirtatious quality of Woolf's letters, seeing it as a confirmation that "children who have been reared in incestuous households tend, in their adulthood, to try to sexualize every relationship."[46]) and to the curious transformation of her speculations into "facts." At one point, for instance, DeSalvo mentioned George's incestuous assaults on Vir-

---

45. Ibid., 34.

46. Ibid., 87.

ginia "and perhaps on Vanessa too." Sixteen pages later, in her chapter on Vanessa, she wrote blithely of "the fact that she was sexually molested." In his review, Quentin Bell referred to this quality as DeSalvo's "mythogenic power." Another passage described Leslie Stephen's selfish, exaggerated mourning after Julia's death and his enlistment of Stella to "assuage his grief and remorse," as Virginia put it. DeSalvo built a convincing picture of Stella's dismal situation as the eldest surviving female in a large middle-class household. Quoting Woolf's memoirs about the constant attention and comfort demanded by Leslie Stephen, she argued that "Woolf implied that her father demanded, and that Stella might have given him, comfort of a sexual nature."[47] Although few would read Woolf's statements in this light, DeSalvo was well within a reasonable—and reasonably qualified—interpretation of the memoir. Ten pages later, however, with no additional evidence, DeSalvo asserted that Stella had become "Leslie's sexual and emotional support."

Quentin and Olivier Bell never recovered from DeSalvo's book. A 1996 issue of the *Charleston Magazine* includes a short essay by Olivier reiterating that Virginia's juvenile story, "A Cockney's Farming Experiences" (which DeSalvo had explored in detail as "an extremely painful evocation of the experience of child abuse and neglect") should be read in the light of its co-authorship by Virginia's elder brother Thoby, then an eleven-year-old schoolboy with a demonstrable taste for sensational reading matter. She described DeSalvo's *Virginia Woolf* as a "farrago," "the product of indefatigable reading, ingenious speculation, imaginative interpretation and psychological extrapolation." The commercial success of DeSalvo's book rankled even more. Not only did it suggest that her bleak vision

47. Ibid., 57.

was gaining ever wider currency, it must have forced the Bells to consider exactly what role they now played in Woolf's posthumous affairs, seventeen years after the official biography had appeared and
five years after the final volume of the diary. Having gradually sold
or donated all the original material in their hands (even the *Hyde Park
Gate News*, now at the British Library) and given permission for the
publication of Woolf's reading notebooks, her early journals, her essays (the complete essays are being edited by Andrew McNeillie, once
Olivier Bell's assistant on the *Diaries*), and more, they could no longer
be considered the guardians of Virginia Woolf's image, nor even the
custodians of her archive. Yet several of Quentin Bell's essays from
the later 1970s and 1980s suggest that he felt responsible for what was
being said of his aunt. His responses to Jane Marcus and Louise De-
Salvo, in particular, were not only defences of his biography but assertions of what had to be considered the estate's position on various
issues. In interviews, as in these essays, he maintained a good-natured,
somewhat courtly tone, relying on humour and the "facts" of
Woolf's life and times to deflate the wilder speculations of scholars.
He stressed the limitations of our knowledge, sedately patrolling the
boundary between orthodox and suspect uses of the written record of
Woolf's life. At one point, however, he sent a consoling letter to Ol-
wyn Hughes, in the thick of her conflicts with Plath scholars, which
suggests considerable depth of feeling regarding the new Woolfians:
"It is in fact amazing how closely these creatures seem to resemble
each other: the leaden prose, the persistent lying, the equivocations,
the crude feminism. I know them all from personal experience. And
the worst is that they teach."[48]

---

48. The Bells have always been uncomfortable with the publicity surrounding their work
on Woolf and Quentin's position as her literary executor. Jane Emery (then Jane Novak),

Jane Marcus, who has avoided critical discussion of the DeSalvo book, offered her own trenchant summaries of the Woolf world in the 1980s and 1990s, observing that just as Woolf's life had served "as the prototypical narrative for the woman artist and for the feminist," so her life and work would "remain a test case for theory."[49] "For us," she wrote, "Virginia Woolf figures as a version of the *fin de siècle* hysteric in which genius, madness, and suicide sensationalize the narrative of her life. Her life is a *musée pathologique vivant*." Marcus had her hands full with the "pathographies" that kept appearing on Woolf, ranging from Thomas Caramagno's award-winning *The Flight of the Mind: Virginia Woolf's Art and Manic-Depressive Illness* (1992) to Alma Bond's *Who Killed Virginia Woolf?* (1989), a well-meaning but goofy production that included sections on toilet training and penis envy. Pathographers were easily labelled and dispatched in comparison with her new antagonists in academe: post-poststructuralist (post-?) postfeminists. Most of their aims for a postmodern Woolf could surely be accomplished, Marcus argued, "without a total repudiation" of a generation of feminist critics.

Beyond the universities, however, the current popular conception of Virginia Woolf is far from postmodern and retains a strong resemblance to Quentin Bell's Virginia Woolf. Added, perhaps, is a cer-

---

an American scholar who has specialized in Woolf since her undergraduate days, when Woolf was still living, remembers her first visit to the Bells in 1971. On her return home, a magazine editor asked her to contribute a short piece on the Bells. She sent them an advance copy and they wrote back that they liked her too much to use her as a publicist, especially as she did not come to see them as a journalist, but as a fellow student of Woolf. She withdrew the article. This marked the beginning of a long friendship.

49. Jane Marcus, "Pathographies: The Virginia Woolf Soap Operas," *Signs* (Summer 1992).

tain maturity and knowingness, exemplified by Eileen Atkins's 1990–91 performances of *A Room of One's Own* (the British-made video of which is enjoying a long life on American public television) and her later, more subtle impersonation of Woolf in *Vita and Virginia*. The new face of Virginia Woolf may indeed be that of Eileen Atkins. Even the painting on the cover of the English edition of the Hermione Lee biography—an image to which Olivier Bell strenuously objected—seems unaccountably disturbing until it resolves itself into a subtle fusion of Woolf's facial features with those of her impersonator, so that Woolf appears a little more sharp and cunning, and vaguely more theatrical, than in contemporary photographs. Not to mention her advancing age. There is something in her having survived the sustained opposition to her writing and her position in English letters (Tom Paulin's 1991 BBC television show on Woolf as an overrated writer is among recent assaults) that makes images of Woolf at the height of her powers, in the series by Man Ray, for instance, or photographs taken at Monk's House in the 1930s, more fitting now than that Beresford portrait of wispy adolescence. Any survey of recent biographically based scholarship—English, American, or French—would reveal that the new Woolf is successful, self-assured, and menopausal.

The Hermione Lee biography—an amazing tightrope walk over the churning waters of Woolf scholarship—embodies the most complete understanding yet of the ways in which our image of Virginia Woolf has evolved over the decades, and of how one can still write the life ("a" life) of such a shifting subject, using Woolf's own ideas about biography. Although the book reads well as a straightforward, if unusually detailed, literary biography, it is in fact a layered text, thoughtfully addressing the events of Woolf's life while keeping up a sotto voce commentary on previous Woolf scholarship.

Her discussion of the Duckworth brothers, for instance, functions as an impassioned refutation of Louise DeSalvo's position, although Lee does not name her target, except in the endnotes. This intense awareness of the posthumous life of Virginia Woolf gives the Lee biography a peculiar, melancholy quality, perhaps in part what Anatole Broyard meant when he spoke of writers arriving late on the scene. "It is impossible to think about this story innocently," Lee remarked at one point, "without being aware of what has been made of it." An observation that now applies to the bulk of Virginia Woolf's life.

THE EMPHASIS ON the Bloomsbury women, which yielded books as strange and powerful as Mary Ann Caws's *Women of Bloomsbury* and as bland as Jan Marsh's *Bloomsbury Women* (1996), has expanded in recent years to an emphasis on couples—not, perhaps, the characteristic formation of Bloomsbury relationships. Nevertheless, Vita and Virginia, Virginia and Vanessa, Vanessa and Duncan, Virginia and Leonard, Lytton and Carrington, Molly and Desmond, Maynard and Lydia, James and Alix each have had their book or play or film, in what may be a search for novelty or a normative urge on the part of writers, an attempt to arrange Bloomsbury into appetizing shapes and bite-size pieces, suitable for mass consumption.

But the commodification of cultural icons is a tricky subject. Virginia Woolf T-shirts, Barnes & Noble shopping bags with the Beresford profile, the Charleston shop, and the film *Carrington* all demonstrate that Woolf and her friends have been "commodified," but since the profits from these endeavours are relatively low—in comparison, for instance, with the profits from the use of Marilyn Monroe's image—we can assume that the much-lamented marketing of Bloomsbury refers principally to the outpouring of books on the subject and secondly, perhaps, to stage and film adaptations of the Bloomsberries' lives and work. Sales figures give some idea of the profits to be made from Bloomsbury-related books and suggest that one shouldn't confuse demand with a lack of resistance. *Deceived with Kindness* initially sold a respectable 6,500 hardback copies for Chatto & Windus. Paperback rights were sublicensed to Oxford University Press, where the book was reprinted at least seven times between 1985 and 1994, and have now reverted to Chatto, who reissued the book under their Pimlico imprint. Biographers make the largest share of money in this particular pie (DeSalvo's success with *Virginia Woolf* yielded a six-figure advance for her next two books), yet Holroyd's revised *Lytton Strachey* had sold only about 2,000 copies of a modest English print run of 2,500 within the first six months of publication. This is about as many copies as the hardback edition of *Selected Letters of Vanessa Bell* sold in England; in America, about 3,000 copies sold before discounting. Though among the more successful efforts of recent years, Melinda Coss's *Bloomsbury Needlework* (1993) was soon remaindered in the United States. So much for gold-digging in Bloomsbury. Books with a largely academic appeal fare much worse, of course. The first volume of Andrew McNeillie's edition of Virginia Woolf's complete essays sold 2,000 copies, for instance, the second volume only 950 copies. On the other hand, the recent one-volume abridgements of Woolf's letters and diaries, designed to entice the general reader, have failed to do so. Only about 800 copies of the *Shorter Letters* were bought in England in the year after publication.

The best way to make money in the field is to own copyright. King's College, Cambridge, to whom Forster bequeathed most of his possessions, charges sizable fees for the use of his work. They also demand the stiff fee of £100 for the right to reproduce Vanessa Bell's

1933 painting of Roger Fry and Julian Bell playing chess, which hangs in a stairwell at the college, and have benefited enormously from the film adaptations of Forster's novels, which began with David Lean's *A Passage to India* (1984) and appeared every year or two thereafter, under the aegis of Merchant and Ivory. Nevertheless, "it is no sinecure being a literary heir," as Olivier Bell wrote, weighing royalties and copyright fees against the responsibilities of managing a literary estate. The Bells' duties slackened as the bulk of Virginia Woolf's private papers were published, and in 1994 Quentin handed over responsibility for his aunt's estate to the Society of Authors. He and Olivier had distributed portions of the Woolf estate to their children, as Angelica had distributed part of what she owned to her daughters. Now that Virginia Woolf is back in copyright in England, due to the adoption of European Community standards, these beneficiaries can count on many more years of royalties with minimal involvement in the day-to-day affairs of the Woolf estate. Cressida Bell, a London-based designer and decorative painter who opened a shop on Prince Street in 1994, owns half of *To the Lighthouse* with her sister Virginia Nicholson. She feels grateful for the legacy and thinks that, considering the message of *A Room of One's Own,* her great-aunt would have approved of the two or three thousand pounds in royalties that come to her annually, which made it possible for her and her partner, Christine Miles, to keep their business afloat through several lean years in the 1980s.

The Bloomsbury grandchildren have not always responded so cheerfully to their connection with the Group. Adam West, Nigel Nicolson's son, apparently refused to read Virginia Woolf until he was thirty-two, having had more than enough of her during his formative years. Angelica Garnett says that of her twin daughters, Frances is interested in Bloomsbury and is fairly well read in the subject, but

Nerissa, while alive to the merits of early Bloomsbury painting, "has drawn right away from historical Bloomsbury, particularly Charleston, which she loved, not wanting to be over-concerned with a past she felt she had nothing to do with."[50] They and their elder sister, Henrietta, share the other half of *To the Lighthouse*. In a 1986 interview entitled "No Longer Afraid of Virginia Woolf," Henrietta recalled that when she was at school in the late 1950s, "Virginia Woolf's reputation was at a very low ebb. Nobody had heard of her, though when I was in the third form at school, my father's book, *Lady into Fox*, was set for A levels." She, too, had wanted to write but did not devote herself to it until her forties.

> The problem really was all my famous relations. I had been put off trying to get anything published because I couldn't help thinking that whatever I did it would never be as good as anything they've achieved. I felt I started off with a built-in handicap.[51]

And yet she felt grateful, too, to have grown up in beautiful houses, without much money but surrounded by artists and writers. It is perhaps worth mentioning that while English reviewers tended to judge Henrietta Garnett's first novel, *Skeletons in the Closet*, on its own merits, Americans took their lead from the book jacket and delved into Garnett's connection with Bloomsbury.

Cressida Bell counts herself, with some amusement, among

---

50. Letter to the author, 13 Sept. 1995.

51. Quoted in Liz Hodgkinson, "No Longer Afraid of Virginia Woolf," *The Times* 24 Oct. 1986.

those who capitalize on their link with the Group. At her first art school, St. Martin's, she had kept her Bloomsbury heritage quiet until a tutor snidely confronted her with: "So. You're one of *those* Bells." Later, at the Royal College of Art, she made a point of quickly mentioning it whenever Bloomsbury came up, to forestall rude comments about her family. When it came time to graduate and start her decorating business, she consulted a journalist friend, who told her she needed an "angle" for her press packet, something to make her newsworthy, and suggested that she play up the connection with Bloomsbury. This proved enormously successful, yielding a two-page spread in the *Observer*, among other articles. She still gets copious press coverage. When commissioned, she can execute convincing Bloomsbury-style decorations, although her preferred style is tighter and more vibrantly coloured. One wealthy Florida couple hired her for a three-month faux-Bloomsbury decorating job: several rooms' worth of furniture, walls, textiles, even a grand piano.

Virginia Nicholson remembers that her sister had been attracted to bright, glittering objects since early childhood: "When she could barely talk she had a part in a family play where the one line she could be guaranteed to utter confidently was 'Lots and lots of Diamonds!' "[52] Of the three Bell children, Virginia is the most involved in the fortunes of Bloomsbury. Since moving to Sussex in 1990 with her husband, the writer William Nicholson, she has become increasingly active at Charleston and now sits on the Council of the Charleston Trust. She is writing the text for a glossy new book on Charleston, from plans made by Quentin Bell soon before his death.

---

52. Essay on exhibition notice for *Quentin Bell, Cressida Bell, & Julian Bell at the Bloomsbury Workshop*, July 1995.

Virginia remembers that in her one year at King's College in the mid-1970s, a few notes arrived in her pigeonhole from people wanting to talk about Virginia Woolf and Bloomsbury. More might have approached her, but there was luckily another student named Virginia Bell, who shared the burden of association.

"It *is* a bloody racket," Cecil Woolf, Leonard's nephew, told an interviewer, in reference to the Bloomsbury industry, "and it's become thoroughly exploitative. The people concerned would be turning in their graves."[53] Starting his publishing business in the early 1960s, Cecil Woolf resisted using the Bloomsbury connection to promote himself. Nevertheless, he and his wife, the scholar Jean Moorcroft Wilson, now see themselves as latter-day Bloomsberries, to the extent that they work together, at home, on their small publishing enterprise (their kitchen table, where they pack books, was once used at the Hogarth Press) and raise five children in a chaotic, haphazardly furnished London house. They are also a minor part of the industry they deplore, through their new pamphlet series, called Bloomsbury Heritage, and through Jean Woolf's writings and lectures. She is the author of *Virginia Woolf's London* (1985), a book inspired by her American students, "who otherwise simply wouldn't know what *Mrs. Dalloway* was about."

Although her link with Bloomsbury is even more tenuous, Clarissa Roche occasionally shows up in Bloomsbury-related articles, by virtue of her marriage to Paul Roche (dissolved in the 1980s) and her long friendship with Duncan Grant. Her home (the subject of an illustrated article, "Bloomsbury Retreat," in *Country Life* in 1988) is filled with his paintings, many of them gifts from Duncan. For sev-

---

53. "Woolfs Still Stalk the Bloomsbury Streets," *Independent* 27 Dec. 1990.

eral years she has been engaged on a biography of Sylvia Plath, whom she knew, and the white plaster walls of her kitchen are scribbled over with ideas that must have occurred to her while she was cooking. One note reads simply: SODOMY.

NO WRITER ON Bloomsbury since Michael Holroyd has really faced a blank page. Recent scholarship and journalism are thick with references to earlier sources, and some works, like the Hermione Lee biography, keep up an anxious running argument with specific antagonists. The simplest statements about Bloomsbury now require complex justification. Not only are new information and original insights increasingly elusive, but the canonical works—the lapidary phrases of Quentin Bell, for instance—sink into our memory like rhymed verse. Phrases that spring easily to mind often turn out to be near quotes from Quentin Bell or Nigel Nicolson or Noel Annan, which must then be laboriously rephrased. The many Bloomsbury-related plays and movies that have surfaced in the past fifteen years may reflect not only the commodification of the Group, which is obvious enough, but an urge to shrug off all this redundance and lifeless exactitude and to return some measure of playful allure to Bloomsbury and its works. Sally Potter's film *Orlando*, for instance, is not a faithful treatment of Woolf's novel—if such a treatment is possible—but demonstrates a defiantly idiosyncratic engagement with its source, the sort of reading a generous writer hopes for.

Passing references to the Group in films like the humourless *Tom & Viv*, in which an unseen "Bloomsbury" is repeatedly blamed for Vivien Eliot's madness, can perhaps be taken as more representative— or at least more traditional—views than those embodied by Christopher Hampton's admiring but somewhat overheated *Carrington*. The story of the making of *Carrington* has distinctly cinematic plotting.

Hampton had been attracted to the story since his first reading of Holroyd's *Strachey* in the late 1960s. In 1976, Warner Brothers commissioned a screenplay, which Hampton spent a year writing under fairly luxurious circumstances. Whenever he needed to consult the Strachey papers, for instance, a large van would arrive filled with photocopies. He delivered the script in late 1977 (Herbert Ross was in line to direct), flew to Los Angeles for the launch party, and then heard nothing. In 1980, London Weekend's South Bank Show asked Michael Holroyd to do a show to mark Lytton Strachey's centenary, and Warner allowed Hampton to use eight minutes of his *Carrington* script for this purpose. Still no word regarding filming. After a student reading of the play, BBC and ITV pursued the script. Eventually, Thames bought it from Warner for ten times the amount Warner had paid Christopher Hampton. In the late eighties Mike Newell agreed to direct the film. He and Hampton then spent many painful months trying to raise £3 million from various European entrepreneurs, riding the success of Newell's *Enchanted April* and Hampton's Best Screenplay Oscar for *Dangerous Liaisons*. Juliette Binoche was cast as Carrington. When executives at Thames tried to replace Mike Newell, however, all the foreign investors dropped out, as did Binoche. Soon after, Thames lost their ITV franchise and could sell only their old successes like *Benny Hill*. Hampton threw himself on the mercies of Hollywood, enduring, as he recalls, "hundreds and hundreds" of meetings, at one of which Harvey Weinstein of Miramax told him that he loved the project but wouldn't get involved: "Let's face it. This is a film about a woman who falls in love with a faggot and kills herself." By 1992, Emma Thompson had become interested (she took painting lessons at the Slade to prepare for the role), which helped attract $6 million from Polygram and two other small French distributors, but Mike Newell left the project. He had directed too many "little British films" that made no money, he told Hampton, and could not imagine that the latest, *Four Weddings and a Funeral,* would be any different. His departure left *Carrington* with everything but a director. Thompson and others urged Hampton to direct the film himself.

The unusual premise of *Carrington,* as well as Jonathan Pryce's unexpected success at Cannes, led to greater publicity than is usually accorded to small English films, and this publicity seems to have directly spiked the prices of Bloomsbury art. (Hampton cleverly bought a Carrington still life at auction before the film's release.) Although *Carrington* is better liked by Bloomsbury enthusiasts than Sally Potter's *Orlando,* press reviews were mixed. The *Times* critic found the film "not especially painful" to watch. A long review by *New Yorker* critic Anthony Lane recalled criticism of the 1930s and suggested that Lane's knowledge of the Bloomsbury Group went little further than the film *Carrington.*

> I tend to regard Bloomsbury as one of the more gruesome plagues ever visited on British culture: all those Partridges and Garnetts, Stephenses and Bells; all that snobbery posing as incisiveness, the willful mistaking of social poses for literary values, the worship of the beautiful which turned out to be simply a fondness for interior decoration.

Many critics complained of Hampton's neglect of Carrington's art, images of which, aside from reproductions of the interiors she painted,[54] were relegated to the end credits. "In showing us so little of Carrington's art," wrote Kenneth Baker in the *San Francisco*

---

54. An artist named Christopher Evans decorated some three hundred murals and household objects for the film.

Chronicle, "Hampton's film ironically respects her privacy only where it matters least." Yet this is an aspect of her life that Hampton says he augmented from earlier drafts of the screenplay.

The script also overlooked Carrington's lesbian affairs, which Hampton feared would only further complicate her already labyrinthine attachments. In a September 1995 interview in the *Advocate*, Emma Thompson let it be known that she regretted this omission. She would have liked to play a love scene with a woman. She would like to enact such a scene in life, as well, but had never met the right woman—someone like Michelle Pfeiffer, perhaps, with those wonderful lips. In fact, she continued, every time she saw Pfeiffer, she ran up and kissed her on those wonderful lips. "Do you ever get love letters from women?" the interviewer asked. "No," Thompson replied, "I never have." "Well, you will now."

Frances Partridge, the last living member of the Ham Spray ménage, had opposed the idea of a film, dreading the inevitable distortions of events and characters, especially that of her late husband, Ralph, who had died in 1960. She had been annoyed by Holroyd's depiction of Ralph, based largely on Gerald Brenan's account of his friend and rival, and thought that the best comment on Holroyd's Strachey came from a friend of hers who blurted out, "Oh, that *book*! When I die I'm going to have SHUT UP put on my tombstone."[55] By threatening to withhold copyright for Carrington's letters and diaries, Partridge effectively killed the BBC's initial plan in the late 1960s to make a film of Strachey's life, directed by Ken Russell. "I mind the idea of the false Ralph they will create very much indeed," she wrote in her diary, "whether rationally or no."[56] Later, she relented, perhaps

---

55. Frances Partridge, *Good Company*, 92.

56. Ibid., 157.

realizing that a biographically based film—of sorts—could still be made without direct quotes from copyrighted material. She declined serving as adviser on Christopher Hampton's project but met and liked Emma Thompson. At an early screening of *Carrington*, she is said to have gasped on first seeing Jonathan Pryce descending from the train as Lytton Strachey, so exact was his impersonation. Afterward, though, while waiting for a bus, she remarked to a friend that the real story of Carrington had yet to be told.

MAKING NARRATIVE SENSE of what happened to Bloomsbury in the 1980s and early 1990s is like trying to contain a large spill of water with one's hands. It is partly that the flow originates from so many sources. There is no guiding spirit, no Leonard Woolf, to pace the appearance of books or control access to documents, and no planned sequence to events. Bloomsbury scholars in Kyoto are convening while Nathalie Sarraute and Alain Robbe-Grillet perform Virginia Woolf's play *Freshwater* in Paris and New York and while an early Vanessa Bell is acquired by the Museum of Modern Art in New York. American scholars design a "Virtual Bloomsbury" database for undergraduates while Tilton, the Keyneses' Sussex cottage, is being rented by the Keynes biographer Robert Skidelsky and while Emma Thompson wins an Oscar for her role in *Howards End*. The events of the moment are so near that it is difficult to pull them into focus, to make coherent images of the fragments that fly at us. This blurred foreground is essential to the "feeling" of the Bloomsbury boom, the sense of something vital and uncontrolled that partakes of other movements, like feminism and the cult of celebrity, but offers its own poignant singularity: a compound of the deadness and the uncanny lingering presence of the Bloomsbury Group.

If there is a still point at the centre of the Bloomsbury universe, it may be a tiny gallery and bookshop near the British Museum, presided over by Tony Bradshaw, a former stockbroker and corporate investment adviser who picked up where d'Offay left off in his promotion of the Bloomsbury artists. Bradshaw first learned of the Group through Nigel Nicolson's *Portrait of a Marriage*, which he found himself reading four or five times when it appeared, fascinated by the ways in which Vita and Harold made their unconventional marriage work. He first saw Bloomsbury pictures at a Sotheby's benefit sale for Charleston in about 1983. Two years later, he and his wife, Frances, purchased a flat in London and were convinced by the developer to lease a small commercial space, about twelve feet square, that was sitting vacant across the courtyard. The Bloomsbury Workshop opened in 1986, with a small selection of new, secondhand, and rare books and a handful of minor works by the Bloomsbury artists. By the late 1980s, having won the approval of the Bells and influential others, the gallery had become the hub of what Bradshaw calls "tertiary Bloomsbury," the network of scholars, heirs, enthusiasts, and eccentrics that constitutes the present-day Bloomsbury world.

As well as books and art, Bradshaw will sell whatever Bloomsbury-related items come his way, from Charleston ceramics once owned by Vanessa's cook, Grace Higgins, to Virginia Woolf's passport photo. His fastest sales were to Tina Brown, editor of the *New Yorker*, whose secretary rang the Bloomsbury Workshop and announced that Brown was in the market for work by Vanessa Bell. "I have a little something here," Bradshaw said and described a drawing he had just acquired. "That sounds good," answered the secretary. She rang back ten minutes later to say that Tina Brown would buy the drawing, sight unseen. Brown was also interested in owning a more important piece by Vanessa, and Bradshaw told the secretary he would show her transparencies of available paintings when he was next in New York. When he called for an appointment, some weeks later, he was told that Ms. Brown had only a few minutes to spare but was eager to see him. She was in a meeting when he arrived. A door opened, Tina Brown emerged for a moment, shook his hand, held the transparency to the light, and said, "I'll take it. Good-bye."

Rash acts are rife in the world of collecting, which inspires emotions akin to those the Bloomsbury fanatic feels when he learns that Michael Holroyd will be lecturing nearby, or that a new biography of Forster is appearing. Jeanette Winterson has described her own joyous possession of Bloomsbury drawings and rare books in her essay "The Psychometry of Books." One volume in particular, *Twelve Woodcuts by Roger Fry*, set and printed by Virginia and Leonard Woolf at the Hogarth Press in 1921, gives Winterson "immediate bodily delight."

> In her diary entry, Virginia Woolf wrote, "150 copies have been gulped down in 2 days. I have just finished stitching the last copies—all but six." Is it the hand-decorated coloured-paper wrappers, or the thick cream insides, or the fact that she stitched this book that I have before me now? It is association, intrinsic worth, beauty, a commitment to beautiful things, and the deep passage of the woodcuts themselves. Passages into other places. A smuggler's route into what is past and what can never be past.[57]

One of the best-known and most devoted Bloomsbury collectors in England is Robert Reedman, a retired architect, who bought

57. Winterson, *Art Objects* (London: Jonathan Cape, 1995), 123.

Woolf's passport entry for 1927 and who owns a complete run of the hand-printed Hogarth Press books, included a coveted copy of *Poems by C. N. Sidney Woolf* (1918), the rarest of Hogarth publications, of which only about ten are thought to exist. (In 1994, Tony Bradshaw sold one of these palm-sized, nineteen-page pamphlets for £11,000. Two years later, he was able to sell another copy to a Belgian collector for £15,000.) Reedman's first purchase of a Hogarth Press book was during the war, when he picked up a copy of Virginia Woolf's *The Mark on the Wall* (1919) for threepence at a bookstall. He had not even heard of the author but was captivated by this little book, now worth over £500. In his Oxford house filled with books, antiques, and English modern art, there is barely room on the walls for his woodcuts by Carrington, many small Duncan Grant drawings and watercolours, a Duncan Grant still life, and a superlative Vanessa Bell oil painting, dating from about 1912, of trees in Turkey, similar to the well-known oil by Roger Fry. One of Reedman's recent finds is a Julia Margaret Cameron print of the first Mrs. Leslie Stephen, below which, on the matte, Virginia Woolf has written two descriptive sentences. No one at the auction house recognized the handwriting, but Robert Reedman did.

Bradshaw has also helped build Bloomsbury collections in America. Craufurd and Nancy Goodwin of North Carolina hope to leave their home and art collection to the town in which they live and are concentrating on acquiring a few more major Bloomsbury pieces. They are writing a book together on Bloomsbury gardens. Another collector, Kenneth Curry, is planning to bequeath his Bloomsbury works to his alma mater, Rollins College, in Florida. He owns a version of Vanessa Bell's *Portrait of Mary Hutchinson* (1915). On the West Coast, the most avid collectors are Lester and Eileen Traub. Like Robert Reedman, the Traubs collect anything to do with Bloomsbury (and a good deal else besides), but they began as book collectors. When their first child was born, Lester presented his wife with a signed limited edition of *Orlando;* for their second child, he gave her *The Waste Land.* Along with many Bloomsbury paintings, they have a small cobalt-blue Omega dish (kept under Plexiglas), a Roger Fry sketchbook, a recent Quentin Bell pot, the stencils for Vanessa Bell's 1921 Christmas card, and a 1923 letter from Lytton Strachey to Raymond Mortimer. Their first piece of Bloomsbury art was a Duncan Grant watercolour of a nude, bought from Anthony d'Offay. A flurry of random acquisitions followed, but these days they weigh every purchase carefully, with an eye to the overall value and importance of their Bloomsbury collection. When I interviewed the Traubs, they had just completed their set of the handprinted Hogarth Press with Stanley Snaith's notoriously elusive *A Flying Scroll* (1928). They asked if Robert Reedman owned a copy, and I was forced to admit that he did.

Bloomsbury art remained stable in value from about the mid-1980s, and it is only now, due to the publicity generated by the film *Carrington,* edging upward again. It is Carrington's work, in fact, that has appreciated most—a trend that began with Holroyd's *Strachey* but gained a firmer footing with a 1978 show at Oxford, organized by her brother Noel Carrington, and its accompanying catalogue. After this show, Anthony d'Offay began to look actively for Carringtons, though they were hard to come by even then. In 1979, David Garnett's edition of her letters was reprinted in paperback. Ten years later the first biography of Carrington appeared, an expansion of Gretchen Gerzina's Stanford dissertation, and in 1987 the Tate Gallery accepted the offer of a Carrington painting from her brother Noel. One of Tony Bradshaw's former assistants, Jane Hill, published *The Art of Dora Carrington* in 1994 and organized the well-reviewed Carrington retrospective at the Barbican Centre in London, timed to coincide with the opening of Christopher Hampton's film in October 1995.

Carrington's work has been difficult to price because of its extreme scarcity. In his first exhibition devoted to her, Bradshaw could offer only five pieces for sale. The highest auction price for a painting by Carrington is £23,000—a striking figure for a little-known painter, but no comparison to Vanessa's record price of £80,000, in the boom 1980s, for a portrait of Lytton Strachey, or Duncan's record of £70,000 for a self-portrait that had belonged to Kenneth Clark and was later to sell privately for nearly double that price. Without question, Bradshaw's best purchase was a Carrington sketchbook that he found at auction in 1993 for an absurd £600. The first drawing he sold from this book went for £1,500, and he estimates his eventual profits from the sketchbook at close to £40,000. By now, he can spot a Carrington from a half mile away. He remembers glancing at a painted mirror at Jeremy Hutchinson's home and feeling a shiver of recognition. Hutchinson had just bought the thing for £25 at a Brighton junk shop. It was later included in the Barbican exhibition.

Bloomsbury book prices have risen predictably, with Virginia Woolf first editions showing steep appreciation since the Quentin Bell biography. In America copies of the limited edition of *Orlando*, which could be had for $15 in 1964 and for about $100 in the early 1970s, now fetch over $600. Similarly, "very nice" copies of *The Voyage Out* sold for about $20 in 1964, $150 in the early seventies, and $1,500 in 1996. Copies of *Jacob's Room* or *Mrs. Dalloway* with the rare Vanessa Bell dust jackets can bring over $4,000. While Forster first editions were worth far more than Woolf in the early 1970s, they are more or less equal at present. Strachey's prices are much lower—$132 for a rubbed copy of *Eminent Victorians* in 1994—but his later books were printed in such large editions that the laws of scarcity fail to apply.

Judith Lowry of the Argosy Bookstore in New York remembers snatching up Hogarth Press books at bargain prices in London in the mid-1960s. At Sotheby's, she bought a copy of Woolf's *Monday or Tuesday* with Lytton Strachey's bookplate and ownership signature. The association had not been mentioned in the catalogue—not through oversight, she thought, but because it was thought to be of little significance. One day the dealer Bernard Stone offered her an archive of letters and photographs that had come from the family of Jack Hills, Stella Duckworth's husband. It included letters from Leslie Stephen to Stella, childhood letters of Stella's to her mother, Stella's diary, a family photograph album with pictures of the Stephen family and friends, and a pencil drawing of Virginia.

> The letters were fascinating, and had a kind of raw immediacy, covering as they did the period just before Stella's marriage and ending with her death. Unfortunately I was unable to convey the importance of these letters to anyone. I offered them to several major university libraries, but none of them showed any interest. When I came back to the U.S. I kept the collection at home.[58]

Sometime in the mid-1970s, Lowry's father was at a dinner meeting of the Old Book Table, a group of New York booksellers who excluded women from their membership (and still do) but who permitted an occasional woman guest speaker. Lola Szladits came that night and spoke about the special collections at the New York Public Library, including the Virginia Woolf material. Lowry's father suggested that she call Dr. Szladits and try to "unload those letters that

---

58. Letter to the author, 27 April 1994.

no one else seemed to want." Szladits was not only interested, she was the first person Lowry had spoken with who knew all about Bloomsbury and understood the significance of the Stella Duckworth archive. "I was happy to sell her the letters," Lowry recalls, "feeling as one does with a favorite puppy that goes to the right home."

The Berg Collection at the New York Public Library contains the bulk of Virginia Woolf's surviving papers—her diaries, most notably, as well as the manuscripts of *Jacob's Room*, *To the Lighthouse*, *The Waves*, *The Voyage Out*, and *Between the Acts*, twenty-three reading notebooks, and a host of related material, including Vanessa's and Vita's letters to her. A visit to the Berg may be the one universally acknowledged rite of passage for Woolf scholars. "I call it a pilgrimage," Ellen Hawkes Rogat wrote in 1973, "because I went as a devoted reader of Woolf."

> I had cleared a space in my life to become totally immersed in hers. Not surprisingly, the journey was wonderful, strange, and sometimes even comic. Because note-taking from the diaries is prohibited, I had to focus exclusively, almost obsessively, on the pages of Woolf's angular handwriting. In a sense, I was spinning out a Woolfian filament, a bond that was not easily broken.[59]

Louise DeSalvo, who spent months on end at the Berg Collection, puts her first visit there into class perspective. Her father had been a

---

59. Ellen Hawkes Rogat, "Visiting the Berg Collection," *Virginia Woolf Miscellany* 1.1 (1973).

machinist, she explains, and there had been no model for intellectual work in her family: "I very much felt as if I was in the presence of important and quasi-sacred objects. . . . I could learn how a creator worked by looking at these documents."[60]

For twenty years, from 1970 to 1990, trips to the Berg Collection were coloured by the premiership of the late, legendary Dr. Lola Szladits, as fierce a guardian of Woolf and her papers as Leonard himself. "Lola was terrifying, and meant to be," recalls Joanne Trautmann Banks, who arrived with a letter of introduction and permission from Quentin Bell, which Szladits read and disregarded, telling her coolly, "I have no idea who you are."[61] Szladits's early history and her work at the Berg were described in a 1984 *New Yorker* profile by Whitney Balliett, the magazine's first profile of a librarian. Something of her devotion to the cause also emerges in a short essay, "A Personal Note," appended to Mitchell Leaska's edition of *Pointz Hall: The Earlier and Later Typescripts of* Between the Acts (1983), in which Szladits recounted the eight months of labour and ingenuity that went into organizing the numerous partial drafts and fragments of *Between the Acts* that had arrived at the Berg in a large unsorted box in the early 1960s, and her great pleasure at Leonard Woolf's approval of her efforts. Szladits was a considerable force in the literary market (Auden's notebooks are said to be her most valuable acquisition) and an unforgettable presence at the Berg. Ellen Hawkes, whose two months of study there coincided with a record-breaking heat wave,

---

60. Interview with the author, 6 April 1994.

61. Joanne Trautmann Banks, "The Editor as Detective," *Charleston Magazine* 13 (Spring–Summer 1996): 6.

remembers Szladits pushing and pulling the fans, opening the roof vents for more air, and even crawling into the attic to inspect the pipes. At one point she could be seen balancing on the ledges of the third-floor hall windows, trying to pry them open.

The Berg's first purchase of Virginia Woolf manuscripts came in 1958, through the Chicago rare book and manuscript dealers Hamill and Barker, with the proviso that Leonard would retain possession of the diaries during his life. He earned about $20,000 from the sale and later gave the Berg several further manuscripts, as they turned up in the course of his slow sorting of trunks and cupboards at Monk's House. Although their methods were less than commendable, Hamill and Barker had a sound instinct for literary futures and were responsible for a large number of modern English manuscripts entering American collections in the 1950s and 1960s. They are said to have watched the newspapers for obituaries of authors, "particularly those associated with Bloomsbury," as Joanne Trautmann Banks learned.

> Soon after a death, the ladies would arrive on the doorstep of the grieving family. They were well dressed. They murmured their deepest sympathy and respect. Then they offered to dispose of the literary remains for (in the case of Woolf's letters to Vita Sackville-West) £1 each.

In 1968, Frances Partridge gave Frances Hamill some letters from Lytton Strachey to Ralph Partridge, along with a list of people she had letters from. She had wondered which of these might be worth keeping. "All," Hamill replied. "There's something disconcerting," Partridge wrote in her diary that night, "about this conversion of human contacts that one has actually been the recipients of into money—flesh and blood into metal. I don't know if it is unrealistic or even sentimental to be disgusted by it."[62]

British scholars can be touchy on the subject, on the one hand irritated that so many manuscripts from this period have ended up across the ocean, and on the other hand inclined to ridicule Americans for overvaluing this material. Between 1956 and 1970, the Harry Ransome Humanities Research Center at the University of Texas was famous for its extravagant purchases: "It had oil money," as Lola Szladits said, "and could buy anything." Hamill and Barker were the conduit for many of their acquisitions. In the mid-1960s, Gerald Brenan earned over $13,000 (in today's terms about $65,000) from sales to Texas through Bertram Rota, a London dealer, and the ladies from Chicago. His biographer reports that he sold "everything they would take—his Carrington correspondence, journals, manuscripts, notebooks, poems—and had fantasies about selling his socks and his toenails."[63] The Texas collection is especially strong in Strachey, Woolf, Carrington, and Ottoline Morrell. For some reason, the Huntington Library in California owns Saxon Sydney Turner's papers. The Lilly Library in Indiana recently acquired the MacCarthy papers, which the British Library had declined to buy at £500,000. Washington State University in Pullman has an excellent Woolf collection, including most of the books from Monk's House.

Although the British Library has considerable Bloomsbury-related holdings, as does King's College, Cambridge, which has the papers of Keynes and Forster, the best Woolf collection in England

---

62. Frances Partridge, *Good Company*, 133.

63. Jonathan Gathorne-Hardy, *The Interior Castle: A Life of Gerald Brenan* (London: Sinclair Stevenson, 1992), 473.

is at the University of Sussex, to which Trekkie Parsons gave the Leonard Woolf Papers, an enormous archive of some 65,000 pieces, including about 400 letters concerning the sale of Virginia Woolf material through Hamill and Barker. It was here, also, that the Monk's House Papers (documents passed from Leonard Woolf to Quentin Bell for use on the biography) eventually settled and, most recently, Nigel Nicolson's correspondence regarding *The Letters of Virginia Woolf*. The university also recently acquired Leonard's stock and share certificates. The Monk's House Papers and Leonard Woolf Papers are by far the most sought-after manuscript collections at Sussex, attracting as many as 140 scholars, most of them American, each year.

EVEN AT THE zenith of the revival—about 1978–1984—it was still uncertain whether "Bloomsbury" was a beneficial or damaging label. It was not only that two or three Bloomsberries had ascended into greatness, leaving the others dangling uncomfortably. Most members of the Group already had, or soon acquired, a faithful following. But their collective identity, that albatross of name and ethos, was faltering. Even Leon Edel, in what purported to be a group biography, had chosen to exclude the less productive Bloomsberries, the Adrians and Saxons, something that went against all previous definitions of the Group. "Bloomsbury," by Edel's standards, was an appellation one had to earn. In an exhibition review from the same period, Richard Shone stated that "on the subject of Bloomsbury I would say only this, that its existence and atmosphere certainly helped liberate a notable talent in English painting . . . and that in later years it prevented Vanessa Bell from maturing into a really considerable painter." The second half of this comment raises more questions than it answers, but we can see Bloomsbury—or whatever is meant by the term—slipping from inspiration to scapegoat.

As early as the 1950s, Clive Bell had complained of the vague nature of the term and that journalists could not decide whether it referred to "a point of view, a period, a gang of conspirators or an infectious disease."[64] Now that the original members are all dead, the concept of "Bloomsbury" floats even more freely through the culture, like a seed cluster snapped from the stem. Rather than wrestle with the many stubborn connotations of the term, critics have continued their strategy of rescuing varying members of the Group by asserting or implying that they were not the real thing. In 1972, for example, a flattering review of Roger Fry's published letters pegged him as a peripheral figure, lacking "some of the more distinctive Bloomsbury traits—the arrogant self-esteem, consciousness of innate superiority and lofty disdain of the unenlightened beyond the pale."[65] In his eulogy for Duncan Grant, Kenneth Clark had said that Duncan was "completely outside the Bloomsbury ethos."[66] Forster had long been considered only a fringe member, to the immense benefit of his reputation during the 1940s and 1950s. Holroyd tried this unsuccessfully with Lytton Strachey. On the other hand, no one has ever argued that Vanessa Bell was not Bloomsbury.

Maynard Keynes proved difficult, but after the publication of the Harrod biography in 1951 it became commonly accepted that his Bloomsbury years were self-contained, ending before his marriage.

---

64. Quoted in S. P. Rosenbaum, *The Bloomsbury Group* (Toronto: University of Toronto Press, 1975), 85.

65. Ralph Edwards, review of *The Letters of Roger Fry, Connoisseur* 182 (Feb. 1973): 112–13.

66. Quoted in Turnbaugh, *Duncan Grant and the Bloomsbury Group* (Secaucus, N.J.: Lyle Stuart, 1987), 108.

(Maynard's wife, Lydia, had neither helped Harrod nor read his book when it appeared, so there was not much detail on the marriage, either, and not a murmur about his homosexuality.) For scholars of Keynes and Forster especially, Bloomsbury became an attribution that could be dropped, when convenient, and just as easily reasserted. An otherwise comprehensive 1975 collection of essays on Keynes relegated Bloomsbury to a few gossipy pages by Paul Levy, but two years later, in the flush of enthusiasm for the Group, the fourth Keynes seminar was devoted to "Keynes and the Bloomsbury Group" and included contributions by Quentin Bell and Richard Shone. In a pro-Bloomsbury environment, Maynard's nephew, Milo Keynes, might even be found asserting that Maynard was "the centre of Bloomsbury. He was such a leading figure all around that he was bound to be the centre."[67] In recent years, the Bloomsbury emphasis has declined slightly, and some have found Robert Skidelsky's massive biographical enterprise *John Maynard Keynes* (1983) to be less than friendly to the Group, although Skidelsky himself has been intimately involved with the Charleston Trust.

Establishing opposition is a primary job of critics and reviewers. This is perhaps why each figure who achieves a reasonable measure of public acceptance—first Maynard and Morgan, later Virginia, Vanessa, Duncan—is felt to be dragged down by his or her association with those lesser Bloomsberries (what F. R. Leavis, who deplored Forster's connection with the Group, often referred to as "a very inferior social milieu"). Slighter members of the Group, however, are buoyed by the association. Hugh Cecil, Desmond MacCarthy's grandson, who wrote a biography of him, has said that although

---

67. Alan MacWeeney and Sue Allison, *Bloomsbury Reflections* (New York: Norton, 1990), unpaginated.

Desmond wasn't of the inner circle, "he is perhaps most frequently thought of as a member of Bloomsbury. That, in a way, is how his name has survived. There are lots of literary figures who are of the same eminence as Desmond MacCarthy who have faded away from memory. I think Bloomsbury and the interest in it, the cult, if you like, has rather helped a lot of people."[68]

This is even more true of more distantly related figures and books than of Desmond MacCarthy. It is difficult to say, for example, whether the artist Nina Hamnett would have warranted a full-scale biography without her link to Roger Fry and the Omega Workshops or whether Dorothy Brett's biography would have been published without the subtitle *From Bloomsbury to New Mexico*. In the absence of a Bloomsbury revival, who would have published (or read) Elizabeth Boyd's *Bloomsbury Heritage: Their Mothers and Their Aunts* (1976)? And would even an academic press have taken on Leslie Stephen's lugubrious *Mausoleum Book* (1978) or a reprint of Leonard Woolf's failed second novel, *The Wise Virgins* (1979), or Julia Duckworth Stephen's *Stories for Children, Essays for Adults* (1987)?

Lady Ottoline Morrell would have attracted notice in any case. She had already appeared in several literary memoirs as a set piece, an occasion for jewel-encrusted prose. The first volume of her own memoirs surfaced in 1963, edited by Robert Gathorne-Hardy. The Holroyd biography devoted so much attention to her relationship with Lytton Strachey, however, that she began to be considered an adjunct to the Group. Insulted by Holroyd's depiction of her mother, Julian Vinogradoff angrily removed two paintings from an exhibition promoting the second volume of the Strachey biography. Six years later, Gathorne-Hardy's introduction to the second half of Ottoline's

---

68. Ibid.

memoirs seethed with irritation at Holroyd, and what remains of the Ottoline camp still resent his portrayal of her and argue that the "Bloomsbury version" of her powerful personality is not to be trusted. The authorized biography, Miranda Seymour's *Ottoline Morrell: Life on the Grand Scale* (1994), was advertised as highlighting "the Bloomsbury's snobbery, malice and deceit."

Most critics have ignored the little tempest over Ottoline. Victoria Glendinning's *Times Literary Supplement* review of *Lady Ottoline's Album* opened with the standard "too much Bloomsbury" line but soon progressed to a witty description of the photographs. Struck by the fashions of the period, she paused to describe André Gide's romantic appearance in a hat: "In an adjacent photograph, hatless, the proportions are lost. Besides, he was bald, and one bald intellectual looks much like another."

The greatest difficulty, perhaps, in maintaining white-hot interest in Bloomsbury as a group after the 1970s was that the more information poured forth in diaries and letters, biographies, and memoirs, the less one could summarize their shared beliefs or behaviours with any grace or certainty. An exception could always be found. The disjunctions and disaffinities between members began to stand out more than their Cambridge roots and Clapham heritage. Bloomsbury threatened to become a defunct category at the same moment that weighty biographies of its individual members began to crowd bookshops: an austerely impersonal life of Leonard Woolf by Duncan Wilson (1978); an equally austere biography of Maynard Keynes by the economist D. E. Moggeridge (1976); P. N. Furbank's long-awaited two-volume life of Forster (1977–78); another biography of Leonard Woolf, this time by Selma Meyerowitz (1981); a collection of essays on Lydia Lopokova, edited by her nephew Milo Keynes (1983);

Desmond MacCarthy: The Man and His Writings, edited by his son-in-law David Cecil (1984); and the first two volumes of Skidelsky's definitive life of Keynes.

Memoirs from fringe figures and family members like Gerald Brenan, Geoffrey Keynes, and Barbara Strachey surged from the presses in the 1970s and 1980s, the best of which without question are Frances Partridge's diaries—writings so startlingly acute that it is a shame Bloomsbury cannot claim her as an original member. *A Pacifist's War* (1978) and *Memories,* published in America as *Love in Bloomsbury* (1980), deal unsentimentally with the years before her marriage, shifting between diary entries and later commentary. They manage to convey, as she had hoped, the texture of her daily existence at David Garnett and Francis Birrell's bookshop in London, where she worked, and at Ham Spray, while Lytton and Carrington still lived. Several later volumes of diaries were reprinted in paperback in England in the early 1990s. Although they are rich with anecdotes of the illustrious dead, Bloomsbury is not the fundamental appeal of Partridge's sane, sad, penetrating works, and they deserve a much wider readership than those who will scan them for mention of Lytton or Carrington.

Nevertheless, like Quentin and Angelica, Frances Partridge has attracted a devoted following among Bloomsbury enthusiasts. "I'm rather like Mrs Dale's Diary," she told a journalist in 1996, "and people are fascinated."

But I am 97 (well, soon will be) and I'm more feeble than I look. Perfectly strange people write to me. All sorts. One of them is an air hostess. The worst are the people who think they actually are Carrington. They tend to have written a play about her, which they are quite prepared to act in. Would I be so good as to read it and comment?[69]

Overexposure to Bloomsbury can bring out a certain strained hilarity, and this must account for a rash of odd, not hugely amusing items that began to emerge in the late 1970s, such as a December 1980 *New York Review of Books* cartoon headed "Bloomsbury Squares," below which the nine principal members of the Group are arranged like the guests of the television show *Celebrity Squares,* and Kenneth Mahood's *The Secret Sketchbook of a Bloomsbury Lady* (1982), a spoof of the Bloomsbury photograph albums that kept appearing, and the most elaborate send-up yet of Bloomsbury and its amours. Michael Holroyd contributed the mock foreword.

There is also a strange, unexplored connection between Bloomsbury and the mystery novel. In Susan Kenney's *Garden of Malice* (1983), an American woman professor travels to England to help edit the private papers of the glamorous Lady Viola Montfort-Snow, whose chief accomplishment was the creation of a series of gardens on the grounds of a ruined abbey. Ellen Hawkes and Peter Manso drew even more directly on Bloomsbury legend in a thriller called *The Shadow of the Moth: A Novel of Espionage with Virginia Woolf* (1983). Readers can sense Hawkes's satisfaction in inventing precisely the plucky, heroic, damned clever Woolf she had hoped to find, years earlier, in the Bell biography.

Outside of book reviews and editorial pages, in which the death of Bloomsbury is frequently announced, there are no signs of a decrease of interest in the Group. Scholars have now organized an annual Virginia Woolf conference in the United States. Vanessa Bell's

---

69. "Frances Partridge, Bloomsbury Diarist," *Country Life* 20 Feb. 1997: 56.

writings on art have been edited by a young Italian art historian, Lia Giachero, and are scheduled to appear in 1997, as is Frances Spalding's long-awaited life of Duncan Grant. Biographies of Clive Bell, Adrian Stephen, and Julian Bell are in the works. Patricia Laurence's book on Bloomsbury and China is being prepared. Mary Ann Caws and Sarah Bird Wright are writing on Bloomsbury and France.

WHAT, THEN, ACCOUNTS for the continuing appeal of the Bloomsbury Group? It may be assumed that having read hundreds of books, articles, reviews, letters to the editor, published remarks, and private letters about Bloomsbury itself and the revival in particular, I should at least be able to explain the fascination with the Group. The truth is that there are too many points of entry to list. Many come to Bloomsbury through a scholarly or biographical interest in a particular member of the Group; others admire the Group's politics or aesthetic theories or lifestyle, or revel in the sexual gossip of seventy years ago. Once introduced to the Group, they find themselves drawn into what Janet Malcolm has called the novelistic appeal of Bloomsbury, whose members

> placed in posterity's hands the documents necessary to engage posterity's feeble attention, the letters, memoirs, and journals that reveal inner life and compel the sort of helpless empathy that fiction compels.[70]

Nostalgia plays a large role, but not, I think, the nostalgia for social privilege that Bernard Bergonzi and others have described. When Bloomsbury fanatics gather on the Charleston lawn each summer or

---

70. "A House of One's Own," 65.

pore over photographs of Carrington and Lytton or dip into their retirement funds to buy an envelope that once passed under the point of Duncan's pen they are not longing for a life of leisure supported by servants and a vast laboring working class. They are luxuriating in a world of inverted values, where friendship, books, and art take precedence over the daily business of moneymaking. The Bloomsberries did require servants and small private incomes to support their long hours of work and conversation, but frozen food and computer-equipped home offices have brought the Bloomsbury lifestyle within the reach of the vast labouring middle classes at least, and there is a sense in which every stencilled wall and teetering pile of paperbacks testifies to the lasting attractions of Bloomsbury.

But make no mistake: "Bloomsbury" remains a dirty word. In fact, it may be more culturally useful as a term of abuse than as a neutral adjective or proper noun. Hence the persistence of "errors" in scholarship and journalism, and the perpetuation of outdated critiques of the Group. "Bloomsbury" can mean almost anything, as Clive Bell argued forty years ago, and this extends the Group's strange power at the same time that it limits the Bloomsbury revival. No other catchphrase so neatly contains the anxieties of modernism: social guilt, sexual anarchy, uppity women, emasculated men. The English have tended to despise Bloomsbury as an elitist clique, what Noel Annan called an intellectual aristocracy and what Raymond Williams described as a breakaway fraction of the ruling class. That the members of the Group were sleeping with one another, in all those sordid and engaging combinations, is felt to add ominous, somewhat gothic undertones to their position as establishment figures in government, publishing, and the arts. Americans, on the other hand, have defined the Group by its sexual irregularities and played up the freakishness of its domestic arrangements. That such people could be productive writers and artists, or attain positions of power, comes as something of a shock to the general reader, who is not helped by the efforts of unfriendly critics to collapse all of Bloomsbury's achievements into its sexual unorthodoxy, the better to stigmatize the Group and dissuade its adherents.[71]

EVERY ONCE in a while a piece of journalism or a phrase in someone's memoir will locate a new focus of fascination with Bloomsbury or point to a hidden flaw in its ethos or reveal something tiny but illuminating that all our rigorous historical and textual reconstruction has missed. In some cases, the writer had only hoped to be funny. A February 1981 "Atticus" column in *The Sunday Times* began: "Hold the back page! I have found someone in the Bloomsbury Group who has no intention of writing her memoirs."

This reticent soul turned out to be Grace Higgins, cook and housekeeper to Vanessa Bell and Bloomsbury for fifty years. Retired since 1970, she then lived on a housing estate outside Lewes. When the reporter arrived, she and her husband were watching a televised item about the Charleston Appeal Fund, which ended with Malcolm Muggeridge describing the Group as Fortnum & Mason anarchists without respect for decent behaviour. "They were not!" Mrs. Higgins exclaimed. "I get angry when people talk like that. We never saw them in each other's beds, did we, Walter? They were very kind people." She had never regarded the Group as especially clever or remarkable, however, and was surprised that people became so interested in them. Virginia Woolf she described as a cheerful woman, recalling that

---

71. The most astute counterattacks on heterosexist reactions to the Bloomsbury Group have been by Christopher Reed. See his "Bloomsbury Bashing: Homophobia and the Politics of Criticism in the Eighties," *Genders* 11 (Fall 1991) and "Critics to the Left of Us, Critics to the Right of Us," *Charleston Magazine* 12 (Autumn-Winter 1995).

she had once sung "The Last Rose of Summer" to her hosts at Charleston. Virginia "went on and on and on. When the taxi came for her, we had to tell it to wait, didn't we, Walter?" Grace reminisced about Lytton Strachey, who may have giggled too much, and about a Welsh collie she had called Morgan, after E. M. Forster, until Vanessa Bell objected. They named the dog Blotto instead. When her husband suggested she write a book about her life at Charleston, she reminded him that Quentin Bell had once offered to help her do so. "But I shouldn't want to do that," she concluded. "I was just happy to spend my time with them. They were my sort of people."

INDEX